*A Secular Faith*

BOOKS BY DARRYL HART

*The Lost Soul of American Protestantism*
*That Old-Time Religion in Modern America*
*The University Gets Religion*
*Evangelicals and Science in Historical Perspective*
(editor, with David N. Livingstone and Mark A. Noll)
*Dictionary of the Presbyterian and Reformed Tradition in America*
(editor, with Mark A. Noll)
*New Directions in American Religious History* (editor, with Harry S. Stout)
*Theological Education in the Evangelical Tradition*
(editor, with R. Albert Mohler, Jr.)
*Religious Advocacy and the Writing of American History*
(editor, with Bruce Kuklick)
*Fighting the Good Fight* (with John R. Muether)
*Reckoning with the Past* (editor)
*Defending the Faith*

# A Secular Faith

## WHY CHRISTIANITY FAVORS THE SEPARATION OF CHURCH AND STATE

## Darryl Hart

*Ivan R. Dee*
CHICAGO 2006

www.ivanrdee.com

Library of Congress Cataloging-in-Publication Data:
Hart, D. G. (Darryl G.)
  A secular faith : why Christianity favors the separation of church and state / Darryl Hart.
    p. cm.
  Includes bibliographical references and index.
  ISBN-13: 978-1-56663-576-9 (cloth : alk. paper)
  ISBN-10: 1-56663-576-4 (cloth : alk. paper)
    1. Christianity and politics—United States. 2. Church and state—United States. 3. United States—Church history. I. Title.
BR516.H257 2006
261.70973—dc22

                                                        2006009506

*To the memory and legacy of J. Gresham Machen*

# Contents

# *Preface*

FOR MANY devout American Christians, the thought of the President of the United States pausing during a time of national peril or uncertainty to pray to the God of the universe is a comforting one. This was certainly the impression I took away from a recent summer seminar at a prominent American university, where scholars had convened to discuss the American founding and legal barriers to religious involvement in the political process. The idea of a president looking for divine assistance appeared to most of those assembled as at least innocent if not becoming. If God doesn't exist, prayer certainly couldn't hurt. But if divine assistance was available to the petitioner, wasn't it better for the most powerful man in the free world to acknowledge his dependence upon powers mightier than his rather than proudly thinking he could manage on his own? In fact, wasn't this the sort of activity in which a long line of reverential presidents engaged, from the Father of the Country to Honest Abe?

Since most of the academics in the room were conservative of some stripe, the thought experiment immediately conjured up images of the current occupant of the Oval Office, George W. Bush. His invocation of divine blessing and acknowledgment of his own faith has appealed to many American Christians who view secularization as one of the chief threats to the well-being of the nation. But complications ensued when this group of conservatives considered the hypothetical of someone like Hillary Rodham Clinton offering a prayer for help in her conduct as chief executive of the United States. At this point the image turned from consoling to annoying, even alarming. Questions about her sincerity, her comprehension of the proper matters for which to pray, her willingness to follow a wise course of action irrespective of any answer to her prayer—all these came to mind. The second version of this thought experiment posed the inconsistency that so often accompanies the way Americans mix Christianity and politics. Just as the thought of Clinton beseeching divine favor drives conservatives crazy, the thought of Bush doing so is equally infuriating to liberals and Democrats. The problem, as American history shows, is that the party in power rarely sees itself through its opponents' eyes; it doesn't consider that its appeal to divinity might not only look self-serving but also make self-delusion more likely.

The point of this book is to try to complicate contemporary understandings of the relationship between Christianity and liberal democracy in the United States. It should challenge both believers who think their faith serves specific forms of political participation, and skeptics who view Christianity negatively because of its recent influence on electoral politics. It starts from the premise that Christianity is an apolitical faith. Its message and means, though not indifferent to civil society, transcend all political rivalries, whether between Republicans and Democrats, big business and labor unions, the right and the left, or even Fox News and CNN. Historically the Christian religion, with the major exception of its American expression, has been concerned not with life, liberty, and the pursuit of happiness but with salvation from sin and death.

For this reason the book is dedicated to the memory and legacy of J. Gresham Machen, a twentieth-century Presbyterian who op-

posed any church pronouncements on the social or political questions of the day because in so doing, he believed, churches were
turning aside from their proper mission: "to bring to bear upon
human hearts the solemn and imperious, yet also sweet and gra-
cious, appeal of the gospel of Christ."

# Acknowledgments

READERS have no one to blame for this book but the author himself. Still, several people were helpful in prompting me to write it. Presenting a paper at a session on religion and the American right, organized by Leo Ribuffo, at the American Historical Association's annual meeting in 2003 gave me the opportunity to unravel and deepen some of my thinking about the religious right and its convoluted appeal to Christian teaching. Ivan Dee read a copy of that paper, eventually published in 2004 in the *Journal of the Historical Society* as "Conservatism, the Protestant Right, and the Failure of Religious History," and encouraged me to develop some of my arguments into a book. I am grateful both to Leo and Ivan for encouraging this effort.

Parts of this book come from papers or essays previously given or published. A brief section of Chapter One comes from the talk "Transformed: Protestants and American Culture," originally delivered at a symposium on "The Importance of Culture," sponsored by the Bradley Institute for the Study of Christian Culture at Belmont Abbey College, Belmont, North Carolina, in October 2004. A short part of Chapter Two comes from an essay, "The Use and Abuse of Christian Liberty," to be published in *The Faith Once Delivered*, edited by Anthony Selvaggio, P&R Publishing. A brief section from Chapter Four comes from "The Tie That Divides: Presbyterian Ecumenism, Fundamentalism, and the History of Twentieth-century American Protestantism," published in *Westminster Theological Journal* in 1998. Finally, several paragraphs from Chapter Five are slightly revised from "Overcoming the Schizophrenic Character of Theological Education in the Evangelical Tradition," in *A Confessing Theology for Postmodern Times*, edited by Michael S. Horton, Crossway Books, 2000.

D. H.

*Philadelphia, Pennsylvania*
*May 2006*

*A Secular Faith*

# Hole in the Wall

Since the election of Jimmy Carter to the presidency in 1976, the wall of separation between church and state in American life has taken a substantial beating from the tsunami of faith-based politics. Some Americans now wonder if the wall ever existed. But to the extent that it did, even if it was more of a parapet than a fortress-sized barrier, the wall dividing the spheres of faith and civil government has suffered not simply from neglect but from outright attack. As a result, American politicians now engage in practices once considered unimaginable.

During the 2000 Republican primaries, for example, George W. Bush delivered a campaign speech at Bob Jones University, a school known as one of the oldest and most strident of fundamentalist institutions. For Bush it was not a difficult decision to speak at the Greenville university whose constituency was crucial to his carrying the South Carolina primary. In fact Bush campaign officials may not have known that Bob Jones was a separatist institution, which meant that it would have nothing to do with those evangelicals who cooperated with the more liberal—so-called mainline—Protestant churches. The symbolic separation of fundamentalists and evangelicals had appeared earlier, during the 1957 Billy Graham evangelistic crusade in New York City. That was the first time the still relatively young evangelist had decided to welcome the help of congregations and pastors from the "modernist" or liberal denominations. Bob Jones renounced Graham's decision, objecting to this theological deviance that in his view had been leading the mainline churches astray since the 1920s.

The Bush campaign may have been oblivious to the Greenville university's links to the less popular side of this division between evangelicals like Graham and fundamentalists like Jones. But its chiefs must surely have known the school's reputation for segregation and the 1983 court case in which Bob Jones University was forced to give up its tax-exempt status because it prohibited interracial dating. Even so, Bush went ahead and spoke at the fundamentalist university. The reaction from John McCain, his opponent in the primaries, and from Roman Catholics forced Bush to write an explanation to Roman Catholic clergy who may have been offended by the university's characterization of the pope as the Antichrist. Nevertheless he suffered no obvious collateral damage, so accustomed had Americans—including the press and scholars become to faith as a crucial aspect of a presidential candidate's success. Thus Bush could win election even after openly courting a faith closer to the adherents of William Jennings Bryan during the Scopes Trial than with enlightened attorneys, scholars, and journalists who had supposedly exposed fundamentalism as at least bizarre if not fundamentally un-American.

In the 2004 campaign the faith-based stakes of the presidential contest were no lower. Evidence came not from Bush's attempt to secure his evangelical base as much as from the religious identity of the Democratic candidate. To many of the nation's values-voters, John Kerry, an observant Roman Catholic, looked to be insufficiently devout. These citizens likely had a point since Kerry, who needed to retain the support of women's and right-to-choice voters, played down his membership in a Christian communion outspokenly opposed to abortion-on-demand court rulings and public policy. But the religion-and-politics valence of 2004 completely reversed the pattern of the 1960 campaign of John F. Kennedy, another Roman Catholic Democratic presidential candidate. Kennedy needed to reassure Protestants that his Roman Catholic faith and practices, some of which included submission and obedience to the pope, would not come before his higher obligation to the U.S. Constitution. Forty-four years later, both Protestants and many Roman Catholics expected a Roman Catholic politician not only to take church teaching into account but to follow it, at least in the matter of abortion. Observers of both the 2000 and 2004 elections could not be blamed for thinking that the wall separating church and state, no matter how wide, deep, or high, had suffered a fate similar to the famous one in Berlin.

Although this is not the first time in American history that religion has influenced the nation's politics, the prevalence of faith in contemporary political discourse is singular. Protestants who once drew upon religious motivation to oppose slavery or the whiskey bottle also relied in the next breath on the separation of church and state to prevent Roman Catholics from gaining political power or access to public funding for education. Clearly the various efforts of Protestants, from the voluntary societies of the Second Great Awakening (1820s to 1830s) to support for civil rights, were inconsistent in distinguishing between their own version of Christianity as the good liberal fit for America's politics, and the unfit Roman Catholic expression. And both kinds of Christianity, in important ways, were incompatible with a view of government free from direct religious influence or ecclesiastical involvement. But the present-day consensus about religion and American politics—that politics needs the ideals, inspiration, and morality of faith—is unprecedented. Not even the election of 1800, when the well-publicized heterodoxy of Thomas Jefferson prompted New England Congregationalists to vote with the Federalists and his defense of religious liberty lured Methodists and Baptists to side with the Democratic-Republicans, could American political discourse match the level of unanimity about religion's value in public life that exists at the beginning of the twenty-first century.

## *What Does the Constitution Allow?*

When James Reichley wrote *Religion in American Politics* (1985), the utility of faith for public life needed to be demonstrated, unlike today when it is generally assumed. At the time, the emergence of religious-based politics seemed strange and in need of a broader perspective. Over time Reichley's treatment became the standard way to evaluate the place of faith in electoral politics, especially after evangelical Protestants became a fixture among the Republican party's most reliable constituents.

In evaluating the religious right's influence, Reichley's instinct was to turn to the American founding to see if born-again Protestants were infringing the accepted boundaries of American politics. He specifically examined the intentions of the Founding Fathers on religion in the new republic and the significance of the Establishment Clause in the First Amendment. In what now reads like an anachronistic description of the different schools of thought, Reichley identified four different positions on the relationship between religion and politics: separationists, social activists, accommodationists, and interventionists. Separationists and social activists both agreed that church and state should be kept strictly separate, but they differed on the role of churches in public life. Separationists wanted to confine religion to spiritual and moral matters; social activists looked for religious support for various political and social reforms. In turn, accommodationists and interventionists were less particular about the institutional separation of church and state but reached different conclusions about the role of churches in politics. Accommodationists believed that religion should set the moral direction for society while interventionists sought direct involvement by religious leaders in the political process of policy and legislation.

By 2000 Reichley's four categories seemed quaint, at least by the logic of the journalists, academics, and politicians who contributed to two different collections of essays, *What's God Got to Do with the American Experiment?* (2000) and *One Electorate Under God?* (2004). According to Alan Wolfe, the debate over religion has boiled down to Americans being unable to "make up their minds whether religion is primarily private, public, or some uneasy combination of the two." The reason for religion's obvious utility for public life, in the words of Richard Wightman Fox, is that it "allows people to grapple with the human mysteries that neither science nor politics can address," and "provides a force that science and politics can call on in the effort to understand and transform the social world." Faith's remarkable helpfulness prompted E. J. Dionne, Jr., and John J. DiIulio, Jr., to observe blithely that "God and arguments about God will always have a great deal to do with the American experiment."

The politicians who contributed to these books were no less sanguine about faith's usefulness, even if they disagreed on the shape that its influence should take. In *One Electorate Under God?* the former governor of New York, Mario Cuomo, who seeks a nonsectarian role for religion in politics, debated Mark Souder, a Republican congressman from Indiana who believes that as a Christian politician he cannot sever his own religious convictions from his duties as a legislator because "most political issues are moral issues." E. J. Dionne, Jr., and Kayla M. Drogosz introduced the exchange with a rather sunny estimate of religion's contribution to American politics. "Religion can certainly be both used and misused in politics," they write, "but secular political ideologies are also subject to use and misuse. . . . If those of strong views whether secular or religious, are ruled out of the public discussion, then democracy will only be impoverished."

And so the debate over the propriety of religion in American politics because of real constitutional questions has developed into the therapeutic dilemma of not wanting to exclude anyone from the political process. As Jeffrey Rosen, possibly the lone voice of dissent, writes in response to the Cuomo-Souder exchange, the danger of contemporary politics is that "all politicians, religious and secular, orthodox and progressive, will be forced to address the public in therapeutic and individualistic terms, which will contribute little to our understanding of the public policies these politicians are likely to enact."

## *What Does the Lord Require?*

Pockets of resistance to this recent wave of interest and respect for faith in public life exist, but they are increasingly rare. People like Lewis H. Lapham, the editor of *Harper's*, can be found among the unconvinced. He writes of the current presence of religion in the public square that "we used to know better, and to clear away the mess of sanctimony that now seeps into so much of the public mumblings about religion . . ." Lapham adds that "the delusional is no longer marginal, and we err on the side of folly if we continue to grant the boon of tolerance to people who mean to do us harm under the conviction" that they are building the kingdom of God. But generally speaking the attitude of secular elites has changed dramatically from twenty-five years ago, when the fundamentalists in Jerry Falwell's Moral Majority seemed a scary intrusion of conservative faith into partisan politics. As David Brooks recently confessed, recovering secularists like himself needed to admit that folks like him, who lived without religious direction and inspiration, are "not the norm." In all the attempts by scientists to explain religion, Brooks lamented, Western scholars had never seemed to consider the need to account scientifically for "those who do not feel the constant presence of God in their lives, who do not fill their days with rituals and prayers and garments that bring them into contact with the divine, and who do not believe that God's will should shape their public lives." So acceptable has religion become because of its presence in American politics that people without belief, not the Religious Right, may be the real oddity.

Still, before traditional Christians become too comfortable with the idea that faith is normal, they may consider two important reasons for being suspicious of the current friendliness to religion in public life. The first is that the apologists for faith-based politics appear to be incapable of recognizing that Christianity has historically been an exclusive and intolerant faith. In other words, because conservative Christians opposed deviance from received truth, a brief for Christian-friendly politics is inherently incompatible with a polity that includes a variety of faiths. Yet Martha Mindow, for example, suggests that any religion seems to provide "rich resources for envisioning a better world and motivating people to strive for it." In this same sentence Mindow concedes that religions may also be divisive and sectarian, therefore the need for a liberal democratic polity that will refine the dross of religion's antagonistic impulses from the gold of its moral and inspirational uplift. Even James Reichley, in the conclusion of his 1985 book, ended with an upbeat appraisal of religion in general. "Republican government depends for its health on values that over the not-so-long run must come from religion," he wrote. For this reason, "The key role of religion in maintaining the health of democracy gives all citizens, including those who are themselves without religious faith, a large stake in the way the churches carry out their roles in secular society." When Reichley ever so subtly shifted from religion to churches in that last sentence, he appeared to circumnavigate the impossibility of separating generic faith from particular creeds, rites, or communions. But despite the elision, the problem remains, both for Christian adherents who believe that their religion is true to the exclusion of other religious traditions, and for recovering secularists who want the moral capital of religion without its sectarian down payment. The faith that appears to offer the most benefits for public life (e.g., religion in general) is also one that has no respect for the particular and exclusive claims of any traditional religion, whether Christian, Jewish, Muslim, or Mormon. David Brooks may indeed believe that Orrin Hatch, the Mormon senator from Utah, is a capable legislator and fine example of the Mormon faith, but the *Times* columnist would also likely turn red if he learned all that Hatch needed to believe about Joseph Smith and the origins of Mormonism. The same would be true for Abraham, Mohammed, and Jesus Christ.

The second reason to be suspicious of the recent openness to religion in public life is that the estimates of specifically Christian contributions to American politics may in fact be dead wrong about the Christian religion. As great an intellectual and practical problem as it is to distill the good generic qualities of the world's religions from a particular faith's less attractive teachings and practices, this book is not about this specific difficulty. Instead it is about Christianity in the United States, and more about Protestantism than Roman Catholicism because of the former's larger involvement in and responsibility for the political developments of American society. The basic argument in the pages that follow is that Christianity in its classic formulations, especially the Protestant traditions of Lutheran, Reformed and Anglican, has very little to say about politics or the ordering of society. This does not mean that Christianity has nothing to say. Clearly, certain notions about men and women being created in the image of God, or about the sinfulness of human nature, or even about the legitimacy of personal property, have implications for politics. But beyond these implications, which may be applied in a variety of ways, Christianity has little to say explicitly about the sort of polity in which Americans have been living for the last 230 years. In fact, when Christians have tried to establish a Christian basis for the planks of political party platforms, or even for broad-based social reforms, they have fundamentally misconstrued their religion.

*A Secular Faith*, then, is a book more about the religious than the political side of the relationship of faith and American politics, like those books already cited. Any number of books explore the theme of religion and American politics. Where this one differs is by taking as its first priority not how Christianity can support the United States and its political institutions, or where it hurts them, but rather what Christianity itself may have to say about liberal democracy, a two-party system, or the separation of powers. Instead of asking what role is permissible for Christians and their religious institutions in a liberal democracy, this book begins with a very different question: What does Christianity require of its adherents politically? In applying this question to the relationship between faith and politics, rather than asking how much religion a liberal democracy can comfortably tolerate, the subject looks decidedly different. At the very least it requires some knowledge, first, of the religious meaning of Christianity. Once you clear this hurdle, negotiating America's political order looks like a piece of cake. This isn't to say that mastering Christianity 101 will solve America's political and cultural contests. It will not. My argument is that the basic teachings of Christianity are virtually useless for resolving America's political disputes, thus significantly reducing, if not eliminating, the dilemma of how to relate Christianity and American politics.

Too often in considerations of religion and American politics, Christianity has been misunderstood. But, more important, where Christians have tried to use their faith for political engagement they have generally distorted Christianity. The editors of the *New Republic* captured part of the distortion that attends politicized Christianity when they wrote of then Texas governor George W. Bush's decision to make June 11, 2000, Jesus Day, a holiday dedicated to Christ's example of "love, compassion, sacrifice, and service." An editorial in the magazine suggested that Bush did not glorify but "cheapened Jesus," because the reason for Christ's specialness is not simply his contribution to social service but his status as the second person of the Trinity. Attempts to employ the sacred and eternal for the common and temporal end up trivializing faith, which is "the certain fate of religion in the public square."

This problem might be simply a function of the generally vulgar style of American democracy and the contortions any candidate must undergo to be successful. A monarch might conceivably use Christianity in much more tasteful and dignified ways. But the problem I raise goes deeper than the tendency to reduce Christianity to bumper-sticker proportions on the campaign trail. The more profound issue is that Christianity is essentially a spiritual and eternal faith, one occupied with a world to come rather than the passing and temporal affairs of this world.

"Otherworldly" is the word usually employed to describe this side of Christianity. It is a characteristic that has generally been criticized by both nonbelievers and Christians themselves, either for underwriting a form of political quietism that ignores social injustice, or for sanctioning a form of spiritual monasticism in which the true believer's aim is to withdraw from the world. This book does not pretend to answer these criticisms, as important as they are. As a Protestant who firmly believes in the importance of worldly vocations as yielding genuinely spiritual rewards, and who just as firmly believes in the fundamental goodness of creation, I suggest that otherworldliness need not be as politically passive or culturally withdrawn as its critics allege. But the worldly assets of otherworldliness are not the point here. Instead I want those advocates of Christianity's public role and political responsibility to take seriously Jesus Christ's own words when he said, "My kingdom is not of this world." At one time in American history, sixty or so years ago, evangelical Protestants knew that those words involved an ambivalence about the rulers and principalities of this world. Now otherworldliness seems a fossil of an older time when faith knew its place. This is why not only evangelicals but Christianity's political allies must consider the otherworldly implications of the Christian religion.

Christ's words about the spiritual and eternal character of his rule may help resolve the perennial political difficulty that even religion's secular allies acknowledge. The trick of successfully employing any faith for public ends is to have access to the socially useful parts of religion while leaving behind its dogmatic and sectarian baggage. Christianity conceived as a secular faith avoids the problem of trying to cut this knot by acknowledging that it is impossible to sever. Christianity is a package that involves both love of God and love of neighbor. The latter love appears to be particularly useful for civil society because it nurtures respect, charity, truthfulness, and various other virtues. Love of God is not so politically utilitarian since it involves sensitivity to and condemnation of idolatry and profanity—in other words, false religion. Christianity is difficult because it has always insisted that unless the love of neighbor is bound up with love of God, the affection is not really Christian. As even H. L Mencken could see, "Religion, if it is to retain any genuine significance, can never be reduced to a series of sweet attitudes, possible to anyone not actually in jail for felony." The love of God, tenacity about worship, defensiveness about sacred rites, aversion to false religion—all are parts of genuine faith that make it impractical if not damaging for public life. The downside of religion in American politics is that the demands of public life tame Christianity's deeper significance and make it conform to standards alien to faith. Even so, what few advocates of faith-based politics seem to remember is that even though Christianity will not yield social or political norms, it does produce individual Christians who are supposed to love their neighbors, obey laws, and submit to the government, and who may be capable of holding public office responsibly. Christianity may be indifferent to life in the polis, but Christians themselves may not be. A fundamental difference exists between the work the church is called to do in proclaiming the message of Christianity and the vocations to which church members are called as citizens.

## The Illusion of Christian Politics

Noah Feldman recently analyzed the standoff over religion in American politics which is useful for the arguments that follow. He identifies two groups of political antagonists in the current debates about religion in American public life. One consists of "values evangelicals," people who themselves are not necessarily born-again Protestants but who are sympathetic to the notion, popularized by the Protestant right, that "the right answers to questions of government policy must come from the wisdom of religious tradition." Because religion provides the best way to live a peaceful and productive life, values evangelicals (which include Jews, Roman Catholics, and Muslims) believe government should "adopt those values and encourage them wherever possible." On the other side of the argument are "legal secularists," people for whom religion is a "matter of personal belief and choice largely irrelevant to government," and who fear that ultimately religion will be divisive socially and politically.

Where each group fails, according to Feldman, is by excluding those on the other side of the argument. Values evangelicals cannot find a set of values broad enough to include secularists, and legal secularists exclude values evangelicals by making religion a matter of personal preference. For Feldman, the talk of secession of blue states from red states after the 2004 election, though half-hearted, "bespeaks a division deeper than any other in our public life, a division that cannot be healed by the victory of either side."

Feldman's identification of these two political constituencies fails, however, to address those Christians who find no home with either values evangelicals *or* legal secularists. These adherents might best be called Christian secularists. They are Christians who dissent vigorously from the notion that government has any role in promoting faith or its moral teaching. The institution charged with this task is the church, through its teaching and worship, along with the instruction and counsel that comes through Christian families. For Christian secularists, the work of government lacks any overtly religious or spiritual purpose. This is not because Christian secularism has a certain political philosophy that involves government's religious neutrality. The Christian secularist who could not admit that history is littered with governments, both Christian and pagan, that used religion to promote social order and unity would be foolish. Instead the reason for keeping Christianity out of the hands of government stems from a particular understanding of the Christian religion and the institutions that bear responsibility for its propagation. Christian secularists disagree vigorously with values evangelicals both about the nature of Christianity and what it means for statecraft.

Where Christian secularists differ from legal secularists is a nicer question. On the matter of religion's role in public life, both sides would agree that faith is properly a private concern—with some qualifications. If private means the category we reserve for private schools, or private social clubs, that is, institutions that are not open to citizens but spring from voluntary associations, then calling Christianity a private affair makes perfect sense. The local congregation, the synod or assembly of a denomination, a parochial school—these are all private institutions, and their separate status from public bodies is an important contribution of the dissolution of Christendom that the American and French revolutions heralded when they disestablished the church. For theological reasons having to do with the role of divine agency in the development of human faith, Christian secularists might not be prepared to go as far as legal secularists in calling belief a matter of personal preference. But even here, in the personal dimensions of religion, calling acts of piety personal and private does seem basically sound from a Christian secularist's perspective. The reason is that the most intimate and sacred acts of religious devotion, those that fulfill the Christian's duty to love God, take place in either personal (the home) or private (the church) settings.

Beyond these similar perspectives on Christianity, Christian and legal secularists will likely agree or disagree on public policy or legislation or electoral candidates on the basis of political philosophy or gut instincts about public life, not on the basis of belief or nonbelief. From the Christian secularist's perspective, this is precisely how politics should proceed. Citizens and public officials should articulate their ideas about the true, the good, and the beautiful, or about the American Experiment, or about the GNP and tax rates, and debate these matters forthrightly. Because the United States is a free country, citizens have the liberty to marshal arguments about these ideals and policies on the basis of their religious convictions. But, as Feldman observes, if anything, the contribution of religion to recent American politics is not to offer unparalleled insights but to make elections, policy debates, and court appointments extremely partisan. Keeping religion out of politics along the lines proposed by Christian secularism may be a welcome relief to the fear-mongering practiced by both sides in the red-versus-blue-state partisanship that dominates so much of contemporary American political discourse.

Still, *A Secular Faith* is not intended as a solution to the culture wars. The arguments that follow may help reduce those hostilities, but the aim here is different. It is to show that efforts to use Christianity for public or political ends fundamentally distort the Christian religion because it is essentially an otherworldly faith.

To say that using Christianity for political purposes is a distortion of the faith is of course to dissent not only from Jerry Falwell or Jim Wallis but also from much more significant church luminaries, from parts of John Calvin to the encyclicals of John Paul II. For that reason the approach in the chapters that follow is more suggestive than assertive. Each chapter takes a popular truism about religion and American public life—from the idea that standards of public decency need a religious foundation, to the idea that faith is a strong aid to charity and humanitarian assistance— offers historical perspective, discusses how the Christian teaching behind this idea may be variously interpreted, and interacts with present-day arguments of relevance. Thus these are explicitly Christian questions about the various assumptions behind the emerging consensus on religion's positive role in American politics. By raising them, *A Secular Faith* may prompt Christianity's political advocates either to find another religion or, better still, avail themselves of the same political and philosophical wisdom that America's founders used to create a *novus ordo seclorum*, a new order for the ages.

# CHAPTER ONE

# *City on a Hill*

Among the succession of nineteenth-century European observers to assess the accomplishments and deficiencies of the United States, the Frenchman Alexis de Tocqueville is perhaps the most astute. More certain is the fact that he, unlike Harriet Martineau, Achille Murat, Frances Trollope, August Levasseur, or James Bryce, is still being read and assigned to students, even to the extent that the two volumes of *Democracy in America* have recently been retranslated and reprinted. Tocqueville marveled at the ability of Americans to create a republican and democratic form of government without the anguish that had afflicted his own nation. Christianity, he thought, was among the notable reasons for the United States' safe arrival as a liberal polity, a conclusion that endears Tocqueville to many American conservatives and may explain the longevity of his book's appeal. He observed, for instance, that "For Americans the ideas of Christianity and liberty are so completely mingled that it is almost impossible to get them to conceive of the one without the other." Tocqueville knew that this tie between religion and politics dumbfounded his "pedants" back home, where the assumption prevailed that "freedom and human happiness lack nothing but Spinoza's belief in the eternity of the world. . . ." But after seeing American democracy at work he was convinced that "Despotism may be able to do without faith, but freedom cannot."

Tocqueville attributed the genius of the American harmonization of Christianity and republicanism to New England's original settlers. Unlike the South, where slavery tainted the region's "mores and social condition," New England established the chief principles of the United States' "basic social theory." In addition to coming from the ranks of England's educated middle class, the region's early settlers "belonged to that English sect whose austere principles had led them to be called Puritans." For Tocqueville, Puritanism was more than simply a set of religious convictions. It also embraced "the most absolute democratic and republican theories." In a string of quotations from early New England sources to establish his point, Tocqueville concluded the section with a paragraph from John Winthrop, the first governor of the Massachusetts Bay Colony whose 1630 sermon, "A Model of Christian Charity," delivered on board the ship *Arbella*, would become a founding document in interpreting the American republic. Tocqueville himself did not render a close reading of Winthrop's sermon. His main point was to establish that New England Puritanism combined "two perfectly distinct elements," namely, the spirit of religion and the spirit of freedom. Although at odds in other civilizations, here they came together to give American society its exceptional character.

If Tocqueville himself paid only passing attention to Winthrop's sermon, political philosophers and historians have scoured its text, seeking the unique ingredients of the American experiment with limited government and popular sovereignty. Michael P. Zuckert regards Winthrop's words on board the *Arbella* as definitive for one major interpretation of America. In contrast to a secular reading of the American founding, Zuckert demonstrates how a prominent strain of political theorizing has traced the ideals of the Revolutionary generation to the seeds planted by Winthrop's conception of the Puritan "errand into the wilderness." According to Zuckert, this line of political reflection has looked to Puritanism for "the truly characteristic features of American politics." "The concern with the individual," he explains, "that is reflected in the American commitment to individual rights . . . had [its] source among the Puritans."

Among historians, Ruth H. Bloch offers a variation on a conventional theme when she addresses the degree to which Puritanism influenced the particular brand of republicanism that informed American independence from England and subsequent constitutional developments. She points out that Calvinistic notions of salvation informed "key" Revolutionary ideas about virtue and liberty. The Protestant doctrine of providence also imbued the American founding with a sense of higher purpose or millennial significance. In addition, the Founding Fathers drew upon older conceptions of a godly community to develop the basic ingredients of American nationalism. Bloch concludes that the historical roots of the American Revolution's ideology lay in seventeenth-century Puritanism. Even the "Lockean theory of the social contract as the basis for civil society was largely derived from Puritan ideas about the covenanted church." Assessments like those of Zuckert and Bloch give all the more credence to efforts to detect the kernel of American politics and identity in Winthrop's sermon that defined the New England experiment.

As grand and noble as his vision may have been just before setting foot in the New World, Winthrop likely had no idea that his reflections on the aims and purpose of Massachusetts Bay Colony would be the subject of so much scholarly scrutiny or the ideological basis for one of the most powerful nations in the history of the planet. Like his fellow Puritans, Winthrop's designs were so spiritual that the thought of establishing a nation that would rival other worldly powers was more a sign of sinful ambition than godly service. According to Francis J. Bremer, the author of a recent study of Winthrop, the sermon had more to do with local realities than with visions of empire. "The loving community [Winthrop] spoke of in 'Christian Charity,'" Bremer writes, "was an extension of the community of mutual aid and comfort he experienced growing up in Groton."

Even if Winthrop's intentions were far different from the meanings later scholars would find in his words, one of his religious references in the sermon would take hold in the imagination of generations of Americans. He believed that the new society across the Atlantic was uniquely the result of divine blessing. The phrase "city on a hill" captured this conviction, at least in conveying the idea that New England was not merely a political experiment but also a society endowed with redemptive significance. Even if Winthrop himself did not envision that holy city to encompass Oregon, Oklahoma, or even Ohio, his employment of this biblical image became the trope that later orators would use to tie the Puritan founding to U.S. expansion, power, and prestige. In effect, Winthrop's sermon became the benchmark for American exceptionalism. For as long as long as Americans have thought their nation to be at the cutting edge of divine providence, they have looked to the first English settlers in New England for inspiration and motivation. But that interpretation of divine favor is precisely the reason why Christians who today engage American public life would do well to decouple their endeavors from the Puritan errand.

## Holy Urbanism

"A Model of Christian Charity" may have been unusual as a Puritan sermon for not having a biblical text (though it was chock-full of scriptural images and quotations), but it was fairly conventional in explaining the religious rationale for the voyage that brought four ships filled with roughly four hundred English Protestants and their belongings to the New World. Winthrop began with a proposition that most Englishmen believed, that God "hath so disposed of the condition of mankind, as in all times some must be rich, some poor, some high and eminent in power and dignity; others mean and in submission." But he likely feared that not all his hearers, no matter their religious zeal or discipline, would long abide such a blunt depiction of the various social ranks and implicit duties to be determined by divine providence. So Winthrop's trick was to go beyond a mere assertion of the duties and privileges incumbent upon the company of emigrés and turn the acceptance of these social stations into something lovable—hence the sermon's title, "A Model of Christian Charity."

As he explained the reasons for such love, the law of nature was insufficient. From it the best one could hypothesize was either a state of innocence where all men and women related harmoniously, or a condition where defense against the assaults of enemies was a reasonable reaction. But the law of the gospel required love even of one's enemies. As such, Winthrop suggested, the Christian society into which these Puritans were about to enter should be characterized by charity. This was no call for sentiment or warm feelings. By charity Winthrop meant a type of social bond in which this Puritan band would share, lend, and provide for one another financially and physically. As members of the church, he explained, "all the parts of this body being thus united are made so contiguous in a special relation as they must needs partake of each other's strength and infirmity; joy and sorrow, weal and woe. If one member suffers, all suffer with it, if one be in honor, all rejoice with it." Winthrop was not discounting the value of "sensitivity and sympathy" to one's neighbors and fellow citizens. But when he asserted that "among the members of the same body, love and affection are reciprocal in a most equal and sweet kind of commerce," he was undoubtedly referring in that last word to more than personal interaction but also to economic and political order.

What has attracted the most attention in Winthrop's sermon, making it in the words of Andrew Delbanco "a kind of Ur-text in

American literature," is less his understanding of charity than his appeal to the idea of the covenant. In the section of his remarks where he applied the general truths about the law of the gospel to the particular circumstances of the Massachusetts Bay Colony, Winthrop appealed to the language of covenant. "Thus stands the cause between God and us," he declared, "We are entered into covenant with Him for this work. We have taken out a commission. The Lord hath given us leave to draw our own articles. We have professed to enterprise these and those accounts, upon these and those ends. We have hereupon besought Him of favor and blessing." At which point followed the standard logic of blessings and curses that biblical covenants always included. For the peace and prosperity of God's blessing, this covenanted people would need to execute a "strict performance of the articles contained" in the covenant. But if the Puritans embraced "this present world" and prosecuted their "carnal intentions," Winthrop warned, "the Lord will surely break out in wrath against us, and be revenged of such a people, and make us know the price of the breach of such a covenant."

On the surface, Winthrop's ideals appear to be remote from the assertions or legislation expressed in either the Declaration of Independence or the U.S. Constitution, but that has not stopped scholars or politicians from appealing to Puritanism as the basis for the American experiment. On the one hand, Winthrop's religious motivation is explicitly ecclesial; the new colony was designed to be a commune for those within the Puritan fold. The references to God in the Declaration of Independence are generic at best, and the republic envisioned during the 1770s and 1780s, though generally Protestant, was scarcely one in which any Founding Father might have plausibly asserted, as Winthrop did, that "we must love brotherly without dissimulation, we must love one another with a pure heart fervently. We must bear one another's burdens. We must not look only on our own things, but also on the things of our brethren." On the other hand, the due form of government that

Winthrop alluded to would hardly serve as a model for the United States, even if some of his ideas may have survived in the state constitutions of Massachusetts or Connecticut. As Gordon S. Wood has observed, the Founding Fathers' intellectual rationale for the new republic was "imprecise, confused, and eclectic." Winthrop's sermon did resonate with the founding generation of patriots, especially those who believed that virtue was necessary for republican government. But no matter how widely disseminated the later account of America's New England roots, Winthrop's Puritanism was hardly a way station on the way to Jefferson's natural rights or the Constitution's checks and balances.

If the Puritan understanding of the covenant appealed to in "The Model of Christian Charity" did not inspire the legal arrangements of the American founding, Winthrop's understanding of the divinely sanctioned character of the endeavor in the New World would nonetheless have considerable meaning for later generations of Americans. The concluding paragraphs of his sermon refer to a part of Christ's Sermon on the Mount that numerous politicians and clergy would also use to describe the exceptional nature if not messianic purpose of the American project. That verse from the gospel of Matthew in the fifth chapter reads: "You are the light of the world. A city on a hill cannot be hid" (vs. 14). The phrase "city on a hill" is the one that many typically associate with Winthrop's sermon. It clearly expressed his own understanding of the Puritan errand, informed later Puritan assessments of the colony's strengths and weaknesses, and would eventually set the standard by which to judge United States domestic and foreign policy.

The whole paragraph in which this phrase is found in Winthrop's sermon is worth considering in order to understand his purpose in appealing to this biblical image:

> Now the only way to avoid this shipwreck, and to provide for our posterity, is to follow the counsel of Micah, to do justly, to love

mercy, to walk humbly with our God. For this end, we must be knit together, in this work, as one man. We must entertain each other in brotherly affection. We must be willing to abridge ourselves of our superfluities, for the supply of others' necessities. We must uphold a familiar commerce together in all meekness, gentleness, patience and liberality. We must delight in each other; make others' conditions our own; rejoice together, mourn together, labor and suffer together, always having before our eyes our commission and community in the work, as members of the same body. So shall we keep the unity of the spirit in the bond of peace. The Lord will be our God, and delight to dwell among us, as His own people, and will command a blessing upon us in all our ways, so that we shall see much more of His wisdom, power, goodness and truth, than formerly we have been acquainted with. We shall find that the God of Israel is among us, when ten of us shall be able to resist a thousand of our enemies; when He shall make us a praise and glory that men shall say of succeeding plantations, "may the Lord make it like that of New England." For we must consider that we shall be as a city upon a hill. The eyes of all people are upon us. So that if we shall deal falsely with our God in this work we have undertaken, and so cause Him to withdraw His present help from us, we shall be made a story and a by-word through the world. We shall open the mouths of enemies to speak evil of the ways of God, and all professors for God's sake. We shall shame the faces of many of God's worthy servants, and cause their prayers to be turned into curses upon us till we be consumed out of the good land whither we are going.

With this peroration Winthrop clearly raised the stakes for his fellow passengers. To "keep the unity of the spirit in the bond of peace" was certainly a sufficiently tall order. Some of the Protestants who stayed behind in England may have considered Winthrop's rendering of Christian charity to be a tad utopian. But to add to this already unattainable standard the extra burden of having the whole world watching was to give no relief to the faith-

ful about to disembark in a land without any of the comforts of settled villages, regular ministers, or English customs. As Edmund S.
Morgan puts it, Winthrop and his Puritan followers "had undertaken to establish a society where the will of God would be observed in every detail, a kingdom of God on earth."

When a few years later Morgan turned to the topic of the
American Revolution and the influence of the Puritans on it, he
virtually ignored Winthrop's desire to establish the kingdom of
God on earth. Instead Morgan stressed—as would many historians
and political scientists—the importance of Puritan notions about
human depravity, civil society as a covenanted arrangement, and a
work ethic that emphasized frugality and looked warily upon luxury. Morgan is entirely persuasive in noting that the "appeal for
restoration of the frugality and simplicity which men of [one] generation thought had prevailed in the preceding one" is a constant
theme in American history and owes much of its resilience to the
Puritans. But equally important was the Puritan conception of the
millennium that Winthrop's sermon tapped. Just as the Puritan errand was a significant episode in God's redemptive plan for his
elect, so too the rise and development of the United States would
have importance beyond the ordinary affairs of kings and states. By
appealing to "the city on a hill," Winthrop fused divine intentions
for the church with human efforts to construct a just and harmonious society. Although America's Founding Fathers and later officials jettisoned Winthrop's theology that distinguished the elect
from the damned, they found it difficult to shake the Puritan conviction that God had chosen to grant to the social order of the
United States special privileges and responsibilities.

## *Nation on a Hill*

Millennialism is a word from the lexicon of Christian theology that
generally connotes strange and obscure teachings about the end of

human history. Periodically throughout the course of Christianity certain believers have ventured predictions about the end of the world, based on either overwhelming instances of human depravity or amazingly beneficent outpourings of personal and social wellness. This sense that the end of the world as we know it is near, either through the agency of divine judgment or the inauguration of the kingdom of God on earth, is what most associate with millennialism. The Millerites of the 1840s became infamous for believing predictions that Christ's return would take place on a specific day in 1844. But millennialism has also taken less time-sensitive forms. For some evangelical Protestants the course of human history is but a stage for the cosmic contest between God and Satan, and the earth's affairs may be read accordingly as pregnant with millennial significance. The phenomenal popularity of the novel series *Left Behind*, by Tim LaHaye and Jerry Jenkins, is the most recent example of millennialism's remarkable appeal. More specifically, however, the word refers to a thousand-year period of Christ's rule. Even without prompting notions about an immediate end of human history, it has inspired Christians to think about the prospects of a world in which sin and suffering have ceased, and when virtue and righteousness will prevail.

Ideas about a millennium have been much more widespread and conventional within American Protestantism than the examples of the Millerites or the *Left Behind* novels suggest. Whether or not someone believes in a literal or figurative thousand-year period of peace and spiritual prosperity, most Protestants have some conception of the relationship between this world and the one to come, when human history finishes. Eschatology is the technical term that theologians use to categorize ideas about the form of life and period of history to follow current patterns. This form of Christian teaching has much more to do with the nature of heaven than with the state of persons after death. The two are obviously related since the status of a person, whether as a believer or unbe-

liever, has almost everything to do with his or her eternal resi-
dence. Eschatology proper concerns not simply the fate of the
person but more broadly the status of the created order (the current heaven and earth) in the next world, that is, the new heavens
and earth. Will the new state of affairs be generally an improvement upon the current patterns of earthly existence? Will it be radically different, involving some sort of cataclysmic event that trans-
forms the existing creation? Or will it be an entirely new form of
existence?

As bizarre as these questions may sound to modern secular
ears, they are common fare for theologians and at once demonstrate how peculiar is the Christian religion despite more than
two centuries of its domestication for American public life. Those
students of divinity who explore these questions have been ab-
sorbed with the direction and goal of human history. Some
schools of Christian theology have been more optimistic about
the influence of Christianity upon historical developments. These
have often been called postmillennial, which means that human
history will continue to improve as the church expands and eventually ushers in the kingdom of God, or the era of Christ's millennial rule. This scheme of eschatology stresses continuity between this world and the one to come. The other eschatological
outlook, one more pessimistic, goes by the name premillennial. It
sees human history generally as a series of failures, after which
Christ returns to establish the kingdom of God. Obviously the
premillennial position emphasizes discontinuity between current
earthly arrangements, because of human sinfulness, and the need
for divine intervention to establish a new and sin-free pattern of
human existence.

This all too simplistic overview of Christian eschatology is necessary for placing in perspective American Protestants' ideas about
their nation's role and place in human history. For most English-
speaking American Protestants, from Jonathan Edwards to Harry

Emerson Fosdick, both chronologically and theologically, postmillennialism was the dominant construction of salvation history. Basic to this conviction was the idea that the millennium, the time prophesied in the Bible as the era of Christ's reign on earth, would emerge from the activities and labors of Christians. Traditionally, as Augustine had conceived it, the millennium was a spiritual reality in which Christ's rule was already evident after the Resurrection within the affairs of the church while Christians awaited Christ's return. But in certain sectors of the sixteenth-century Protestant movement, excitement about the prospects of reformation, combined with Roman Catholic opposition to reform, generated speculations about the dawn of the millennial age. The Puritans who accompanied Winthrop to New England carried with them hopes for the millennium that colored the understanding of their own mission. The New Englanders' sense of being a covenanted people, a new Israel, ordained to accomplish a significant work in the coming of the new heavens and new earth, waxed and waned throughout the seventeenth century, depending in part on the political fortunes of the the Puritans both in the old and new worlds. But in the eighteenth century the revivals of the First Great Awakening breathed new life into colonial Protestant hopes for the coming of God's kingdom in the New World. These millennial hopes proved to be useful to the colonists, who were overwhelmingly Protestant. Later in the century they mixed biblical imagery and political philosophy to conceive of the American Revolution and the formation of a new nation as part of grand millennial accomplishment that would establish a new order for the ages. According to James Maclear's survey of millennial ideas during the American Revolution, the Founding Fathers had no trouble conceiving of the new nation as a new Israel, "with all its implications of special election, vocation, and guidance." He adds that Christian patriots "saw nothing incongruous in linking Moses and Winthrop and Washington, who 'with his worthy companions and valiant band, were instrumental in the hand of JESUS, the King of Kings, to deliver this American Israel from their troubles.'"

Although millennial hopes inspired religious eccentrics as diverse as Joseph Smith or the Jehovah's Witnesses, ideas locating the coming of the kingdom in the United States also found respectable outlets in the various institutions that American Protestants founded. One example comes from Francis Wayland, at the time president of Brown College (later university). In a sermon delivered in 1830 before the American Sunday School Union meeting in Philadelphia, "Encouragements to Religious Efforts," Wayland believed he discerned in American affairs the dawning of an age even more glorious than the Protestant Reformation. The spread of education combined with technological advances had resulted in a historic transformation. "Never have there been presented so many or so great encouragements," he declared, "for a universal effort to bring the world into cordial subjection to Jesus Christ." With a little more religious effort the millennium might indeed arrive with the United States inaugurating the new age. If a revival of religion occurred,

> the principles of the Gospel may be made to regulate the detail of individual and national intercourse; and high praises to God may be heard from every habitation; and perhaps before the youth of this generation be gathered to their fathers, there may burst forth upon these highly-favored States the light of Millennial Glory. What is to prevent it? . . . I do believe that the option is put into our hands. It is for us . . . to say, whether the present religious movement shall be onward, until it terminate in the universal triumph of the Messiah, or whether all shall go back again. . . . The church has for two thousand years been praying, "Thy kingdom come." Jesus Christ is saying unto us, "It shall come if you desire it."

So widespread was Protestant optimism about the United States role in the dawn of the kingdom of God that inventions like the telegraph could elicit from editors of women's magazines sentiments like the following:

> This noble invention is to be the means of extending civilization, republicanism, and Christianity over the earth. It must and will be extended to nations half-civilized, and thence to those now savage and barbarous. Our government will be the grand center of this mighty influence. . . . The beneficial and harmonious operation of our institutions will be seen, and similar ones adopted. Christianity must speedily follow them; and we shall behold the grand spectacle of a whole world, civilized, republican, and Christian. Then will wrong and injustice be forever banished. Every yoke shall be broken, and the oppressed go free. Wars will cease from the earth. Men "shall beat their swords into plough shares, and the spears into pruning-hooks. Nation shall not lift up sword against nation; neither shall they learn war any more"; for each man shall feel that every other man is his neighbor—his brother. Then shall come to pass the millennium, when "they shall teach no more every man his neighbor, and every man his brother, saying Know ye the Lord; for all shall know him, from the least of them unto the greatest."

The mix of biblical teaching, republican politics, and technological innovation was indeed a potent elixir that turned otherwise sober Protestants tipsy with visions of America as *novus ordo seclorum*.

After the Civil War the binge of this kind of optimism about the fortunes of America forced a reaction of millennial pessimism. The doctrines of dispensational premillennialism (the ones informing the *Left Behind* novels by LaHaye and Jenkins) originated before the war between North and South but gained popularity in the aftermath of that military contest. What this form of millennial speculation yielded was a gloomy reading of the United States and its place in salvation history. Instead of believing that the advance of republican forms of government, technological progress, and the gospel would usher in the kingdom, dispensationalism taught that divine judgment and retribution would characterize the inauguration of Christ's millennial rule. This reading of human history appealed to Protestants who saw the Civil War as a defeat for the cause of Christian civilization. Dispensationalism's attraction also extended to Protestants outside the South who sensed that the technological and industrial progress of the late nineteenth century was not a sign of the kingdom's dawn but rather a demonstration of apostasy. The threat of imminent judgment also proved to be a boon to evangelism, in the form of large-scale urban revivals like those led by Dwight L. Moody, Billy Sunday, and Billy Graham. To be sure, in the dispensationalist scheme, God still had a special covenantal relationship with the United States. But instead of being the site of his special favor, it had degenerated into a nation deserving judgment.

These two Protestant versions of the millennium, inherently antagonistic, were responsible in large part for the fundamentalist-modernist controversy of the 1920s. Where liberals through their Social Gospel–colored glasses saw progress and cultural advance, the squint of fundamentalists noticed only the wages of America's infidelity and immorality. Beyond the fundamentalist-modernist controversy, rival millennial visions would continue to inform the differences between liberal or mainstream Protestants and fundamentalists, also known as evangelicals in the more recent kinder and gentler iteration. Of course the cultural upheavals of the 1960s forced each side to reassess its eschatological outlook. The anti-Americanism of the left prompted liberal Protestants to adjust America's place in God's plan, often to the point of substituting global notions of civilization for formerly national ones. Likewise, the cultural contests of the 1960s became the lever that pushed evangelicals out of their religious ghettos and into the public square, where the temptation of electoral victory sometimes got the better of their cultural pessimism. Still, the competing outlooks that divide what liberals and evangelicals bring to politics is the legacy of a millennial outlook that either optimistically or pessimistically has endowed the United States with redemptive significance.

Practically no American Protestant would ever confuse America with heaven on earth. But the United States as a chosen nation has been a common notion, one with fairly direct ties to the sort of logic that helped John Winthrop describe Puritan efforts in the New World as the establishment of a city on a hill. As Abraham Lincoln, in an 1861 address to the New Jersey state legislature, said of his intentions to preserve the Union and defend the Constitution, "I shall be most happy indeed if I shall be an humble instrument in the hands of the Almighty, and of this, his almost chosen people, for perpetuating the object of that great struggle." Honest Abe may have hedged on the degree to which the United States was a site of divine election, but the widespread acceptance of America's redemptive role was sufficient for even a doubting president to affirm it. Sentiments like Lincoln's continue to inspire believers and nonbelievers alike.

## *Which City?*

The specific phrase "city on a hill" comes in a well-known but variously interpreted biblical passage, Christ's Sermon on the Mount. It runs for several chapters in the gospel of Matthew and is supposed to contain some of the most practical and profound teaching about the Christian's responsibilities in the real world. In this string of maxims and exhortations are some of the most popular expressions of Christian duty and devotion, such as the Golden Rule and the Lord's Prayer. The imagery of a city on a hill appears early in the discourse and follows immediately the equally well-known Beatitudes. After identifying the blessed people in the kingdom of God—the poor, the mourners, the righteous, the merciful, the pure, the peacemakers, and the persecuted—Christ employs two metaphors to help his disciples understand their responsibilities. These are salt and light: "You are the salt of the earth," and "You are the light of the world." The idea of a city on a hill elaborates the metaphor of light: "A city set on a hill cannot be hid. Nor do men light a lamp and put it under a bushel, but on a stand, and it gives light to all in the house. Let your light so shine before men, that they may see your good works and give glory to your Father who is in heaven." Following as it does the Beatitudes, this particular instruction confirms the earlier point that the disciples should persevere in well-doing even if persecuted or beleaguered, because such good works will ultimately either be vindicated or have a salutary effect. In other words, not even obscure acts of kindness or humility are insignificant; they have the potential of demonstrating the power of true religion.

For John Winthrop to appeal to this biblical passage was not particularly remarkable for the Puritans found themselves in a situation not entirely unlike the first followers of Christ. They felt persecuted and needed encouragement to persist on the straight and narrow path. To find such aid in a familiar passage that granted a higher purpose and meaning to good works no matter how insignificant or arduous made perfect sense. The history of Christianity is rife with similar invocations of this part of the Sermon on the Mount.

Where Winthrop and later American followers may have misunderstood the idea of a city on a hill was in identifying the city of which Christ spoke with the society that the English would establish in the New World or, even as Lincoln had it, with the persons identified in the Constitution's opening line, "We the people." Commentators on the Sermon on the Mount have long recognized that the import of Christ's instructions was not political but ecclesiastical. For instance, Martin Luther believed that the particular phrase "city on a hill," and the metaphor of shining light that accompanied it, referred specifically to the apostles first and then to those would follow them in the office of the Christian ministry. In his commentary on this section of Matthew's gospel, Luther wrote, "Therefore, it surely is and remains the office of the apostles alone both to rebuke aright the real internal vices, and again to heal, comfort and cheer up all poor distressed consciences, and allow no one to go unrebuked in wrong-doing or uninstructed and unencouraged in what is good." He added that Christ's intent here was to appoint and consecrate preachers who would be "salt and light," meaning that they would publicly proclaim the the gospel. Luther asserted:

> . . . because Christ means that this office shall be exercised not secretly or in only one place, but openly, throughout the world; and he shows them plainly enough, what they have to expect from the world, when he says: "A city that is set on a hill cannot be hid. Neither do men light a candle and set it under a bushel," etc. That is as much as to say: He who wants to be a light must see to it that he do not creep into a corner, but stand forth publicly and be not afraid. For so it goes, as we said before, that those who are called to be apostles, and shine, do not like to come to the front, allow themselves to be frightened off by threats, danger, persecution, or are befooled with friendship, favor, honor and worldly good, so that they do not come forward and open their mouths, but creep into corners, hide behind the hills, and shut up their whistles.

Luther's rendering of the city on a hill stemmed from his own perceptions of the abuses in the church of his day and the reforms he believed were necessary. But even discounting the circumstances of sixteenth-century German Christianity, Luther's reading of this passage was decidedly free from nationalistic overtones, a feature all the more remarkable since the Protestant reformer's arguments were often tinged with appeals to German liberation from Roman tyranny (e.g., captivity).

Another example of reading the city-on-a-hill metaphor in churchly rather than political or nationalistic categories comes from Luther's junior contemporary, John Calvin. The Geneva pastor was more concerned than Luther with the personal implications of this metaphor. For Calvin, both images of salt and light had direct bearing on the character of Christ's hearers. They were to live exemplary lives. "The doctrine, which has been entrusted to them," Calvin wrote, "is shown to be so closely connected with a good conscience and a devout and upright life, that the corruption, which might be tolerated in others, would in them be detestable and monstrous." Even so, he is no less explicit in stating that these instructions from Christ have direct reference to ecclesiastical rather than political affairs. Calvin conceded that all Christians should conduct themselves in a commendable way. But because "the preaching of the Gospel was committed to the apostles above others, and is now committed to pastors of the Church," Christ placed them "in this rank on the condition that they shall shine, as from an elevated situation, on all others."

Of course Winthrop and the Puritans were closer to the interpretation of Luther and Calvin than those later Americans who applied the city-on-a-hill metaphor to their nation. Winthrop conceived of the new society in New England as a band of Christians, so holding it to the standards that Christ had established for the church was neither implausible nor unreasonable. Only after the difficulties of passing on the Puritan faith to the second generation emerged did Puritan leaders begin to hedge on some of those church requirements, wondering how to incorporate nonbelievers into a godly community. Still, the Puritans' eventual compromises were not so much an indictment of their cause, or a diminution of their city on Beacon Hill, as they were an exposure of the anomaly that afflicted their mission from the outset. Like Christians since the conversion of Constantine, Puritans conflated many of the norms for the church with those of civil society. In effect Massachusetts Bay was an effort to perpetuate Christendom. The godly commonwealth of New England, however, turned out to have as many difficulties in execution as it did in Christian Europe. But the American Revolution breathed some vigor into the old Puritan vision. Granted, the political order of the Constitution was a long way from the Holy Roman Empire. But the fusion of political and religious ideals was still pronounced. It became more pronounced in the idea of the United States as a chosen nation whose mission was to spread the gospel of Christianity and liberal democracy first across the continent and then around the world.

The redemptive urbanism of the Puritan founders and their American Protestant descendants may have repeated the errors of Christendom, but as Augustinians they might well have reconsidered the significance of the city they hoped would be a beacon, whether religious or political, for the rest of the world. The American invocation of the city-on-a-hill metaphor has been at considerable odds with the old urbanism of the Bishop of Hippo, who had to make sense of Christianity's alleged responsibility for the fall of the Roman Empire. When the tribes from northern Europe, formerly known as barbarians, sacked Rome during the early fifth century and broke the back of imperial rule in the western half of the empire, a variety of critics blamed Christianity for Rome's demise. If Constantine had not converted and established the church as the state religion, thus turning his back on the variety of Roman and Greek deities that had apparently blessed the empire, Rome might have endured. The invasion of the barbarians, in effect, was the revenge of the other gods. To this argument Augustine responded with *The City of God*, a book he began writing soon after the Vandals had raided Rome.

On one level, Winthrop's idea of the Puritan errand into the wilderness of the New World as a city on a hill accurately followed Augustine's own configuration of cities in the grand scheme of salvation. For the Bishop of Hippo, two cities competed for human allegiance and devotion, the earthly and the heavenly, and these two cities corresponded to the state of human existence either outside or under the influence of divine grace. Augustine explained, "Two cities have been formed by two loves: the earthly by the love of self, even to the contempt of God; the heavenly by the love of God, even to the contempt of self." "The former," he added, "glories in itself, the latter in the Lord. For the one seeks glory from men; but the greatest glory of the other is God, the witness of conscience. The one lifts up its head in its own glory; the other says to its God, 'Thou art my glory, and the lifter up of mine head'" [bk. 14, ch. 28].

The spiritual difference between these cities had obvious consequences for the politics of each. According to Augustine, "In the one, the princes and the nations it subdues are ruled by the love of ruling; in the other, the princes and the subjects serve one another in love, the latter obeying, while the former take thought for all." The self-love of the earthly city, consequently, exalted "its own strength, represented in the persons of its rulers." In contrast, the citizens of the heavenly city were characterized by saying to their God, "I will love Thee, O Lord, my strength." Clearly Winthrop and his fellow Puritans were hoping to endow their godly commonwealth with the attributes of the heavenly city, and in certain circumstances were particularly gifted in spotting those qualities of the earthly city exhibited by English political and ecclesiastical authorities.

But as antithetical as the two cities were in Augustine's mind, and as much as that antagonism might separate believers from nonbelievers, he had no illusions about dispensing with the need for the earthly city this side of heaven. In fact, despite being characterized by self-love, the earthly city was also capable of producing much good. Augustine affirmed that "the things which [the earthly city] desires cannot justly be said to be evil, for it is itself, in its own kind, better than all other human good." The reason for such a positive estimate was the peace and prosperity that the rule of the earthly city procured for its citizens. Although often secured by war, the resolution and peace to follow were "good things, and without doubt the gifts of God." Augustine did not confuse this earthly good with the higher good that characterized the heavenly city. In fact he warned that if the earthly city neglected "the better things of the heavenly city, which are secured by eternal victory and peace never-ending," it would be marred by covetousness and would confuse the blessings of this life with those of the life to come. Such a pursuit of earthly good would result only in "misery." Even so, simply because self-love characterized the earthly city, Augustine still recognized the goodness and usefulness of its accomplishments.

Nor did the basic selfishness of the earthly city prevent the Bishop of Hippo from acknowledging the legitimate duties that citizens of the heavenly city had as members of the earthly city. Simply because of their allegiance to the kingdom of heaven, Christians were not exempt from earthly responsibilities and cares for the societies in which they lived. According to Augustine, "So long as [the heavenly city] lives like a captive and a stranger in the earthly city, though it has already received the promise of redemption, and the gift of the Spirit as the earnest of it, it makes no scruple to obey the laws of the earthly city, whereby the things necessary for the maintenance of this mortal life are administered." Of course, this could sound like a grudging acceptance of earthly politics, and for a host of Augustinian theologians throughout church history this pilgrim perspective on the social order functioned as an important hedge upon the temptation to identify the cause of the empire or the nation with the ultimate purposes of God. But as reluctant as Augustine's acknowledgment of earthly citizenship may have appeared, it was not a renunciation, as some mystics, pietists, and fundamentalists would have it, of the world and its politics. Here Augustine made a fundamental distinction between cult and culture, or between religious and secular affairs. In the former, Christians and non-Christians would have to part company and exist with varying degrees of antagonism, or as Augustine put it, the heavenly city would have to be "obnoxious" to the earthly city. But in secular affairs, including politics, Christians would not scruple about "diversities in the manners, laws, and institutions whereby earthly peace is secured and maintained, . . . recognizing that, however various these are, they all tend to one and the same end of earthly peace." The only restriction upon Christians observing the laws and customs of the earthly city was whether such observance injured "faith and godliness." Otherwise believers were free to be good citizens of the earthly city by desiring and maintaining "a common agreement among men regarding the acquisition of the necessaries of life."

From an Augustinian perspective, then, the city on a hill that the Puritans hoped to build and that later American Christians believed their nation to be, was an impossibility. The Puritan vision was guilty of confusing the earthly and heavenly cities, hoping that Boston or later Washington, D.C., would function as the Jerusalem of the new heavens and the new earth. The reason for this confusion had much to do with a failure to grasp Augustine's important distinction between the sacred and the secular. The Achilles heel of many Christian politicians, American or not, has been the failure to recognize the impermanence of secular politics, that it is a temporary arrangement to restrain evil and promote justice until the dawn of a new period in the history of salvation. Even though the politics of the earthly city may proceed from selfishness or irreligious motivation, its authority is still legitimate and something in which believers may participate.

On the flip side of this distinction is Augustine's recognition that a partial manifestation of the heavenly city already exists in this age of secular rule, and it can be found in the church. As Luther and Calvin recognized, the church, with its clerical duties of preaching and worship, was the city on a hill that Christ apparently had in mind in the Sermon on the Mount. This city's politics merely foreshadowed the heavenly city because the church in this stage of history was primarily a means to the consummation of history, the second coming of Christ, and the dawn of the new heavens and new earth. The ultimate peace of the heavenly city, as Augustine explained, would not arise until "this mortal life shall give place to one that is eternal, and our body shall be no more this animal body which by its corruption weighs down the soul, but a spiritual body feeling no want. . . ." In the present, Christians enjoyed this peace only by faith; in the next phase of history they would know it by sight.

## Promised Land

As much as the imagery of city on a hill may appear anachronistic, a worn-out metaphor used for the last time by the likes of Ronald Reagan during the cold war, for a handful of thoughtful academics and pundits Winthrop's phrase still has value in describing the United States. Recently Samuel P. Huntington argued that the United States has a distinct identity which the advocates of multiculturalism, cosmopolitanism, or internationalism cannot revise no matter how much they might discredit or ignore it. At the core of American identity is a creed that is deeply rooted in the Anglo-American Protestant culture planted by Winthrop's Puritan comrades and watered by succeeding generations of citizens and believers. According to Huntington, the "American Creed" stands for such cultural landmarks as "the English language; Christianity; religious commitment; English concepts of the rule of law, the responsibility of rulers, and the rights of individuals; and dissenting Protestant values of individualism, the work ethic, and the belief that humans have the ability and the duty to try to create a heaven on earth, a 'city on a hill.'" This creed deserves much of the credit for making the nation it unified great: it attracted "millions of immigrants" and made possible a society full of "economic opportunities."

One of the remarkable aspects of Huntington's book is its defense of Protestant contributions to the United States at a time when Protestant leadership, whether mainline or evangelical—the folks in the pews are a different story—is much less confident about American Protestantism's record. Without a single gesture of irony, Huntington summarizes Protestant influence upon America as follows:

> In the seventeenth and eighteenth centuries, Americans defined their mission in the New World in biblical terms. They were a "chosen people," on an "errand in the wilderness," creating "the new Israel" or the "new Jerusalem" in what was clearly "the promised land." America was the site of a "new Heaven and a new earth, the home of justice," God's country. The settlement of America was vested, as Scavan Bercovitch put it, "with all the emotional, spiritual, and intellectual appeal of a religious quest." This sense of holy mission was easily expanded into millenarian themes of America as "the redeemer nation" and "the visionary republic."

One suspects that official Protestants dissent from Huntington's summary less because they believe Christianity is irrelevant to a just and egalitarian society than because such Protestant chauvinism comes across disrespectfully to non-Protestant Americans who sometimes suffered when dissenting from the American creed. But to the leaders of the Protestant right, any number of radio-talk-show hosts, and a large portion of red-state Americans, Huntington's depiction of Protestant America has great appeal because it resuscitates an older set of religious and cultural assumptions held before 1970 by most Anglo-American Protestants.

The trouble with Huntington's argument is not historical but theological. The idea that a heavenly city could be established within the confines of an earthly city was one that gave pause to Christians throughout church history, Constantinople, Rome, Christendom, or the Holy Roman Empire notwithstanding. Jerusalem was for the Israelites one city that might lay claim to a heavenly origin. But the coming of Christ for Christians meant that the city of which their savior spoke transcended any single city or any specific nation. Unlike Judaism, Christianity entered the history of religions without claims to any particular land or region. And although it clearly had historical roots in the Mediterranean world of antiquity, one of Christ's most beloved injunctions to his followers was to go into the whole world and make disciples. As Augustine recognized, the relationship between creed and place was dramatically different for Christians than it had been for the Old Testament saints. After the coming of Christ, the political arrangements that characterized a truly chosen nation moved to an institution, namely the church, whose mission was to draw members from every race, tribe, and state. These Christians were not required to move to a Christian-run land but instead were supposed to remain where they lived, existing in the hyphenated status implied by Augustine's two cities. They were to be citizens both of the heavenly city, conferred through church membership, and of their earthly cities, whether Corinth, Rome, Ephesus, or eventually Paris, London, or Boston. Only with the second coming of Christ, at the end of the church's history, would another shift in the relations between the earthly and heavenly cities occur, one more like that of Old Jerusalem, where the differences between secular and sacred politics would be inconsequential.

Of course Huntington has little stake in Christian constructions of the millennium since his concern is explicitly with the American city on a hill, not with the ultimate New Jerusalem. *Who Are We?* does raise other difficulties, such as whether a religion retains its integrity once it has been commandeered for purposes other than those for which it was designed. Still, Huntington is clear that a domesticated or tamed Christianity is not a problem for him. After quoting one religious historian who wrote that "It's difficult to disentangle what is Protestant from what is liberal in the United States," Huntington adds that the American Creed "in short, is Protestantism without God, the secular credo of the 'nation with the soul of a church.'" A religion without God suggests an earthly city without heavenly reference. That line of development, from a city on a hill to a nation with the soul of a church, does not trouble Huntington. But for Americans who would like to believe that the city prophesied at the end of the Bible in Revelation will not suffer the cost overruns or traffic delays of Boston's Big Dig, the identification of the United States as the promised land may well give them pause.

# CHAPTER TWO

# Whose Freedom, Which Liberty?

John Witherspoon stands out notably in the narratives of American and Presbyterian history. As the only minister to sign the Declaration of Independence, Witherspoon is a noteworthy case for anyone hoping to decipher the inherent harmony between conservative religion and political liberty. To contemporaries, despite being "an intolerably homely old Scotchman," he was the kind of man of whom legends are made. One of his students, Ashbel Green, who would go on to succeed Witherspoon as president of the College of New Jersey (later Princeton University), recalled that "in promiscuous company, [Witherspoon] had more the quality called *presence*—a quality powerfully felt, but not to be described—than any other individual with whom the writer has ever had intercourse, Washington alone excepted." Moses Coit Tyler, one of America's first intellectual historians, rendered this estimate of Witherspoon: "This eloquent, wise, and efficient Scotsman—at once teacher, preacher, politician, law-maker, and philosopher, [was] upon the whole not undeserving of the praise which has been bestowed upon him as 'one of the great men of the age and of the world.'" Partially because of Witherspoon's influence, one of the soldiers fighting against American independence, a captain of Hessian troops in Pennsylvania, wrote, "call this war . . . by whatever name you may, only call it not an American Rebellion, it is nothing more or less than an Irish-Scotch Presbyterian Rebellion."

Witherspoon's influence on the creation of the American republic was striking if only because he came to New Jersey a mere eight years before the drafting of the Declaration of Independence. He arrived in North America after twenty-three years of ministry in the Church of Scotland (the Kirk), most recently in Paisley. What made him attractive to the board of trustees at the College of New Jersey was his reputation as a theological conservative. Although trained at the University of Edinburgh and conversant with the latest developments in Scottish philosophy, Witherspoon emerged as a leading critic of the Moderate party in the Kirk, a group that tended to reduce Christianity to its ethical precepts. His conservative convictions, familiarity with contemporary intellectual developments, and potential to transcend antagonisms among colonial Presbyterians made Witherspoon the unanimous choice of the college's board. The Presbyterians overseeing the young collegiate institution in central New Jersey had no idea that their choice for president would soon put the struggling school on the national stage.

In Scotland the established church had since its founding in 1560 been a pawn in political struggles between England and Scotland, and similar ones between the Crown and the English Parliament. In that context Witherspoon had been vocal in defending the prerogatives of the church against the state, a stance that in the eyes of the American colonists put him on the side of religious liberty. In fact James Madison, Sr., sent his son to study at the College of New Jersey in 1769 primarily because of Witherspoon's reputation as an advocate of liberty. Yet his was by no means a radical commitment to the politics of freedom, because Witherspoon always tethered it to religious fidelity. Even so, he shifted the college from its previous orientation as a school training ministers who would continue to stoke the fires of revival (the school was founded to support the First Great Awakening) to one that trained public servants for the cause of liberty. Not only did Witherspoon rearrange the curriculum to give priority to Scottish philosophy, but during his tenure the college's graduates overwhelmingly pursued careers that provided military, diplomatic, religious, or legislative aid to the Revolutionary cause. In fact, of the 355 students to study with Witherspoon, only five retained loyalty to the British Crown. Beyond his educational labors, which earned the college the nickname "seminary of sedition," Witherspoon instructed fellow Presbyterians on the dangers of British tyranny, served in the Continental Congress, and in 1783 made the college's Nassau Hall available to Congress.

Despite Witherspoon's energetic support for liberty and his robust conviction that political freedom was intimately connected to true religion, the gap between faith and America's political system was fairly evident even in Witherspoon's day. Had his supporters been less partisan in their politics, they might have noticed that the relationship between civil and religious liberty was not as directly proportional as Witherspoon alleged. At the same time, without the aid of Christian zeal the cause of independence might not have achieved the millennial importance that many devout American patriots attributed to it.

## The Sacred Cause of Liberty

"The Dominion of Providence over the Passions of Men" was perhaps the most important argument the Princeton president ever made. It was a sermon based on Psalm 76:10 ("Surely the wrath of men shall praise thee; the remainder of Wrath shalt thou restrain") and delivered on Friday, May 17, 1776, a day designated by the

Continental Congress to be set aside for prayer. That Witherspoon delivered this sermon on behalf of American independence on a Friday, as opposed to a Sunday—the Lord's Day, as Presbyterians called it—was a concession to the differences between the affairs of men (politics) and the ways of the divine (piety). He even admitted in the sermon that his bringing politics into the pulpit was odd. "You are my witnesses," Witherspoon declared to the Princetonians gathered in the town's Presbyterian church, "that this is the first time of my introducing any political subject into the pulpit." Even so, the sermon, which must have lasted for more than an hour, proved to be so useful for the purposes of independence that it was published the next month in Philadelphia where the Continental Congress was then meeting. Its popularlity also accounts for Witherspoon's election in late June 1776 to serve in Congress as a representative from New Jersey, a post that placed him in good stead to sign the Declaration of Independence. The timing of the sermon in Witherspoon's own career and in the conception of a nation about to be born no doubt accounts too for the decision to make it the first text in the multivolume edition of Witherspoon's works. Still, for all the circumstances that help to explain the legendary status this sermon achieved, the logic of Witherspoon's devotional discourse was equally powerful in giving voice to a conception of liberty that would prove to be enduring among American Protestants.

On the surface the text from Psalm 76 was an odd one for the points the Presbyterian college president would hope to make. In the first part of the sermon Witherspoon wrestled with the idea that human evil, "the wrath of men," could in fact glorify God. Without directly addressing the question of theodicy—the defense of divine goodness in light of human wickedness and suffering—he did attempt to do justice to the paradoxical character of divine will, that is, how ultimate good could emerge through proximate evil. Some of his examples were unimaginative, such as the idea that without suffering people tend to grow complacent; or the even more obvious notion that the wrath of men noted in the psalm "clearly points out the corruption of our nature," a point seldom missed by ministers of Calvinistic persuasion like Witherspoon. But when he turned to the positive effects of suffering, the relevance of his sermon to the cause of American independence became more difficult to discern. For instance, the death of Christ and its larger theological significance as a triumph over sin and death was for Witherspoon indicative of the lesson that "Persecution has been but as the furnace to the gold, to purge it of its dross, to manifest its purity, and increase its lustre." Not only was the martyrdom of the early church "the seed of Christianity," but at the time of the Protestant Reformation "nothing contributed more to facilitate its reception and increase its progress than the violence of its persecutors."

The trouble with these illustrations and the reasoning behind them was that the paradoxical quality of suffering could work against independence as much as for it. If the wrath of man actually contributed to divine glory, and if the Parliament and king were treating the colonists unfairly by taxing them without adequate political representation, could not the pain caused by such treatment be interpreted as adding to God's praise? Or if suffering and persecution had historically increased the resolve of Christians, would not the slights from London endured by believers living in the British colonies bolster their trust in and dependence upon God? Witherspoon's reasons for appealing to this biblical text made some sense; he was, after all, attempting to nurture the resolve of patriots about to enter a difficult struggle with one of the more powerful nations on earth. Still, employing the logic of Christian suffering to justify political rebellion was an argument that could just as easily backfire.

Even more strained was Witherspoon's reasoning when he turned to the topic of religious liberty. In the second part of the sermon, where he applied the meaning of the psalm to the political situation in the colonies, Witherspoon attempted to inspire his listeners to patriotic greatness by exhorting them to trust in God and hope "for his assistance in the present important conflict." The patriots could, he believed, have confidence in divine assistance if their cause was just, their principles pure, and their conduct prudent. Although the character of the patriots' principles and conduct gave Witherspoon room to conclude his sermon with admonitions to greater selflessness and virtue, he had little doubt about the nature of the patriot cause. "[T]he cause in which America is now in arms," he declared, "is the cause of justice, of liberty, and of human nature." Witherspoon explained this assertion by noting that the colonists had not been motivated by "pride, resentment, or sedition." Instead the desire for independence from England arose from "a deep and general conviction" that religious and civil liberty, as well as "the temporal and eternal happiness of us and our society," depended on political autonomy. Here Witherspoon was not simply regarding religious liberty as one part of a broader set of civil liberties, as if civil liberty would guarantee freedom of conscience. He had in mind a more precise relationship between civil and religious liberty. "The knowledge of God and his truths," Witherspoon elaborated, "have from the beginning of the world been chiefly, if not entirely, confined to those parts of the earth, where some degree of liberty and political justice were to be seen . . ."

In effect Witherspoon was articulating the logic of many American Protestants after him, which assumed that true religion, that is, Protestant Christianity, flourished only where civil magistrates protected civil liberties. The flip side of this assumption was the similar belief that Protestantism was the best soil from which civil liberty could grow. Witherspoon made this relationship crystal clear when he asserted that "There is not a single instance in history in which civil liberty was lost, and religious liberty preserved entire."

For this reason, if the colonists were to "yield up our temporal property" to Parliament through unfair taxes, they would also be delivering their consciences "into bondage."

The religious basis for political freedom allowed Witherspoon to end his famous sermon with a call for greater religious and moral zeal. "[H]e is the best friend to American liberty," the Presbyterian concluded, "who is most sincere and active in promoting true and undefiled religion, and who sets himself with the greatest firmness to bear down profanity and immorality of every kind." This did not imply political preference for the theological descendants of John Calvin. Witherspoon's brief for true religion did not include great concern for the "circumstantials of religion, or the contentions of one sect with another about their peculiar distinctions." Debates then about the mode of baptism, the frequency of observing the Lord's Supper, or even the extent of Christ's atonement were not at issue in this notion of "true and undefiled religion." Roman Catholicism would eventually emerge as a problem for the advocates of religious and civil liberty in part because the papacy would reveal itself as fairly hostile to those notions as they developed in Europe after the French Revolution. But most Protestants were welcome—the Church of England being an obvious exception—as long as they were morally upright or, in Witherspoon's words, felt "more joined in spirit to a true holy person of a different denomination, than to an irregular liver of his own." A combination of moral integrity, fear of God, obedience to divine law, and resistance to the temptations of vice was the religious recipe for civil liberty. What this list meant for the nonreligious was of course a problem that Witherspoon avoided, especially when signing Thomas Jefferson's "Declaration of Independence." But a month or so before the distribution of that document, the difficulties raised by the presence of nonorthodox Protestants could be set aside.

Of course Witherspoon's assertions were explicitly political in the sense that his understanding of the relationship between religious and civil liberty had a direct bearing on the issue of political independence from Britain. But his ideas had much broader significance for the way Anglo-American Protestants would understand the place of faith within the political and cultural institutions of the United States. Witherspoon was just one voice in a much wider development that characterized Congregationalists in New England and Presbyterians in the middle colonies, and that eventually would permeate Baptists and Methodists who were setting up churches as fast as the frontier pushed south and west. In particular, Witherspoon's ideas on Christian liberty were foundational for what Mark A. Noll has recently called Christian republicanism. Politically, according to Noll, this constellation of ideas featured two main themes: "fear of abuses from illegitimate power and a nearly messianic belief in the benefits of liberty." As such the best form of government was one that preserved freedom, which would in turn nurture human flourishing. The obvious corollary to the ideal of liberty was that any form of political interference with freedom would degrade persons and inhibit national prosperity. As Noll writes, the "critical oppositions" in Christian republicanism were "virtue against corruption, liberty against slavery." Of course the danger of liberty was libertinism, and that is why religion was so crucial to liberty's success. Witherspoon the Calvinist might have reservations about giving sinful human beings unprecedented political freedom, but as long as these free citizens were devout the excesses of liberty did not need to be feared. For the logic of Christian republicanism concluded that virtue ("defined as disinterested public service") promoted freedom and social harmony while vice (that is, "luxury, self-seeking, idleness, and frivolity") yielded tyranny and social unrest.

If Christian republicanism nurtured a distrust of unchecked power and the need for limited government, it also spawned a specific set of expectations about American cultural life. In this conception of the United States, Protestantism and its historic struggle with Roman Catholicism since the sixteenth-century Reformation was key. As George M. Marsden has described it, "the Whig cultural ideal" drew directly on the synthesis of Puritan theology and republican political philosophy that developed in seventeenth-century English politics, had great appeal among America's founders, and dominated nineteenth-century American culture. In this outlook, Protestantism was chiefly responsible for the advancement of political liberty and Western civilization. In other words, Protestantism stood for freedom, open inquiry, learning and impartiality while Roman Catholicism symbolized the opposite—tyranny, ignorance, superstition, and bigotry. The Whig ideal was especially important for the construction of the public school system, the establishment of colleges and universities, and the high estimate of the powers of ideas to make virtuous citizens. According to Marsden, a religiously informed education was "the best means of taming an unruly populace and assimilating diverse peoples into a common culture with shared ideals." Knowledge and Protestantism went hand in hand because both stood for "free inquiry versus prejudice and arbitrary authority."

With such a central place in the intellectual origins of the American founding, the mutual blessings of Protestantism and liberty would become a recurring theme in American Protestant arguments about the identity and purpose of their nation. One notable example of Christian republicanism's potency was Lyman Beecher's *A Plea for the West* (1835). The father of a remarkable set of children, including Harriet Beecher Stowe and Henry Ward Beecher, the Boston Congregationalist in the mid-1830s found himself on the Western frontier, Cincinnati to be precise, presiding over Lane Seminary, a joint endeavor of Congregationalists and Presbyterians. Out in the wilds of Ohio, uprooted from the stability of New England's Puritan culture, Beecher worried about the future of the United States. Specifically he was alarmed by the large number of European immigrants who were surging into the

American heartland and who had no familiarity with the nation's political institutions and ideals. Among them, Roman Catholic immigrants posed an even greater threat to America's future. To say that Beecher's short book about the Western United States was an early expression of nativism is to miss how much the unhealthy fear of foreign inhabitants was a result of the respectable concoction of Christian republicanism.

One of Beecher's main objections to Roman Catholicism was the papacy's refusal to acknowledge the separation of church and state. He did insist that the "civil and religious rights" of Catholic adherents not be "abridged or violated." But as free as they might be to practice their religion, the Roman Catholic understanding of the church and the pope's authority yielded no civil palette for the free institutions of the American political system. Finding instances of Rome's objections to republicanism was not a difficult assignment for Beecher, nor was he guilty of misreading the nineteenth-century papacy's conservative rejection of the American and French revolutions. But Beecher did not appear to be troubled by the odd mix of church and state also under American Protestant aegis. For this reason *A Plea for the West* abounds with examples of the Whig cultural ideal, such as the following:

> The Sabbath, and the preaching of the gospel, are Heaven's consecrated instrumentality for the efficacious administration of the government of mind in a happy social state. By these only does the Sun of Righteousness arise with healing in his beams; and ignorance, and vice, and supersition encamp around evangelical institutions, to run in whenever their light and power is extinct.

In some sense Beecher and Rome had the same understanding of the relationship between religion and politics, each side insisting that true religion was essential to the good ordering of society. But for the transplanted New Englander, Protestantism underwrote a modern form of government that promoted human freedom rightly understood; Rome's faith, because it was rooted in arbitrary power, was inherently tyrannical.

Beecher addressed the political meaning of Christianity in response to his imaginary interlocutor's questions about one faith being "just as good as another." His answer was to defend Calvinism, a religion he admitted was often denounced as "severe, unsocial, self-righteous, uncharitable, exclusive, persecuting . . . dealing damnation round the land . . ." The grounds for Beecher's defense were entirely anecdotal, even if it was obvious that the Calvinistic system "has always been on the side of liberty in its struggles against arbitrary power." This assertion led Beecher into a litany of Whig-Calvinistic accomplishments:

> . . . through the puritans, it breathed into the British constitution its most invaluable principles, and laid the foundations of the republican institutions of our nation, and felled the forests, and fought the colonial battles with Canadian Indians and French Catholics, when often our destiny balanced on a pivot and hung upon a hair.

In fact, Beecher added, "it wept, and prayed, and fasted, and fought, and suffered through the revolutionary struggle, when there was almost no other creed but the Calvinistic in the land."

Still, on the precise point of Calvinistic theology that naturally lent itself to republicanism or the cause of civil liberty, Beecher was basically silent. For him, as for Witherspoon, the connection between Protestantism and political liberty was so close as to be obvious. This explains why Beecher had confidence that if Roman Catholic immigrants to America would simply breathe in the fresh air of liberty without having it filtered through the papacy's tight regulations, they would choose freedom. Here is how Beecher put it:

> If they associated with republicans, the power of caste would wear away. If they mingled in our schools, the republican atmosphere

would impregnate their minds. If they scattered, unassociated, the attrition of circumstances would wear off their predilections and aversions. If they could read the Bible, and might and did, their darkened intellect would brighten, and their bowed down mind would rise. If they dared to think for themselves, the contrast of protestant independence with their thraldom, would awaken the desire of equal privileges, and put an end to an arbitrary clerical dominion over trembling superstitious minds.

Beecher was not the only American Protestant to let the connection between political and religious liberty go assumed rather than proved. Fifty years later Josiah Strong, another Congregationalist minister, asserted the dependence of American liberty on the right kind of faith in his popular book *Our Country: Its Possible Future and Its Present Crisis* (1885). A native of Illinois, Strong was a vindication of Beecher's earlier concern for the future of Protestantism in the West. He first studied at Western Reserve College before preparing for the ministry at Lane Theological Seminary, after which he held a variety of ministerial and administrative posts in the postbellum Social Gospel movement. Strong had learned the lessons of Christian republicanism well and identified immigration, Roman Catholicism, Mormonism, intemperance, socialism, wealth, and urbanization as the seven perils threatening religious and political liberty in the United States. Like Beecher, he paid particular attention to social developments in the West. His solution was broad: to convince Anglo-Saxon Americans of their "commanding influence in the world's future" and their need to choose the spiritual and Christian course instead of a materialistic and atheistic one. But this imperative was no less ambitious than the effects of Anglo-Saxon efforts, namely, hastening "the coming of the kingdom wherein dwelleth righteousness."

As distended as Strong's verbiage may have been, he continued in the familar and safe path set out by Witherspoon and Beecher before him regarding the relationship between religious and civil liberty. On the one hand, the connection between faith and political freedom worked to the decided disadvantage of Roman Catholicism. In his chapter on "Romanism," Strong outlined the basic antagonism between "the fundamental principles of our government" and "those of the Catholic church." Here he piled up quotations from the pope as well as other church officials and publications indicating Rome's opposition to freedom of conscience and free schools ("one of the cornerstones of our Government"), and subjection to the laws of the United States as opposed to loyalty to the pope himself. On the other hand, Strong continued to assert that civil liberty followed wherever Protestantism flourished. The two greatest characteristics of Anglo-Saxons were political freedom and spiritual Christianity, thus explaining why the English, the British colonists, and the people of the United States were both the most free and the most devout. "It is not necessary to argue," Strong wrote, "to those for whom I write that the two great needs of mankind, that all men may be lifted up into the light of the highest Christian civilization, are, first, a pure, spiritual Christianity, and, second, civil liberty." Such confidence may have made complete sense to Strong's Anglo-American Protestant readers. And it clearly reflected the older political and religious calculus of Christian republicanism. But it hardly explained the precise relationship between Protestant devotion and political liberty. Even so, assumptions that Protestantism guaranteed America's political institutions and ideals were sufficiently strong to make Strong's book a best-seller.

Witherspoon, Beecher, and Stong's faith in the links between religion and political liberty persisted all the way into the twentieth century. The mid-century struggle against fascism and communism provided an obvious rationale for reiterating the ideals of Christian republicanism, but the extraordinary nature of those circumstances should not be used to discount Protestant convictions about the relationship between religious and civil liberty. After all,

this was a time when Americans flocked to churches and syna-
gogues in record numbers, and when Congress added the phrases
"under God" to the Pledge of Allegiance and "In God We Trust"
to American coins, all because of that older Protestant belief that
faith was essential to the preservation of civil liberty. It may have
been a wider, less dogmatic, and non-Calvinistic understanding of
faith, one that some would call Judeo-Christian, but it nonetheless
preserved the older Protestant outlook that rooted political liberty
in religious devotion.

One example from the mid-twentieth century comes from
Ralph Henry Gabriel, the Yale University historian who wrote the
highly acclaimed *The Course of American Democratic Thought* (1940).
One of the pieces of Gabriel's argument was that Protestantism
had been a major source of democratic ideals in American history.
His book attracted the interest of program officers at the Edward
W. Hazen Foundation, which during the 1940s was sponsoring a
series of pamphlets on the importance of religion for American society. Upon being asked to give one of the foundation's lectures
(which turned into a Hazen Pamphlet) on the "Spiritual Origins of
American Culture," Gabriel boiled down parts of his book to add
further heft to the surge of interest among educators and social
elites in recovering the religious premises of America's political
ideals. The Yale scholar listed four basic components of the nation's democractic faith: "the free, rational and responsible individual"; social order rooted in "fixed principles"; the idea of
progress; and national destiny. This civic faith was the direct result
of religious conviction. From the Puritans America received "an
emphasis on the fundamental law and the disciplined individual."
From the Quakers came notions of individual liberty, "the dignity
and worth of man and universal brotherhood." And from Founding Fathers such as Thomas Jefferson, a man who had "little use
for the conventional creeds of his day" but whose philosophical
core was "faith in God as the Author of Nature," sprang American

beliefs about progress and national destiny. Gabriel closed with several of the quotations carved on the walls of the Jefferson Memorial, one of which linked the sacred cause of liberty to religious devotion, even of Jefferson's novel kind: "I have sworn upon the Altar of God eternal hostility against every form of tyranny over the mind of man. . . ."

Gabriel's rendering of the connection between civil and religious liberty was different in important respects from Witherspoon's. In fact, over the course of its usefulness, each iteration of the Whig cultural ideal would become scantier in its affirmation of the benefits of John Calvin's teaching. Nevertheless an echo of Witherspoon's Christian republicanism could still be heard in Gabriel's democratic faith. It was the notion that true freedom in the public arena was impossible without religious faith. What Gabriel also perpetuated was Christian republicanism's greatest weakness—that is, failing to spell out the exact nature of the ties between religion and political liberty. Like Witherspoon, Beecher, and Strong before him, Gabriel took it as a given that faith promoted civil liberty. But the looseness of logic did not prevent Protestants and later proponents of the Judeo-Christian heritage from attributing the roots of America's political ideals to Protestant faith.

## *Christian Liberty*

The Protestants who defended the cause of American independence had good reasons for thinking their version of Western Christianity, as opposed to Roman Catholicism, was on the side of liberty. One of the important features of the Protestant Reformation was the idea that Rome had cluttered the Christian faith with a host of man-made rules about holidays, relics, and rituals that obscured the correct teaching of the Bible. So, for instance, when Protestants reduced the number of sacraments from seven to two, they did so because they believed Scripture required observance of baptism and the Lord's Supper. In contrast, Rome had imposed confirmation, marriage, ordination, penance, and last rites upon beholden church members. The idea behind this reform of church practice was that of Christian liberty—namely, that believers were free from those teachings and customs that church officers, no matter how good their intentions, might require without the clear warrant of biblical guidance. Or to take another example, no matter how valuable the practice of receiving the sign of the cross on one's forehead on Ash Wednesday, Protestants refused to make this a requirement for Christian devotion precisely because it sprang from pious intentions rather than explicit scriptural teaching. This is not to say that Roman Catholics have no biblical basis for their practices. The point here is simply to illustrate how the idea of Christian liberty became an important conviction among the earliest Protestants.

Although Protestantism thrived upon this notion of Christian liberty—Martin Luther's early treatise "On the Freedom of a Christian" (1520) being a singular example—the idea did not receive official endorsement as part of a Protestant creed until the Westminster Assembly composed the Westminster Confession of Faith. This council of English and Scottish clergy met from 1643 to 1648 at the instigation of a Parliament that was asserting its perogatives against a king, Charles I, whom the ministers of Parliament believed to be tyrannical. Because the Westminster Assembly met at the behest of Parliament during one of the least politically stable decades in English history, its theological, liturgical, and ecclesiological formulations were charged with political significance, even signaling the rising power of Puritans in Parliament and England's brief experiment with republicanism from 1649 to 1660 during the reign of Oliver Cromwell as lord protector. One might expect that in such a context the Westminster Confession of Faith's statement on Christian liberty would foreshadow in important ways the chief features of Christian republicanism. After all, the

Confession's authors were writing for politicians who were part of the Whig party in England and whose views would later inspire the American patriots. If any church creed might spell out the theological grounds for connecting religious and civil liberty, the Westminster Confession of Faith might be the place to do so.

Yet the Westminster Assembly surprisingly offered no theological justification for either mid-seventeenth-century Whigs in England or late-eighteenth-century Christian republicans in the American colonies. In fact, in a separate chapter on the subject of Christian liberty, the Westminster divines paid no attention to politics. They insisted that the liberties enjoyed by Christians were far removed from the affairs of monarchs, republicans, or democrats. In the first paragraph of Chapter Twenty of the Westminster Confession, the divines were crystal clear in regarding Christian liberty as completely spiritual in nature, without any political implications. It reads:

> The liberty which Christ hath purchased for believers under the gospel consists in their freedom from the guilt of sin, the condemning wrath of God, the curse of the moral law; and, in their being delivered from this present evil world, bondage to Satan, and dominion of sin; from the evil of afflictions, the sting of death, the victory of the grave, and everlasting damnation; as also, in their free access to God, and their yielding obedience unto him, not out of slavish fear, but a childlike love and willing mind. All which were common also to believers under the law. But, under the new testament, the liberty of Christians is further enlarged, in their freedom from the yoke of the ceremonial law, to which the Jewish church was subjected; and in greater boldness of access to the throne of grace, and in fuller communications of the free Spirit of God, than believers under the law did ordinarily partake of.

In other words, the primary consideration in understanding Christian liberty was the ultimate salvation of persons from sin and death. Freedom, accordingly, was a status enjoyed by Christians ir-respective of their political circumstances. The liberation signified by Christ had only to do, in the minds of the Westminster divines, with whether the law of God still had claims upon a person. Would a man or woman face condemnation on Judgment Day on the ba-sis of obedience to divine law? What the Confession taught first of all was that salvation freed Christians from the penalty of sin, promised eternal life, and liberated them from following the laws and customs of the Old Testament.

The spiritual nature of Christian liberty would become a major bone of contention during the American debates over the institu-tion of slavery. Without trying to justify a clearly racist and perni-cious way of ordering society and economic production, trying to understand elements of the pro-slavery argument is useful for at-tempting to grasp what the Westminster divines had in mind. The South Carolina Presbyterian theologian James Henley Thornwell defended well this spiritual conception of Christian liberty when he endeavored to distinguish the politics of slavery from the liberty of the gospel. From an 1850 sermon based on Colossians 4:1 ("Masters, give unto your servants that which is just and equal; knowing that ye also have a Master in heaven"), Thornwell de-clared that Christian liberty was "independent of the decrees of kings or the mandates of States." In keeping with the Westminster Confession, he explained that the freedom of the Christian con-sisted "essentially in the dominion of rectitude, in the emancipa-tion of the will from the power of sin, the release of the affections from the attractions of earth, the exemption of the understanding from the deceits of prejudice and error." But this freedom had nothing to do with politics because it was as much the privilege of the "martyr at the stake, the slave in his chains, the prisoner in his dungeon, as well as the king upon the throne." Of course Thorn-well had a measure of self-interest in resolving the issue of liberty and slavery in this way. He was, after all, a son of the South and preached to powerful men who owned slaves. Even so, his understanding of Christian liberty was close to that elaborated by the Westminster divines, whose spiritual conception of freedom was distinct from the politics of England or the United States. It even transcended those of the Roman Empire under which many of the first Christians were slaves and received the gospel not as a way of overthrowing their masters or the emperor but as a means of escaping the spiritual chains of sin and death.

The apolitical nature of Christian liberty, Calvinistically understood, became even clearer in the remainder of Chapter Twenty of the Westminster Confession. In the second paragraph the divines outlined the traditional Reformed understanding of liberty of conscience in which they explained that Christians were in religious matters obligated to obey teachings only based expressly upon the Bible as opposed to "the doctrines and commandments of men." But they were quick to qualify the implicit rebelliousness in such a conception by pointing out in the third paragraph that anyone using Christian liberty to justify the "practice of any sin" or to "cherish any lust" was destroying the very purpose of such freedom, which was, namely, to serve God without fear of being punished. Only in the last paragraph of the chapter did they come round to the political or social implications of such a spiritual notion of Christian liberty. Here they made sure that the spiritual freedom Christians enjoyed could not be used to justify any sort of threat to social order.

> And because the powers which God hath ordained, and the liberty which Christ hath purchased, are not intended by God to destroy, but mutually to uphold and preserve one another, they who, upon pretense of Christian liberty, shall oppose any lawful power, or the lawful exercise of it, whether it be civil or ecclesiastical, resist the ordinance of God.

Clearly part of the divines' concern was to protect the "external peace and order" of the church. In other words, the liberty of the Christian did not include freedom from church authorities. But this restriction also involved the state. As they went on to explain in the twenty-third chapter of the Confession on the civil magistrate, Christians had a duty to "be subject to [magistrates'] authority, for conscience's sake." Even in the case of unbelieving or infidel rulers, Christians and church officers were still duty bound to submit to all political authority. These political and social hedges upon Christian liberty highlight even more the spiritual character of the freedom that the Westminster divines believed to be a benefit of faith in Christ.

Of course the Westminster Confession of Faith was no more binding upon Thomas Jefferson than it was on Josiah Strong. But it was actually normative for Presbyterians like John Witherspoon, whose 1776 sermon "The Dominion of Providence over the Passions of Men" stirred many American colonists, whether Presbyterian or not, to regard independence from Britain as a manifestation of Christian liberty. When he wrote *A Plea for the West*, Lyman Beecher was also a minister in the Presbyterian church thanks to a somewhat awkward arrangement in 1801 between Congregationalists and Presbyterians to cooperate in the establishment of churches in the West. The Calvinist champions of religious and civil liberty, both during the excitements of the the Revolutionary Era and the period of national expansion, should have known better than to link the freedom of the Christian with the liberties of the American. The failure to connect precisely the relationship, to assume it rather than argue for that link, looks all the more glaring in the context of the Westminster Confession's clear instruction that Christian liberty is far removed from political freedom. So even if the creed of American Presbyterians was a document with no binding authority upon most citizens of the United States, it did possess at least a measure of relevance for the consideration of folks like Witherspoon and Beecher. And yet, despite the apolitical account of Christian liberty by the Calvinists who assembled in London during the

1640s, Calvinists on the other side of the ocean a century and a quarter later did precisely what the Westminster divines forbade, namely, opposing the lawful power of the English monarch "upon pretense of Christian liberty."

## Religious Freedom and the Separation of Church and State

If Witherspoon misappropriated the notion of Christian liberty for revolutionary ends, present-day reflections on the freedoms enjoyed by believers are even more beside the point. Religious liberty continues to be a matter of lively debate in American politics. But the terms of such disagreements emerge not from consideration of Christian teaching but from the wording of the U.S. Constitution. This is not at all inappropriate since American law should set the norm for discussions of American polity. But since Christian believers invariably comprise one of the sides debating the nature of religious liberty, Christian ideas about freedom might well be a factor in current disputes. Instead, sober reflection on the apolitical character of Christian freedom is virtually nonexistent.

When the framers of the Constitution drafted the First Amendment, Christians like Witherspoon could well have thought and argued that the language of religious liberty, the first of two references to religion in the entire document, stemmed from arguments that devout patriots had made. The entire amendment reads: "Congress shall make no law respecting an establishment of religion, or prohibiting the free exercise thereof; or abridging the freedom of speech, or of the press; or the right of the people peaceably to assemble, and to petition the government for a redress of grievances." Because this hedge on legislative power prevents coercion of belief and guarantees the liberty of individuals to decide religious questions for themselves, the First Amendment does on the surface have a certain affinity with the idea of Christian liberty that the Westminster divines affirmed. Liberty of conscience, according to the Westminster Confession, holds that the fundamental basis for faith is individual and personal, not something that can be coerced by human authorities, no matter how legitimate they may be. Of course the Presbyterians who assented to the Westminster Confession did not believe that religion was individualistic and so subject to personal preference. Instead they were simply attempting to articulate a point that the framers of the Constitution also affirmed, namely, that for religious faith to be genuine it needed to be demonstrated and affirmed freely by men and women, without fear of penalty or for personal or social advantage. In this sense the Constitution drew upon Protestant conviction by recognizing the danger to faith produced by laws requiring religious conformity or church membership.

Yet protecting the rights of individual conscience is a far cry from the substance of most current discussions about the framers' intentions regarding religious liberty. Instead of being on guard against any governmental infringement of citizens' efforts to practice their faith, the primary disagreement is now the degree to which believers may engage in public displays of devotion, from erecting the crèche in front of town hall during Christmas season to appealing to religious convictions in political debates.* A recent example of this rather narrow construction of religious liberty comes from the exchange between Mario Cuomo, a practicing Roman Catholic, and Indiana congressman and evangelical Protestant,

---

*The Religious Freedom Restoration Act, passed in 1993 and ruled unconstitutional in 1997, is one exception to this assertion, though the relatively quick turnaround on this legislation may indicate how limited this line of consideration was. The RFRA prevented state restrictions on the free exercise of religion without proof of a "compelling" government interest in such constraint. The law was passed in response to the Supreme Court's ruling in *Employment Division v. Smith* (1990), which upheld Oregon law preventing two workers from receiving unemployment benefits after having been fired for their religious use of peyote.

Mark Souder, in the Pew Charitable Trusts–sponsored forum on religion and public life. Cuomo appealed to the First Amendment's protection of religious minorities from "the official preference of one religion over others." This is a view in general agreement with organizations such as Americans United for the Separation of Church and State, an outlook that stresses decoupling religion from public life. Souder, in contrast, reads the First Amendment differently. He acknowledges that its language clearly prevents government from sponsoring "an official sectarian religion." But he argues that it does not prevent religious citizens from exhibiting their faith in public, whether in public schools or in legislatures. The Indiana congressman's views are representative of such organizations as the Rutherford Institute, which provides legal advice and services to religious Americans for whom the First Amendment is a barrier, rather than an aid, to the free expression of religious conviction.

One plausible option for cutting through the impasse surrounding the First Amendment's implications for relating religion to public life has come from Stephen L. Carter in his book *The Culture of Disbelief*. He argues that the chief purpose of the First Amendment historically was "the protection of the religious world against the secular government." But this pattern of protection reversed course with the series of Supreme Court rulings culminating in *Lemon v. Kurtzman* (1971), in which the "secular intent" of a statute became one of the chief criteria for determining its constitutionality. According to Carter, "the idea that religious motivation renders a statute suspect was never anything but a tortured and unsatisfactory reading" of the First Amendment. It also implied that the Constitution's rendering of church-state relations was to protect the government from religion. This understanding not only reverses the clear meaning and history of the First Amendment but also fails to render plausible the way that most Americans operate. Because they are a religious people, their "religious beliefs tend to be deep and, on many moral issues, seem to be controlling." In other words, those who would construct the wall of separation such that religious convictions may play no role in public debate, political motivation, or civic life, misread the framers' intentions as well as human psychology. The situation requires flexibility. Saying that government "must not advance the interests of one religious tradition over another" is one thing, but saying that "religious conviction" is "a ground for invalidating law" is another. Church and state should be separate, but not religion and politics.

A different response to the current predicament comes from Isaac Kramnick and R. Laurence Moore in their book *The Godless Constitution*. They concede that a prevailing "culture of disbelief" may marginalize religion. At the same time the benefits provided and damage done by politics on religion are "ludicrously overstated." Religion should have the same rights in the public square as General Motors, "no more and no less." But these rights do not include the legitimacy of a form of "religious correctness" that ignores and, worse, opposes government neutrality by insisting that the United States "is an instrument of divine providence." The wall of separation is a political good that needs to be reinforced. "Politicians who run for office claiming God's backing and who urge voters to make their decisions on the basis of a candidate's religious beliefs are treading on ground that the Constitution did not want entered." Contrary to Carter, Kramnick and Moore believe the First Amendment involves an understanding of political life in which government should be sequestered if not protected from religion. It has as much to do with the liberty of believers to practice their faith as it does with government officials to act independently of religious conviction.

One of the ironies of current disputes about the nature of those liberties protected in the First Amendment is that the "secularist" position of Kramnick and Moore is closer to the understanding of Christian liberty articulated by the Calvinist clergy at the Westminster Assembly than contemporary Christians are. For advocates of a secular public square on the one side and the Westminster divines on the other, theology and political philosophy are two different realms of human reflection and pertain to different parts of human existence. Faith and public policy have little to do with each other. This is not to say that ideas about human nature, the character of political power, and other such abstract notions are outside the debates of theologians and political philosophers. But as the example of religious liberty makes clear, when Christian theologians historically discussed freedom they were invoking categories with no clear import for politics. Nor should the point here be read to suggest that seventeenth-century Calvinists shared with modern-day secularists a similar conception of politics. Clearly the Westminster divines would have thought about the ordering of society in ways significantly different from Kramnick and Moore. Nevertheless the understanding of Christianity developed at London during the 1640s, especially the doctrine of Christian freedom, made clear that political arrangements had nothing to do with the attainment of the spiritual liberties enjoyed by believers.

Also worth noticing here is how far present-day notions of religious liberty are from those of historic Christianity. Some Christians feel that if they may not express their faith in public openly, they lack religious liberty. But if Christian freedom of the kind described by the Westminster divines is primarily a liberty to worship and serve God without fear of eternal condemnation, how is the liberty of American Christians restricted by not being able to pray in public schools, enjoy a crèche in front of town hall, or appeal to the Bible in political debates? Or even if such Christian freedom involves liberty of conscience, so that a believer must have enough political liberty to worship in a way pleasing to God, when or where exactly have the secular authorities in the United States attempted to regulate the worship services or private devotional exercises of Protestants and Roman Catholics?* The United States affords Christians remarkable freedom to worship according to the demands of their religion and the dictates of their conscience, a freedom unparalleled in the records of human history. To conceive of those instances where Christians do not receive public affirmation or state sanction for their convictions or practices as treatment bordering on tyranny is to trivialize the many instances throughout church history of persecution and martyrdom.

If Christian freedom has mainly to do with freedom to worship apart from coercion by state authorities, why are today's Christian conservatives alarmed? If they believe they need prayer in public schools, why aren't the devotional exercises of the Christian home or the mid-week services of their local church sufficient? If they think the local mayor should support the construction of a crèche during the holiday season, why isn't a Christmas tree prominently displayed in their living room and on their front lawn good enough to show their recognition of Christ's birth? And if America's religious conservatives need their faith to have a public outlet, if it is somehow a sign of perfidy to keep belief private, why isn't owning a public house of worship free from real estate taxes sufficient for this necessity? But if Christian freedom is principally about freedom from the penalty of sin and eternal punishment, if it is a spiritual as opposed to a political reality, and if it is something enjoyed as much by Christians in a liberal democracy as by believers once persecuted by Roman emperors, why all the fuss about the infringement of religious liberty?

---

*Readers with some knowledge of the battles over Roman Catholic parochial schooling in the United States may be tempted to cite these episodes as examples of religious repression by the state. But I do not believe they qualify, no matter how much I believe the treatment of Roman Catholics was wrong both politically and religiously. Education in the three Rs is not a requirement for Christian devotion the way that participating in worship is. For more on religion and public schools, see Chapter Three below.

# For Goodness' Sake

When Thomas Jefferson, the third president of the United States, ran for that office in 1800 his candidacy unleashed a firestorm of protest from Protestant clergy. The reasons for religious opposition to the Virginian were not difficult to find. Although his advocacy of the 1785 bill supporting religious freedom in Virginia endeared him to various dissenting Protestants, particularly the Baptists whose views on the separation of church and state resembled Jefferson's, the specific language of that statute offended many believers. It began with the phrase "Almighty God hath created the mind free," a sentiment in accord with the Protestant notion of liberty of conscience, but without specific reference to Christianity. When pressed to add "Jesus Christ" to the language, Jefferson resisted and eventually won. As he later explained, this insertion would have contradicted his own intention that religious freedom include not simply Protestants but "the Jew and the Gentile, the Christian and the Mohometan, the Hindoo, and the infidel of every denomination." Other statements by Jefferson from the 1780s came back to haunt him during the 1800 presidential campaign. In his 1786 book *Notes on the State of Virginia*, Jefferson had written of his indifference to the religious opinions of his neighbor. Whether or not a person believed in one

72

god or twenty was of no consequence to him because "it neither breaks my leg, nor picks my pocket." According to one of his clerical critics, John Mason, Jefferson's nonchalance would produce a society "where fiend would prowl with fiend for plunder and blood." Another objectionable passage from Jefferson's *Notes* referred to the history of Christianity as a chief argument against state support for religion, since it made "one half of the world fools, and the other half hypocrites."

Ironically, Jefferson's opponent in the 1800 election, John Adams, was no more orthodox than he, but the Massachusetts Federalist was less strident about his infidelity. In fact most of the so-called Founding Fathers, from Jefferson and Adams to George Washington, Benjamin Franklin, and James Madison were generally indifferent to most of the claims of the denominations, from the vicarious atonement to the real presence of Christ in the Lord's Supper. At the same time they uttered or wrote any number of assertions in favor of religion, a significant factor in keeping alive the argument that the United States was founded as a Christian nation. For instance, in his second inaugural Thomas Jefferson uttered sentiments that may have been conceived to defang his religious critics but that have also given hope to Christian proponents of a religious basis for the United States:

I shall need, too, the favor of that Being in whose hands we are, who led our forefathers, as Israel of old, from their native land and planted them in a country flowing with all the necessities and comforts of life, who has covered our infancy with His Providence and our riper years with His wisdom and power, and to whose goodness I ask you to join with me in supplications that He will so enlighten the minds of your servants, guide their councils and prosper their measures, that whatever they do shall result in your good, and shall secure to you the peace, friendship and approbation of all nations.

John Adams was no less reluctant to resort to religious ideals in his understanding of the United States and its peculiar place in the history of republics. In a letter to Thomas Jefferson in 1813, Adams wrote:

> The general principles, on which the Fathers achieved independence, were the only Principles in which that beautiful Assembly of young Gentlemen could Unite. . . . And what were these general Principles? I answer, the general Principles of Christianity, in which all these Sects were United: And the general Principles of English and American Liberty, in which all those young Men United, and which had United all Parties in America, in Majorities sufficient to assert and maintain her Independence. Now I will avow, that I then believe, and now believe, that those general Principles of Christianity, are as eternal and immutable, as the Existence and Attributes of God; and that those Principles of Liberty, are as unalterable as human Nature and our terrestrial, mundane System.

Determining whether these affirmations of Christianity were genuine is a problem that depends greatly on the eye of the determiner. To the defenders of a Christian America such statements at the very least expose the anti-religious motives of present-day secularists who claim that religion has no proper place in the public square; if Jefferson and Adams could claim a divine benediction for the United States, how could it be inappropriate for politicians today to invoke religion on behalf of the nation and its affairs and conclude speeches with the familiar "God bless America"? In contrast, to those fearful of mixing religion and politics, such assertions about religion by the Founding Fathers can be written off as a product of the time or a concession to the overwhelmingly religious public, but surely should not be taken as a model for articulating public policy in the twenty-first century. The actual disposition of the Founding Fathers is somewhere in the middle of these antagonistic views, with religion clearly mattering to them in ways that generally contradict either a secular or Christian reading of the American founding.

Jefferson and Adams were supporters of religion, even describing Christianity as the best faith of all. For instance, the former wrote that "Of all the systems of morality, ancient or modern, which have come under my observation, none appear to me so pure as that of Jesus." Likewise, in his diary John Adams admitted, "The Christian religion is, above all the Religions that ever prevailed or existed in ancient or modern times, the religion of Wisdom, Virtue, Equity, and Humanity . . . it is Resignation to God, it is Goodness itself to Man." But Jefferson and Adams, like many liberal Protestants after them, believed the church and clerics had corrupted the ethical instructions of Christ and so, as Jefferson put it, "engrafted Platonisms" onto the original simplicity of Christianity. In other words, Jesus was the quintessential ethicist, but the rest of the biblical account involving his deity, miracles, and the significance of his death were distractions from the moral core of Christ's teaching. Not until the early twentieth century would mainstream biblical scholars recognize the difficulty (if not impossibility) of extracting Christ's ethics from the supernatural and redemptive components of the New Testament, though Jefferson's Bible was precisely an unembarrassed effort to perform this hermeneutical feat. But the high value that founders like Jefferson and Adams placed on religion, even Christianity, was always some distance from either the emotional religion of revivals or the scholastic faith of the Protestant creeds.

At the same time Jefferson and Adams's pronouncements on religion stemmed as much from utility as from spiritual insight. The United States and its system of government were an experiment without precedent in human history, not because of their genius, good fortune, or noble ideals but precisely because of their peculiar treatment of religion. In the history of the West the United

States was the first nation to attempt a form of government without an established religion. And even before Constantine bestowed upon Christianity the obligations and temptations of a state church, the older republics of Greece and Rome had relied upon the blessing of pagan deities for social stability. Without the aid of an established faith, then, leaders like Jefferson and Adams argued that the United States needed some kind of religious influence to cultivate the public and private virtue necessary for a free republic to survive. As the third article of the Massachusetts constitution put it, ". . . the happiness of a people, and the good order and preservation of civil government, essentially depend upon piety, religion and morality." Arguments like this explain the persistence of established churches at the state level in places like Adams's home state. They also account for the continuing interest in religion by the likes of Adams and Jefferson who, though indifferent to Christianity's fine print, were clearly intent on preserving its moral authority.

As most students of American history know, the established churches that the founders delegated to the state legislatures eventually phased out of existence. Massachusetts's Standing Order in 1833 was the last state church system to fall. The difficulty of giving preferential treatment to one denomination over the others became so burdensome that the benefits of public religion no longer offset collateral damage. But the need for public morality survived the demise of state churches, which in turn underwrote a free society's need for faith. If the churches could not supply a sufficiently common faith for public virtue, America's schools would have to fill the vacuum. As a result, debates over religious liberty and virtue shifted in the first half of the nineteenth century from the sphere of religion to education. Although these conflicts would not be resolved constitutionally until the twentieth century, the nineteenth century contests over religion in the public schools demonstrated the difficulty of attempting to make even Jesus' simple ethical teaching the basis for public standards of morality.

## *Common Faith, Uncommon School*

Founding Fathers like Jefferson and Adams had little difficulty accommodating Christian diversity, but cultural diversity proved to be a taller order. No matter what the different doctrines and practices that separated Baptists from Presbyterians, Reformed from Lutheran, or Episcopalians from Roman Catholics, all these denominations (an objectionable term to Rome, which still claimed to be the only true church) could agree with the founders' conception that Jesus' ethical teachings were superior to all others. But when it came to the ethno-cultural differences among immigrants to the United States who were unfamiliar with Anglo-American Protestant norms, the ideal of the universal equality of all persons ran aground on the shoals of British provincialism. For instance, in his *Notes on the State of Virginia*, Jefferson observed that "It is for the happiness of those united to society to harmonize as much as possible in matters which they must of necessity transact together." But immigrants were a different matter because they would "bring with them the principles of the governments they leave, imbibed in their early youth; or, if able to throw them off, it will be in exchange for an unbridled licentiousness." These foreign families, who would maintain customs and languages different from those of the country, would eventually participate in the legislation and government of the United States "in proportion to their numbers." As such, "They will infuse into it their spirit, warp and bias its direction, and render it a heterogeneous, incoherent, distracted mass."

The demand for a common cultural framework, combined with a free republic's need for a sufficient moral basis, led many of the founders to look to the school as the institution to inculcate a common standard of virtue. Those like Jefferson and Adams disagreed about the nature of the religious instruction that schools should provide. Adams, for instance, was more willing than Jefferson to speak of the religious basis of the republic as "the *general principles* of Christianity." Jefferson, in contrast, talked more about "natural religion" or the God revealed in nature by the ordinary powers of rational reflection and empirical observation. Nature's God was a neutral idea that for Jefferson avoided the problems of sectarianism. Nevertheless the second president of the United States was no less reluctant to include this neutral faith in the curriculum of the nation's schools than Adams was to do the same for a generic Christianity. As Gordon Wood concluded, "the most obvious republican instrument for eliminating [ancient] prejudices and inculcating virtue in a people was education," which in turn launched a series of proposals for establishing a system of instruction, from grade schools to colleges and universities, to instill the morality crucial to the survival of the new nation. If Americans were not inherently virtuous, education would teach them the morals necessary for a republican form of government.

Before the 1830s when various states established tax-supported systems of public or common schools, most educational institutions were Protestant in origin, character, and curriculum, a system that proved incapable of providing adequate instruction for the increasing diversity of the American population. The common school was an alternative to the churches because it might serve the public while teaching the morals necessary for republican virtue. This dual demand for a school that was publicly accessible and yet religious placed the common school leaders in an awkward position. To advocates for religious education, the common school looked like a slippery slope to an education without religion. But to a diverse public, the common school appeared to be too religious. This dilemma posed a real problem for the United States: where would the nation find a shared basis for virtue if not in some form of education that acknowledged God as the giver of morals?

Interestingly enough, Massachussetts, the last state to abandon tax-supported churches, was the first to implement a state-run system of education that attempted to supply society with the morality formerly provided by the church. The debates that had revealed the awkwardness of taxing Methodists and Baptists to pay for Congregationalist ministers (some of whom happened to be Unitarian, thanks to theological laxity within the Standing Order) were similar to ones that prompted state officials to prohibit the use of sectarian instructional materials "which are calculated to favour any particular religious sect or tenent" in the schools. The legislation that forbade sectarian textbooks also burdened Massachusetts schools with a curriculum that extended well beyond the three Rs: "the principles of piety, justice, and sacred regard to truth, love to their country, humanity, and universal benevolence, sobriety, industry, and frugality, chastity, moderation, and temperance, and those other virtues, which are the ornaments of human society, and the basis upon which the Republican Constitution is founded." The man who as secretary of the state board of education eventually oversaw this republican project of instilling nonsectarian religion and virtue in pupils was Horace Mann (1796–1859). A Massachusetts native, he had been reared on the hard truths of New England Calvinism and had left them for the more comforting notions of Unitarianism.

One of Mann's first tasks was to find textbooks and literature with the right balance of republican-affirming virtue and inoffensive religion. This effort drew him into a protracted conflict with the Massachusetts branch of the American Sunday School Union, which offered to churches, families, and schools a "Select Library" of 120 volumes designed to instill piety and the consequent virtues. Mann, however, objected to the teaching contained in certain of its titles as sectarian. It did not help the American Sunday School Union's case that some of its books promoted Calvinistic themes or that Mann found such teaching inappropriate for adults like himself, let alone public school students. This textbook controversy provided the backdrop for Mann's ideas about the place of religion and morals in public education. While children were not always virtuous they could, through the proper influences, receive the rudiments of good character through education. Mann's belief in the relative goodness of human nature drew support from a progressive view of history that regarded the American Revolution and the new nation as an instance of epoch-making significance for human potential. In Mann's view the common school was the one institution that would "enhance individual and social well-being for generations to come."

Stemming from these basic convictions about human nature, the direction of history, and the mission of public education was Mann's understanding of religion and the three Rs. Education, he believed, was fundamentally concerned with the moral capacities of children, not merely the acquisition of knowledge. For this reason religion was essential to the mission of the common school. But the faith of the common school needed to be a generic one since the particularities of denominations had to be avoided. Taxes and the coercive nature of the state were important factors in keeping the common school free from sectarianism. "If a man is taxed to support a school," Mann supposed, "where religious doctrines are inculcated which he believes to be false, and which he believes that God condemns; then he is excluded from the school by the Divine Law, at the same time that he is compelled to support it by human law." The solution to this "double wrong," as Mann called it, was to train students "up to the love of God and the love of man; to make the perfect example of Jesus Christ lovely in their eyes; and to give to all so much of the religious instruction as is comparable with the rights of others and with the genius of our government." The means that Mann advocated to instill this religious and moral training was the reading of the Bible. The choice of verb was important to the Massachusetts official because *studying* the Bible would be more complicated than simply reading the sacred book, especially reading without comment. As Robert Michaelsen has observed, Bible reading had a "magical quality" for Mann, akin to the Roman Catholic view of the sacraments in which the efficacy of the activity stemmed from the act itself, not from the moral disposition of the one performing it. To let the Bible speak for itself through daily readings in the public school was somehow a sufficient basis for the religion and morality a republican government needed.

A similar arrangement for teaching religion in public education emerged in Virginia at roughly the same time as Mann's administration in Massachusetts. This development was more significant than coincidental, given the very different religious and political leanings in the two states. After all, Puritan designs for a godly commonwealth overturned by the forces of liberal democracy might well have resulted in a pattern of public education fairly different from a moderate Anglican establishment upended by a coalition of revivalists and Deists. But the legacy of both the Puritan Standing Order and the Episcopalian establishment were no match for the demands of republican virtue. In both cases the need for a generic religion dissolved fairly rapidly the vestiges of Christendom that the state churches in Massachussetts and Virginia had kept alive.

In the case of Virginia, Thomas Jefferson's plans for a system of public schooling took longer to receive support from the state legislature. Before his service as president, he had promoted successfully bills that would have provided for the establishment of schools whose instruction was essential, he believed, to liberty and the public good. But the financing of this system fell to county governments, where the idea of raising taxes on the wealthy was almost as objectionable as monarchy. After his tenure in Washington, Jefferson returned to the cause of public education, culminating in his establishment in 1819 of the University of Virginia in Charlottesville. Still, by the time of his death in 1826, Jefferson's plans for a system of common schools had yet to receive the necessary public support.

This strategy for public education, like Mann's in the North, was to provide a curriculum thoroughly grounded in religion. But the faith taught in the public school would be nonsectarian. Like Jefferson's Bible, which highlighted the teachings and moral example of Christ, religious instruction in the public schools would provide the ingredients of a common morality minus denominational commentary or inferences.

Two Protestants were crucial to implementing Jefferson's vision, a further indication that the Founding Father's generic Christianity had significant appeal among Protestants with ties to British dissenting churches. In an 1841 address before the state legislature, Alexander Campbell, the founder of the Disciples of Christ, one of the new denominations to emerge from the Second Great Awakening, explained that Christianity contained a common core of religious teachings upon which Christians could "unite, harmonize and co-operate in one great system of moral and Christian education." He advocated that this common religious instruction, available through Bible reading and moral teaching, be included in public schools on a daily basis. Without such a religious and moral foundation the common school would become a "curse to each and every community." Campbell's views emerged as the foundation for a statewide system of education in Virginia that by 1871 led to the appointment of William H. Ruffner, a Presbyterian minister, as the state's first superintendent of schools. A graduate of Princeton Seminary and a chaplain for two years at the University of Virginia, Ruffner would become known as the "Horace Mann of the South." Over the course of his eleven annual reports, he charted a path between those who wanted the public school free from religion and those who wanted more religious instruction. He argued that the state had a responsibility to "teach the recognized morality of the country, and the will of God as the standard and ultimate authority of all morality." But for the specific teachings and practices of the denominations, the people would have to go to "volunteer agencies."

The common school religious instruction endorsed by state officials in both Massachusetts and Virginia was a compromise for devout Protestants like Ruffner and enlightened or liberal Christians like Mann and Jefferson. The former needed to overlook "details of theological belief and narrow denominational loyalty." The latter had to tolerate more explicit Christian sentiments than they would have preferred. But the settlement yielded solid support for the public morality necessary for virtuous citizens and the longevity of the American republic. As a compromise position, the religion of the common school also lacked the strength that principled consistency usually provides. Like Jefferson's Bible, it tried to turn the Jesus of faith into a model citizen, a figure several steps removed from the revered second person of the Trinity but also not exactly welcome to non-Christian Americans for whom Jesus had no special appeal. Nevertheless, as long as the United States was predominantly a Protestant country, the arrangement encouraged the members of most English-speaking denominations to regard Christianity as the only basis for republican virtue.

That Catholics would object to the program of religious instruction in public schools comes as no surprise to anyone aware of the assimilationist and anti-Catholic views that accompanied the rationale for public education in the United States. Despite centuries of antagonism with Protestantism, Roman Catholicism was a good test for the possibilities of generic Christianity since both Protestants and Catholics claimed to be Christian and to follow the ethical teachings of Christ, and yet could find no basis for religious cooperation. Obviously more was involved in Christianity if both sides of its Western exponents were unwilling to embrace a Christian faith gutted of everything but its moral convictions.

A particular incident from 1859 on Mann's home turf illustrated the objections that some Christians would raise against their own religion when adapted for moral ends. The practice in this specific Boston school was for students to recite the Ten Commandments as part of the daily religious instruction, an unsurprising practice since the Decalogue had for more than eighteen hundred years been a source for Christian moral reflection, whether Eastern Orthodox, Roman Catholic, or Protestant. Yet one of the Eliot School's Roman Catholic students, Thomas Wall, refused to participate in the recitation of one of Christianity's most widely acknowledged essential teachings. The reason for Wall's dissent was that the school used the Protestant form of the Ten Commandments, which divided the first commandment in the Roman Catholic version into two and combined the last two of Rome's form into the tenth commandment. The local Roman Catholic bishop, who complained to the Boston School Committee on the student's behalf, explained that a member of his church could not participate in the religious exercise because "He cannot present himself before the Divine presence in what would be for him a merely simulated union of prayer and adoration." In other words, what for Boston's public school officials and teachers was simply a generic, unobjectionable reading from an age-old source of Christian morality, to Roman Catholics was an act of religious devotion that needed to be performed in a setting properly reserved for worship. On the surface, form was an obvious matter of concern for Roman Catholics because the Bible they were directed to use was the one approved by the church, the Douay version, which was a translation from the Vulgate and included material (i.e., the Apocrypha) not found in Protestant versions of the Bible. But beneath this formal matter of difference between Roman Catholics and Protestants over the holy book was a more basic question: could the Bible be used outside a religious setting for public purposes? Directly related to this question was whether Christian morality could be separated from Christian doctrine, church polity, or worship.

Roman Catholics precipitated similar controversies over religion in the public schools. The two most notable episodes were the school wars of the 1830s in New York City and of the 1870s in

Cincinnati. In each case Roman Catholic objections demonstrated what public school officials might have reasonably considered without opposition—that the Bible was not a neutral piece of religious writing or that its moral instruction could not be so easily extracted from its partisan structure. Roman Catholic arguments against Bible reading in public schools proceeded along two lines. First, the very act of reading the Bible without interpretation was out of bounds because it inherently favored what many regarded as the Protestant hermeneutic of individual interpretation or private judgment. As one Roman Catholic official put it, "The Catholic Church tells her children that they must be taught their religion by *authority*. The Sects say, read the bible, judge for yourselves. . . . The Protestant principle is therefore acted upon, slily inculcated, and the schools are Sectarian." For Catholics, then, the Bible was never neutral but always interpreted, and those with authority to interpret Scriptures were ordained clergy. The second prong of the Roman Catholic critique was that nonsectarian Christianity was an impossibility. According to New York City's Bishop John Hughes, "if you exclude all sects [from public schools], you exclude Christianity." "Take away the distinctive dogmas," he added, "of the Catholics, the Baptists, the Methodists, the Presbyterians and so on, and you have nothing left but deism." Two implications followed. One was that if religion and education were indeed inseparable, the only option was a scheme of parochial or denominational schools where religious instruction would be integral and explicit. The other was that if partisanly religious schools were at odds with the state's duty to provide an education for its citizens, the public schools would have to offer a curriculum void of religious content, that is, a religiously neutral public school.

Roman Catholics were not the only American Christians to face this set of predicaments. A number of Protestants also recognized the deficiency of Christian morality stripped of its doctrinal foundation and looked the question of parochial education straight in the eye. Many of these Protestants were immigrants, such as German Lutherans or Dutch Reformed, for whom language and ethnic identity were intimately bound with religion. But a number of Anglo-American Protestants also disliked the religious compromise involved in the common faith of the public school. These Protestants fell into two camps, those still committed to the common enterprise of the public school and those, like Roman Catholics, willing to abandon the public setting for a parochial school.

In the first group, those committed to teaching religion in public school, the issue was whether the common religion proposed by state officials was truly Christian. Here the conservative Congregationalists who opposed Mann's proposals in Massachusetts leveled a series of astute criticisms at the idea that the Bible provided generic religious ideals. Frederick A. Packard, the head of the American Sunday School Union, based in Philadelphia, objected to Mann's exclusion of Union books because they were sectarian. Packard argued that Mann fundamentally misconstrued human nature, failing to understand that without the threat of eternal punishment Christianity's moral imperatives were easily ignored. Without saying it explicitly, the Sunday School Union chief was intimating that Christian morality was effective only for those who also believed in the rest of the Christian religious tenets, namely, those about God, man, Christ, and the afterlife.

Another of Mann's critics, Matthew Hale Smith, a Congregationalist minister in Massachusetts, raised doubts about how friendly the public schools really were to religion. For Smith, generic Christianity was really no Christianity since it excluded "books as sectarian that inculcate truths, which *nine-tenths of professed Christians of all names believe*," and since it propagated a Christian heresy, namely "universal salvation." By twenty-first century standards, after decades of squeamishness about any mention of religion in the public schools, Smith may seem to be tilting at windmills. But by the lights of Protestant teaching he had a point: promoting generic religion could send the wrong signals and ultimately undermine religion, at least the Christian one. Here his argument about Bible reading was particularly telling. "No plan can so effectively get the Bible, ultimately, out of Common Schools," he declared, "as that which rejects a part as not true, and another part as not fit to be read." By teaching only those parts of the Bible agreeable to officials like Mann, public schools were in effect teaching the particular religion of Mann, not a common religion. (Behind Smith's argument lay a vigorous critique of Mann's Unitarian faith.) What Mann's critics failed to address, however, was the problem of incorporating the exclusive and dogmatic claims of Christianity into a religiously mixed and open setting like public education.

Someone who did wrestle with Mann's recognition of Christianity's sectarian character was Robert Lewis Dabney, a Presbyterian theological educator in Richmond, who was perhaps the most vigorous critic of Ruffner, Mann's counterpart in Virginia's educational system. As one of the Southern Presbyterian church's most conservative (politically and theologically) intellectuals, Dabney was unmistakably an advocate of religion. This was particularly true in his theory of education. "True education is," he wrote, "a spiritual process, the nurture of the soul." Because of the deep ties between mind and soul, Dabney concluded that "the theological and educational porcesses appear so cognate that they cannot be separated."

Yet because of the profoundly religious character of any valuable education, Dabney also favored as a necessary evil a public education stripped of all reference to Christianity. Here he appealed to the religious neutrality involved in American politics and the states that controlled public education. The American ideal of religious liberty stipulated that "no man's civil rights shall be modified or equality diminished by any religion or lack of any." As officials of the state, public school teachers needed to refrain from favoring or promoting religion as much as any legislator, judge, or executive. Consequently Dabney recognized the fundamental legitimacy of Roman Catholic complaints about religion in the public schools, no matter how nonsectarian. He even wondered how Protestants would like the use of the Roman Catholic version of the Bible in public schools, translating specific verses to support Catholic notions of salvation. To say that their translation was inaccurate compared to the King James version was "doubtless true" theologically. But politically the accuracy of Bible translations was moot. "In the State *arena*," Dabney asserted, "we shall respect papists' religious views, precisely as we require them to respect ours."

To the predicament of religion in the public schools, four possible solutions presented themselves by Dabney's count. The first was to impose the religion of the majority on the minority, a plan obviously at odds with American polity. The second was a system, like England's, where the state funded all schools, common and denominational. Dabney listed several problems with that system, the chief of which was the state's lacking the authority "to indicate of either the creeds that it is, or is not, true and valuable." Religious neutrality in government meant the state was deaf, dumb, and blind in evaluating theological propositions. The third option was to include an hour of religious instruction in public schools at the beginning of the day, from which dissenting parents could withdraw their children by sending them to school at the beginning of the second hour of teaching. But this plan also violated the separation of church and state in America by giving the state authority, through its educational officials, to "select a religion, as the true and useful one, for anybody, willing or unwilling." The only option remaining, then, was to "secularize the State's teaching absolutely, limiting it to matters merely secular, and leaving parents or the Church to supplement it with such religious teaching as they may please, or none."

The underlying religious conviction driving Dabney to a conclusion that twenty-first century conservative Protestants would find inscrutable—that is, secular public education—was the totality of Christianity's claims. For Christians who worried about the integrity of their faith, whether Roman Catholic or Protestant, the notion of reserving the ethical content of the Bible for public consumption while deleting the sectarian bits was an absurdity. From the English translation used for daily readings to the proper understanding of Christian morality, the pieces of Christianity were shot through with profound theological meaning. "The only teaching adequate" for genuine virtue from a Christian outlook was *"redemption,"* not, as Mann or Ruffner proposed, ethics minus the doctrines of salvation. Of the doctrines of salvation, Dabney concluded, the state "knows nothing."

If Christians of the most devout and theologically astute kind were objecting to prayer and Bible reading in public education, obviously something was amiss. As Dabney and Roman Catholic critics indicated, part of the problem was the proper institution to provide education. Some conservative Protestants and most Roman Catholics believed that the state had no authority to provide education even of a secular kind: for the former it was the responsibility of parents, for the latter the duty of the church. But aside from arriving at the proper structures, the deeper issue was one of moral duty. As much as Christians and the advocates of republican government might agree on the need for virtuous citizens, they disagreed profoundly on the adequacy of Christianity to supply this need. Critics like Dabney went one step further and concluded with a proposition that reads more like a conundrum than a syllogism: to read the Bible in public schools was not religious but in fact anti-Christian.

## The Dilemma of Christian Goodness

One of the more compelling puzzles of American Protestant history is the way these heirs of the sixteenth-century Reformation came to regard the Ten Commandments, the assumed source of virtue and morality for decent Americans. Even Thomas Jefferson recognized that the Jewish origins of the Decalogue complicated their applicability for citizens of a modern republic, thus preferring the simplified teachings of Jesus. But aside from the sizable theological difficulty of harmonizing the Old and New Testaments, something that helps account for the variety of Christian churches, the requirements of the Ten Commandments lead to a larger point about the place of ethics in Protestant theology, which in turn calls into question the idea that religious exercises in public schools produce virtuous citizens.

Without putting too fine a point on it, Protestants differ from Roman Catholics precisely on the question of good works. For Protestants, the way to salvation is through faith in Christ, not by trying to meet a moral standard and merit divine favor. This accounts for the sloganeering that used to inform Protestant–Roman Catholic polemics, namely, that of justification by faith versus justification by works. Because Protestants insisted that believers could obtain divine mercy only through trust in Christ's saving work, and not through their own efforts to lead moral or blameless lives, Roman Catholic officials invariably charged Protestantism with antinomianism (i.e., against the law). If Protestant doctrine taught that nothing a person did could qualify him or her for salvation, but instead depended entirely on the saving work of Christ, Protestantism would inevitably result in licentiousness or lawlessness. In other words, the notion of justification by faith instead of works supposedly removed all incentive for living a moral and decent life.

The Protestant response to this accusation was a doctrine called the third use of the law. The first two uses of the law concerned, first, the recognition of one's guilt and, second, the need for salvation. The third use of the law was as a guide to the Christian life. Accordingly, the believer did not follow the law in order to merit God's favor since human depravity was so great that not even the good works of a Christian could satisfy divine justice. Instead the law became a way of displaying gratitude for the grace of salvation. According to the logic of both Martin Luther and John Calvin, for instance, the good news of salvation in Christ became the basis for a life of gratitude that would inevitably involve some measure of conformity to the duties entailed in the law. For this reason, Protestant pedagogical devices like the Heidelberg Catechism (1563), a doctrinal standard for the Reformed churches of the Netherlands and Germany, elaborated the duties involved in the Ten Commandments only after explaining the work of Christ. This Catechism opens a section on the Decalogue by explicitly teaching that good works for a Christian are only a means of expressing gratitude, not a way to gain further mercy from God. Question 86 asks, Since Christians have been delivered from misery by God's grace alone "and not because you have earned it: why then must we still do good?" This was precisely the question that Roman Catholics were asking of Protestants. The heart of the answer ran as follows: we do good so that "we may show that we are thankful to God for all he has done for us, and so that he may be praised through us." Then a few questions later (91), the authors of the Heidelberg Catechism want to make sure that their students will not miss the connection between grace (faith) and gratitude (good works): "What do we do that is good?" The answer is, "only that which arises out of true faith, conforms to God's law, and is done for his glory." The important lesson here, and one that drove a wedge within Western Christianity, was the relationship between faith and works. For Roman Catholics the two were interwoven, with grace and virtue assisting and building upon each other. For Protestants faith and works were clearly separable, with the former preceding the latter, and with works being good only when proceeding from trust in (as opposed to a desire to earn) divine mercy.

This all too brief summary of one of the major issues at stake in the sixteenth century helps explain why some American Protestants had important reservations about religion in the public schools, or the related idea that religion produces virtuous citizens. Obviously they did not favor a secular education. But a classroom free from all religious influence was preferable to one in which the Bible was read, a hymn sung, and a prayer offered, because the logic of public school religion ran directly counter to historic Protestant ideas about faith and good works or virtue. The religious exercises proposed by the Manns and Ruffners of the emerging educational establishment promised to make students moral and responsible with guidance from the Bible's ethical teaching but without scriptural instruction about sin and grace, or about the absolute necessity of divine mercy. Roman Catholics, who disagreed with Protestants about the relationship between faith and good works, even recognized the problem because their religion also held that holiness was intimately related to grace. Likewise conservative Protestants saw the impossibility of teaching either the Ten Commandments or Christ's ethics to students who were not already believers in the Bible. This was not simply a matter of politeness. It was more profoundly a matter of Christian theology: Christian morality proceeded from divine grace; to reverse the order was to betray Christianity. As the distinguished historian of Christianity who taught at Yale for much of his career, Jaroslav Pelikan, so well put it in an obscure report to which he contributed for the National Council of Churches in 1963:

> For historical reasons alone, and according to the Bible itself, for more than historical reasons, biblical morality is inseparable from biblical doctrine and biblical doctrine is inseparable from the community of believers. If the faith is broken off from its context in the community, and if the morality is broken off from its context in the faith, the result is a double fracture.

What is remarkable is that more Protestants did not see the problem, and that present-day Protestants who advocate religion in pubilc schools do not understand the way in which their religion is abused when used for only its ethical norms while neglecting the centrality of its redemptive message. One plausible explanation for the disparity is that the believers who desire a common morality for public institutions like schools are actually better republicans than they are Christians. For the impulse behind public school morality stems much more from republican ideology about restraining liberty with virtue than it does from Christian teaching about a religious standard for ethical conduct. In both the Old and New Testaments, the ethical instructions given to Jews and Christians were for the believing communities themselves, not blueprints for public morality among the Chaldeans, Philistines, Romans, or Greeks. To follow either the law of Moses or the teaching of Christ, a person first had to affiliate with the Jews and Christians respectively, by worshiping their God and renouncing all others. That American Protestants thought their exclusive faith could provide the moral standard for a republic conceived in religious neutrality is one of the more surprising twists in the history of biblical religion. Not only was the misunderstanding of religious liberty in the United States glaring, the distortion of the Christian religion was enormous.

## Ungracious Goodness

Although the belief that faith is the only adequate basis for American morality ran aground on the nation's experience with public schooling, it contiues to inform those who lament the failure of secular politics and in turn advocate a recovery of America's religious resources. Nowhere is this conviction more explicit than in a book like *Why America Needs Religion: Secular Modernity and Its Discontents* (1996), by Guenter Lewy, a retired professor of political science at the University of Massachusetts, Amherst. As the title indicates, Lewy connects contemporary arguments about faith's public benefits to older republican and Protestant assertions about religion promoting individual and public virtue. At one point he asserts that "Society needs a morality that will curb the antisocial tendencies of human beings." He then deduces that since such morality is not available simply on "rational grounds," and since it "cannot be created," it "requires the support of a tradition, and this tradition is generally linked to religious precepts."

Lewy follows this logic with empirical data—a survey conducted by Robert Wuthnow, a Princeton University sociologist of religion, which finds that Americans who knew the story of the Good Samaritan were "far more likely than those ignorant of the parable to be involved in charitable activities, donate their time to voluntary organizations, care for someone who is sick, give money to a charity, and so on." Lewy concedes that the cause-and-effect in this chain is not straightforward, since it could be the case that those who first become involved in charitable activities then find that the Good Samaritan parable justifies their participation. But whichever way the influence goes, religion is crucial to "nourishing and replenishing the moral capital of of our society." Lewy also appeals to the fairly well-known example of a person walking at night through a bad urban neighborhood. If, as this illustration has it, this person were to encounter several young men walking toward him, would he be more at ease if he knew that these young men had just come from a Bible study? The point here is that religion not only appears to supply the motivation for humanitarian endeavors but also for personal moral behavior.

As reassuring as this may be to American Christians—and surely arguments like Lewy's, who admits to being not a traditional religious adherent even though holding "strong moral convictions," were comforting to Protestants in Jefferson's day—his case is scarcely an endorsement of Christianity, not to mention its cognizance of the significant differences between Roman Catholics and Protestants. He admits that America is not unique in exhibiting a relationship between religion and morality. "No society anywhere . . . has managed to build a culture devoid of religion." For that matter, all the "great universal religions" have affirmed that "disinterested goodwill, social responsibility, and individual moral integrity" proceed from faith, the very virtues "without which no society can flourish." At this point the fourth word in Lewy's title, "religion," becomes clear while also throwing a damper on Christian efforts to claim that their religion is necessary to the United States' well-being. In fact Lewy is fairly explicit that any religion will work as long as it is a faith that promotes virtue. So why would Christians who are jealous for the truth and integrity of their own faith put themselves in a logical sequence in which any of the great world religions would supply as much intellectual consistency as the religion of Christ? Have they forgotten that the Ten Commandments start with four (by Protestant numbering) governing divine worship? Even in the Bible's moral teaching, separating love of God (theology) from love of man (ethics) is virtually impossible and hermeneutically irresponsible.

The difficulties in Lewy's logic go even deeper. The problem is not only that any religion will do but also that irreligion could conceivably be acceptable if it supplied the right moral capital. Lewy's sweep of human history leaves him with no examples of virtue springing from a nonreligious source. But to alter his illustration about the pedestrian in the dangerous urban neighborhood, imagine the relief this person would experience if he discovered that these young men had just come from a meeting of the Rotary, the Masons, or the Overachievers of America. This example is not far-fetched and suggests that ideas, organizations, and associations other than religious ones also encourage the virtues that Lewy thinks America needs. Political liberalism itself has not been shy in displaying moral seriousness throughout the history of the modern West. As some have argued, its skeptical premises about metaphysics prevent liberal intellectuals from providing a universal foundation for liberalism's understanding of virtue and morality. But this perceived weakness in no way leaves political liberalism without recourse to moral imperatives. Indeed, the recent antagonism between the so-called religious right and the so-called secular left is suffused with moral claims, with, for instance, pro-life and pro-choice advocates appealing equally to moral principles, even the righteousness and justice of their side. If American politics had not been so steeped in the republican and Protestant conceptions of religion, morality, and the public good, perhaps the nation's political debates might not be as shrill as they are. The legacy of virtue politics and the accompanying moral superiority it encourages may be more of a political curse than a national blessing.

Aside from liberalism's contested moral legacy, Christians should be reluctant to have their faith used as Lewy does. One reason has to do with the concerns nineteenth-century Christians voiced about prayer and Bible reading in the public schools; to encourage children, whether Christian or not, to believe they can be good without divine grace is a serious misunderstanding, if not betrayal, of the Christian religion. In other words, as favorable as arguments like Lewy's appear to be for Christians who believe religion will lead to a better America, they are actually a threat to the truth of Christianity.

Another reason for being more circumspect about arguments like Lewy's is that his logic is ultimately unbecoming for Christians. American Christians would agree that pride is a sin. Yet many of those same believers fail to notice that by claiming religion makes people virtuous, they are implicitly (if not sometimes explicitly) calling attention to their own righteousness. After all, they are devout and so, by their logic, they must be virtuous. Several words come to mind for this set of circumstances. Self-righteous is one;

sanctimonious is another. Of course most advocates for religion as the basis of morality do not mean to call attention to their own ethical goodness. Even so, they may have forgotten a lesson that survives at least in Presbyterian teaching, namely, that even the good deeds of Christians are tinged with selfishness and pride. As the Westminster Confession of Faith teaches in its chapter on Good Works, the morality of Christians is "defiled, and mixed with so much weakness and imperfection, that they cannot endure the severity of God's judgment" (16.5). This is simply another reminder of the importance of mercy to Christian accounts of morality. The ability to perform good works arises not only from grace; those deeds themselves need grace ultimately to be acceptable to God. In other words, a Christian understanding of morality should yield in believers a sense of gratitude, not one of self-righteousness. No matter how they parse the relationship between faith and good works, if contemporary Christians could remember that divine mercy, not their own goodness, made them virtuous, and that such goodness is different from the civic virtue available to citizens and necessary for social stability, they might abandon the boast that Christianity is what made the American republic great and especially good.

# CHAPTER FOUR

# Under God

Almost a century before the United States Congress amended the Pledge of Allegiance to include the words "under God," Abraham Lincoln gave currency to that phrase in his memorable speech of 1863 that was part of the ceremony to dedicate the national cemetery in Gettysburg, Pennsylvania. A man as eloquent as he was succinct, the sixteenth president employed these words close by a phrase that was more popular and apparently more ripe with meaning than "under God," until faith became such a contentious part of the nation's politics:

> It is rather for us to be here dedicated to the great task remaining before us—that from these honored dead we take increased devotion to the cause for which they gave the last full measure of devotion; that we here highly resolve that these dead shall not have died in vain; that this nation, under God, shall have a new birth of freedom; and that government of the people, by the people, for the people, shall not perish from the earth.

From the late nineteenth century until the middle decades of the twentieth, Lincoln's point about the sovereignty of the people would inspire many who looked to the United States as the standard-bearer for democracy. Little did Lincoln know that by invoking the idea of divine sovereignty he would eventually become part of a national debate about the religious sources of the American government's legitimacy.

As much as the Gettysburg Address and Lincoln's own stature may have granted the words "under God" currency in American political discourse, the original circumstances of this part of the speech were as ambiguous as the president's own affirmations of belief. As James Piereson admitted in a recent article, the phrase "under God," despite the dominance of Protestants in the national culture, was rarely used before Lincoln's famous speech. In fact the president inserted the words only at the last minute, perhaps as late as while sitting on the podium waiting to deliver his remarks before the gathered throng. These words did not appear, for instance, in the manuscript he had prepared before embarking for Gettysburg, nor did they make it into the text from which Lincoln spoke while at the cemetery. For that matter, the first Republican president's faith offers a variety of ways for interpreting its meaning since Lincoln was a God-fearer who refused to join a church and so defied the conventions of any particular Protestant denomination. Try as they might after his tragic death to turn Abe into a model Christian saint, the Protestant biographers of Lincoln could squeeze out at most vague affirmations of divine providence, justice, mercy, and ethical imperatives. For that reason this phrase remains a mystery in Lincoln's usage. For someone like Piereson, "under God" must have referred to Lincoln's belief that the United States existed not only under divine protection but also "under His judgment," an idea that carried the consequence of divine retribution for failing to conform to God's will. Other commentators have speculated on Lincoln's aim in preserving the Union and using "under God" as a code for a civil faith that would bestow upon the nation a sacred and indissoluble character.

No matter Lincoln's intentions, the phrase entered mainstream American political discourse thanks to Lincoln's address at

Gettysburg. The culmination of its popularity was Congress's 1954 decision to amend the Pledge of Allegiance by adding the phrase after the words "one nation." Originally written for the four-hundredth anniversary of Columbus's discovery of America by the Baptist minister and educator Francis Bellamy, the Pledge was designed to instill in the schoolchildren who would recite and memorize it the lesson that Lincoln wanted the nation to learn from the Civil War, namely, that the Union was indissoluble and that its foundation was justice for all citizens regardless of skin color. Congress's revision also served political purposes and honored Lincoln's invocation, no matter how ambiguous, of the nation's civil religion. Because of fierce rivalry with the Soviet Union and a concomitant struggle between liberal democracy and communism, American officials attempted to seal the antagonism of the cold war by contrasting the religious roots of American freedom and capitalism with the atheistic origins of Marxism. "Under God," then, was a way for Americans, from the Civil War to the cold war, to enlist divine sovereignty for decidedly political and national ends.

As reassuring as it may be to religious adherents in the United States that their country is "under God," a speech by a very important president or a pledge recited daily by the land's schoolchildren does not make it so. For instance, the Constitution makes no reference to God, thus suggesting that the republic for which it functions is not legally under God. The Declaration of Independence, a document clearly important to the American founding but without clear legislative force, refers to a Creator; but the "Nature's God" also in view is not the Protestant deity that Congress likely had in mind when revising the Pledge of Allegiance. For this reason, nonreligious Americans might well object to efforts to turn a nation founded on Enlightenment ideas into a religious entity by asserting that the United States is "under God." On the other side of the divide are legitimate concerns by religious adherents who argue the folly of conceiving of America as not existing "under God." For one thing, even if unacknowledged, God, as a being than which nothing greater can be conceived, will always be "above" America or any nation and so does not require a pledge to affirm such divine existence. More important to religious adherents, though, is that being under God implies a higher standard to which the nation must conform. It suggests that America cannot be a law unto itself—always a wise restraint given the hubris that generally afflicts politicians.

Is it possible to get beyond this apparent impasse? In other words, is the under-Godness of America a zero-sum game that either demands religion in the public arena (as believers have it), or is it a violation of the Establishment Clause of the Constitution (as strict constructionists regard it)? Perhaps we could settle for it being beside the point (as agnostics and atheists might have it). Perhaps this either-or approach is actually the wrong way of construing the problem. After all, when Christ told his disciples to render to Caesar what was Caesar's, and to God what was God's, he was not holding a coin that read "In God we trust." He was raising the theological and even legal possibility of a nation or empire having legitimacy even if it did not acknowledge that it was "under God." In other words, to conceive of Christ as a rival authority to the state, as the Athenians did in the New Testament (Acts 17:7), may be to misunderstand divine authority. Instead of being the basis for political judgments and social order, perhaps the rule that Christ taught his disciples was fundamentally different from that of the state—spiritual, not civil; eternal, not temporal. In which case, if Christianity is a religion less concerned with statecraft than with soulcraft, Christian attempts to place the United States "under God" are unnecessary and may actually be a departure from the original teachings of Christ.

## In God's Kingdom

Walter Rauschenbusch (1861–1918) was only two years old when Abraham Lincoln uttered the words "under God" in Gettysburg. The so-called father of the Social Gospel was a German American who grew up in Rochester, New York, the son of a Lutheran pastor. Despite circumstances that seemed to place considerable distance between Lincoln's meaning and a young immigrant's life, or between the fields of central Pennsylvania and the ethnic neighborhood of an industrial town in upstate New York, Rauschenbusch would emerge to offer one of the most influential interpretations of what it meant for American Protestants to live under God.

Studies at the University of Rochester and Rochester Theological Seminary acclimated Rauschenbusch to American religion sufficiently to turn him into a Baptist. His first call to the ministry took him to a German Baptist congregation in New York City in the vicinity of Hell's Kitchen, a neighborhood characterized by the worst features of the new industrialization, urbanization, and immigration. After an eleven year stint at this church, a period that profoundly shaped Rauschenbusch's understanding of the social crisis, he traveled to Germany to engage in advanced studies in the Bible and sociology and became familiar with some of the leading theologians of Protestant liberalism. Upon his return to the United States, he went back to his home city of Rochester to teach at the seminary from which he was a graduate, where he taught for the rest of his life.

Rochester Theological Seminary also functioned as the site for Rauschenbusch's sustained reflection on the kingdom of God. During his academic career he wrote three widely read books on the subject, which prompted the church historian H. Sheldon Smith to conclude that Rauschenbusch was "the foremost molder of American Christian thought in his generation." His influence also trickled down to Reinhold Niebuhr, who called Rauschen-busch the "most brilliant and generally satisfying exponent" of the Social Gospel, and to Martin Luther King, Jr., who received a large measure of inspiration from the Rochester theologian's "sense of social responsibility."

Of the three substantial books that Rauschenbusch devoted to the social crisis of a modernizing America, the third, *A Theology for the Social Gospel* (1917), was the most systematic. Fittingly, it cul-minated his efforts to move the church in America to do its part in Christianizing the social order. Essential to Rauschenbusch's argument was the contrast he drew between the kingdom of God and the church. The former extended beyond the church, its do-main was wider, its significance broader. The church, in fact, ac-cording to Rauschenbusch, was not originally part of Jesus' teach-ing. He argued that in the New Testament accounts of Jesus' utterances, the word "church" appeared only twice, and these were in passages of dubious authenticity. In effect, Jesus' purpose was to establish the kingdom of God, not a church. But because the church was a practical reality for early Christians, while the kingdom was only a future hope, the "Kingdom of God shriveled to an undeveloped and pathetic remnant in Christian thought." In other words, the kingdom of God was intended as nothing less than a social gospel, a conception of divine will and righteousness that embraced "the whole social order." In Rauschenbusch's own words, it was "the Christian transfiguration of the social order." In contrast to the church, whose ministers proclaimed an individual-istic gospel, one whose aim was personal salvation and the future life, the kingdom of God was concerned with the elimination of religious bigotry and intolerance, political corruption, injustice, mob action and violence, militarism, and racism. Without the the-ology of the kingdom, the church "became a conservative social influence and increased the weight of the other stationary forces in society." But with the kingdom of God as its guiding principle, the church could provide "the movements for democracy and so-cial justice" with a fitting "religious backing."

Between the lines of Rauschenbusch's challenge to American churches was a sense of exasperation that Protestants in the United States had yet to wake up from their socially conservative slum-bers. "Even today," he wrote, "many Christians can not see any re-ligious importance in social justice and fraternity because it does not increase the number of conversions nor fill the churches." To be sure, if pollsters had been in business during the decade of World War I and had asked church attendees if they shared Rauschenbusch's list of social evils, the percentages would have been low, especially because the Social Gospeler's pacifism was an acquired taste at a time when Americans had just fought a "war for righteousness." But Rauschenbusch's impatience with American Christians was well wide of the mark in light of religious develop-ments between the Civil War and World War I. For the actual tra-jectory of American Protestantism during this era showed a pro-nounced shift from an individualistic to a social gospel. The logic may not have matched Rauschenbusch's premise for premise, but the reasoning of mainstream Protestantism reflected a similar ef-fort to extend the standards of divine rule beyond the narrow con-fines of the church to all of society.

After the Civil War, Protestants in the largest denominations found they had more in common than they had imagined, even if worshiping in separate Protestant traditions. Intellectual and reli-gious historians have stressed mounting divisions between so-called liberal and conservative Protestants over Darwinism and new scholarship on the Bible. But at social and political levels, Protestants of British descent, and those on their way to assimila-tion, engaged in a broad program of cooperation and church unity. This cooperative impulse carried through all the way to World War I when after the Armistice mainline denominational leaders proposed an umbrella organization for all American Protestants.

That these ecumenical efforts coincided with war was not an accident of history. Throughout the American experience, Protestants discovered in times of war that their political and social ties were often stronger than their identities as Presbyterians, Baptists, Congregationalists, Methodists, or Quakers. Observers of these church members, or people unaware of the various nuances of Protestant theology and worship, might unsurprisingly also fail to see the importance of denominational differences. That Protestants themselves were so willing to set aside their differences even while saying religion was crucial to the republic is at least puzzling if not contradictory.

The sources of Protestant unity rarely proceeded from church councils commissioned to explore, for instance, the subtleties of sacramental theology or the finer points of ecclesiastical polity. Instead the rationale for greater cooperation stemmed from a perceived common enemy, one that usually had the religious character of the United States in its sights. Consequently Protestants rallied to preserve the Christian (read: Protestant) character of their country, and in doing so they believed they were, to use Rauschenbusch's language, securing one of the most significant provinces of God's kingdom. The perils posed to Christian civilization in late-nineteenth-century America were standard fare from the perspective of folks like John Witherspoon, Lyman Beecher, or Josiah Strong. Violation of the Sabbath, intemperate consumption of alcoholic beverages (prompting an emphasis on abstinence), and assaults on the sweet harmony of the Christian family were some of the reasons why Protestants might disregard the importance of particular baptismal or ordination vows; for these believers, Christian identity stemmed more from familial or social mores than from denominational teaching or practice. These concerns for what Princeton University president James McCosh called "the moral improvement of mankind" only intensified in the decades after the Civil War as large-scale industrial development and the cheap labor such industry required made urban centers appear to be in even greater need of Christianity's civilizing influences than they had been before the war. The fact that many of the new immigrants to the United States were Roman Catholic, combined with papal pronouncements against democracy and religious liberty in the *Syllabus of Errors* (1864), gave more Protestants greater incentive to join forces against the perceived tyranny of the papacy. Rome's formidable countenance received reinforcement during the First Vatican Council (1869–1870) and demonstrated the apparent weakness of Protestant divisiveness. How could Protestantism, many church leaders wondered, ever hope to retain its grip on the American soul if it was divided into so many different denominations? In sum, the dangers to the United States of materialism, skepticism, infidelity, and Roman Catholicism persuaded Protestants of the importance of finding common ground and forming outlets for such togetherness.

Even before Roman Catholics convened in Rome for the First Vatican Council, American Protestants rallied to the cause of Protestant unity, and with it greater influence and efficiency, forming in 1867 the American branch of the Evangelical Alliance. Originally founded in London in 1846 by British Protestants, the Alliance failed to gain American support until almost three decades later. Its purpose was to bring "individual Christians into closer fellowship and cooperation on the basis of the spiritual union which already exists in the vital relation of Christ to the members of his body." Despite these pious overtones, American participation in the Alliance drew upon nationalistic sentiments stemming directly from the Civil War. Many Northern Protestants who advocated the Alliance regarded it as a fitting outlet for the defense of Christian civilization in the United States. The Evangelical Alliance was the first institutional expression, then, of a series of Protestant cooperative ventures to emerge between the Civil War and World War I.

But the Alliance was important not merely for its primacy among interdenominational organizations. It also gave expression to a relationship between religion and society that would color Protestant cooperation and nurture a receptive audience for Rauschenbusch's Social Gospel. The Evangelical Alliance's sixth general conference, held in New York City in 1873, convened members from around the world and especially Western Europe. The presiding officer, William E. Dodge, opened the meetings with a summary of the Alliance's purpose that reflected the fusion of religion and society that drove Protestant cooperation. He hoped the conference would "give an impulse to the growth of religious liberty everywhere," "bind together Christians of every name more closely," "forward the growing sentiment in favor of arbitration in the settlement of international difficulties," and "lift up among all people a victorious standard in the face of modern skepticism, rationalism, the claims of the Papacy, and every other false system."

With a mandate that broad, the surprise may have been that the Alliance met for only ten days. Delegates were able to hear a full slate of reports on the state of Christendom, from descriptions of church life in different nations, and the progress of church union and Christian missions, to assessments of Christianity's relationship to civil government and social reform. In these latter categories Americans were particularly prominent. Here the themes were the hand-me-downs from the antebellum era, with speakers from prominent New England colleges defending Sabbath observance and legislation, and temperance, as well as continuing to link the blessings of civil liberty to the fundamental right of religious liberty. Squaring these lecturers' obvious delight over Protestantism's contributions to such liberties with the legalism that informed Sabbath and temperance legislation was not a subject that many addressed and might have required another day of proceedings.

But as predictable as the American delegates' talking points were from the perspective of antebellum Protestantism, they did highlight a conception of the kingdom of God that was indicative of Protestant notions that the United States existed under divine authority. In this regard the talk on "Intemperance and Its Suppression," by Henry A. Nelson, a professor at Lane Theological Seminary in Cincinnati, was revealing. He identified two problems that remained for a movement that over the course of the nineteenth century had made great strides in alerting the American public to the dangers of alcohol, both for the individual drinker and for the community at large. The first problem was legislative. Nelson conceded that there were a range of proposals for the best means of eliminating alcoholic consumption, from taxation and licenses to fines for drunkenness and resulting injuries. But whatever the merits of various local experiments, Nelson was upset with a rising assumption that drunkenness was "only a misfortune" and the consequent preoccupation with imposing penalties and sanctions upon the vendor or distributor. "The Word of God," he insisted, "plainly treats intemperate indulgence of appetites as a sin—the appetite for intoxicating drink as surely and as sternly as any other." This made the drunkard not merely a "sinner against God" but a "criminal toward civil society, withholding from its interests his due contribution of productive industry. . . ." No matter how difficult the task of finding in the Bible a prohibition against alcohol, especially since wine was an element of one of Protestantism's two sacraments, Nelson's painless transition from divine will to the arrangement of society was a telltale sign of a mind-set that looked to divine law as the norm for civil law.

Legislation was only one problem confronting the temperance campaign. The other was an outlook within the churches that restricted the influence of Christianity to the religious sphere exclusively. Nelson regarded it as obvious that Christianity "must elevate the public sentiment of the world above the groveling maxims

and tendencies of materialism." For that reason, legislative and political solutions to intemperance would be inadequate apart from
communities that were "pervaded by spiritual, Christian influences." Nelson was aware of objections from Christians who might
argue that "Christ's kingdom is not of this world" and that preachers should not go beyond a narrowly religious message in their
public proclamation. But his path around this minor obstacle was
the example of the apostle Paul, who preached to the magistrates
of his day (the governor Felix in particular) of "righteousness, temperance, and the judgment to come," and who lectured the Christians at Corinth about materialistic indulgence. For this reason,
"we believe that pre-eminently from the Christian pulpit must be
sounded forth those mighty truths which work in the bosom of society, and move at length the whole body along pathways of beneficent reform." For Nelson, to regard the kingdom of God as "not
of this world" was to misread the Bible itself.

This talk before the Evangelical Alliance came almost a decade
before a theological struggle at the nation's oldest Protestant theological institution, Andover Seminary, which demonstrated the degree to which the social consequences of Christianity had captured
the American Protestant soul. Oliver Wendell Holmes may have
dated the shift sometime around 1855 in his oft-quoted poem
"One-Hoss Shay." But when Congregationalist theologians at Andover in the early 1880s began to transfer their loyalty from the
Calvinist Jonathan Edwards to the father of American Protestant
liberalism, Horace Bushnell, the bubble of Protestant orthodoxy
had, as Holmes put it, clearly burst. The specific doctrinal truths to
come in for revision made up a long list. Most of them pertained to
overturning the old orthodoxy's dualisms that strongly contrasted
the church and the world, divine and human, supernatural and natural, and sacred and secular. Still, behind these theological revisions
was a shift far more radical than the history of theology sometimes
suggests. The figures responsible for the changes at Andover may

have been less responsible for rejecting Protestant orthodoxy than for attempting to transform theology itself from a fairly abstract esoteric endeavor into one that was directly practical. In an essay that introduced Andover's "Progressive Orthodoxy," Egbert C. Smyth insisted that the school's teaching was better understood as "real" rather than "new." The reason was that it dealt with "beings more than with abstractions, with actual processes and the rational contents more than with *a priori* assumptions, with laws of life and organic forces more than with mechanical combinations, . . . with things more than with words, and with persons more than with things."

In several respects, then, the shift in Protestant thought at the end of the nineteenth century, represented by the Andover initiative, was a process that allowed theologians to engage in the sorts of subjects that animated speakers at the Evangelical Alliance. One way to do this was through an expansive view of Christianity and the Bible that saw its application to all aspects of life as necessary to genuine devotion. As William J. Tucker explained it, in its relationship to the world Christianity could be "organic" and "vital" without becoming "formal." It could recognize that Christians were members of families, factors in society, and citizens of the state. All aspects of life needed "the intentional and well-considered application of Christianity." This was as true for the Christian in business as it was for the health of society. Here Tucker singled out recent legislative initiatives "for the protection of the family" and "for purity in political life." A comprehensive Christianity, as opposed to an exclusive one, a faith that was not confined merely to churchly or spiritual matters, was one that gave theologians, preachers, and church members access to a host of human endeavors for the sake of "communicating Christianity" to the world. Religious devotion had morphed into reform.

Another path to practical Christianity led through the notion of the kingdom of God. In 1897 Shailer Mathews, a professor of

New Testament at the University of Chicago Divinity School, published *The Social Teachings of Jesus*, a book that deployed the language of God's kingdom in ways comparable to Rauschenbusch some thirty years before the father of the Social Gospel made it a shibboleth for reform-minded Protestants. Mathews's project, which was not a technical but still a responsible piece of biblical research, originally appeared in the pages of the *American Journal of Sociology*, a circumstance indicating the religious roots of professional sociology in the United States and of the desire by seminary faculty to venture outside the constraints of their own narrowly religious field. In a book devoted to sociology, the chapter on "society" would logically hold the key to the author's main objective, even if he presented his material as though merely reporting what Jesus thought and taught. Interestingly enough, this was the chapter where Mathews gave sustained attention to the kingdom of God. The Chicago professor believed it obvious from the biblical data that Jesus' conception of the kingdom was not political (i.e., theocratic) or individual (i.e., personal morality). Less certain was whether the divine kingdom was a present or future (that is, eschatological) reality. Here Mathews's definition of the kingdom, italicized so that readers could not miss it, held the right balance between the here and now and the age to come while also providing the comprehensive vision that practically minded Protestants desired. "By the kingdom of God," Mathews announced, "Jesus meant *an ideal . . . social order in which the relation of men to God is that of sons, and therefore to each other, that of brothers.*" Explanations like this were responsible for later caricatures of liberal Protestant theology as the Fatherhood of God and the Brotherhood of Man.

As Mathews developed this notion, the specifics of the kingdom were sketchy but left sufficient room for Christianity to seep into every aspect of human relations, whether welcome or not. The kingdom that Jesus had in mind, according to Mathews, was largely a moral and spiritual phenomenon. "In the new social order of Jesus," he wrote, "those men who have satisfied the deepest possibilities of their nature are living in union with God. . . ." Or, put differently, the kingdom was "no mere collocation of dissimilar, repellent individuals, but a union of men similarly righteous, all alike possessed of a consciousness of noble possibilities, seeking the good one of another, with moral impulses springing from their religious life." Mathews conceded that this could sound utopian, especially when he argued that the means by which to implement this kingdom "do not concern us here." The reason for this nonchalance owed as much to the lack of specificity in Jesus' own teaching as in Mathews's conviction that the kingdom was not a blueprint for implementing a new range of institutions and progressive plans. Where the Chicago professor would differ from Rauschenbusch was in his belief that the path of social transformation toward the kingdom of God lay "along the line of conversion or, more exactly, the regeneration of the individual." Unlike Rauschenbusch, who argued for social or institutional conceptions of sin and salvation, Mathews was content with a gradual appropriation of Christian ideals through the lives of individuals and small associations of persons.

Still, Mathews was not indifferent to social realities. In fact *The Social Teachings of Jesus* had far more to say about secular affairs than it did about religious ones, though like other theologians of the era Mathews was fighting mightily against such dualisms. As a result, his book featured chapters on the family, wealth, the state, and social life. Again, in each of these sections Mathews presented an impressionistic rendering of the kingdom. But the cumulative effect was to indicate that the ramifications of Christianity were far reaching. Indeed, the consequences of Jesus' teaching extended well beyond traditional religious structures. Here Mathews's silence about the church was as curious as it was significant. He did advocate that the church had a genuine role to play in the moral regeneration of men and women. But ultimately the kingdom of God far surpassed the narrow confines of ecclesiastical affairs or responsibility. "The new social order," Mathews asserted, "was to be religious," and its progress depended upon religious institutions like the church. "But it is as much grander than the church as an ideal is grander than the actual; as much wider as social life is wider than any one institution; as much more catholic as Christianity is more catholic than ecclesiasticism."

The breakdown of distinctions between religious and secular spheres, an expansive view of Christianity's responsibilities combined with an older strain of Protestant moralism—all these trends contributed to twentieth-century American Protestants' sense of responsibility for the welfare of their society, not simply as citizens but as Christians. If Mathews lacked specificity in his articulation of the kingdom, church leaders would soon make up for the deficiency. After approximately four decades of cooperative efforts like those of the Evangelical Alliance, thirty-one of America's largest denominations joined in 1908 to form the Federal Council of Churches, an agency designed to harmonize differences among and improve the efficiency of its member communions. Although the Federal Council, and its later revised form, the National Council of Churches (1951), never amassed the authoritative muscle to become more powerful than the church bureaucrats who ran the denominations belonging to it, the agency did speak for and embodied the twentieth-century Protestant establishment, later called mainstream Protestantism after the 1960s when Protestantism was no longer synonymous with American religion. One of the first items of business in 1908 was to address the social conditions that many white Protestants believed were unraveling the fabric of American society. The only legitimate authority to which to appeal was not to the Declaration of Independence or the Constitution but the Lordship of Christ, a phrase generally synonymous with the Kingdom of God.

The agenda for the Federal Council at its first meeting was not substantially different from the program of the Evangelical Alliance three decades earlier. The list of pressing subjects was identical— divorce, temperance, Sunday observance, family life, "the immigrant problem," education. But one item stood out: "The Church and Modern Industry," a topic that prompted the Council's members to write and adopt its first creedal statement, in this case a Social Creed, a further indication of religious leaders' willingness to jettison the ir- relevant world of the spirit for the practical affairs of everyday life. In the statement preceding the creed, the Council recorded "its pro- found belief that the complex problems of modern industry can be interpreted and solved only by the teachings of the New Testament, and that Jesus Christ is the final authority in the social as in the in- dividual life." American Protestants had just expanded the territory of God's kingdom significantly. To this end the Council commended a spirit of reconciliation and goodwill in finding a "common plat- form" among employers and workers. But its Social Creed was less sympathetic to the interests of the bosses than it was to the plight of American labor. Its affirmations ran as follows:

> For equal rights and complete justice for all men in all stations of life.
>
> For the right of all men to the opportunity for self-maintenance, a right ever to be wisely and strongly safeguarded against en- croachments of every kind.
>
> For the right of workers to some protection against the hardships often resulting from the swift crises of industrial change.
>
> For the principle of conciliation and arbitration in industrial dis- sensions.
>
> For the protection of the worker from dangerous machinery, oc- cupational disease, injuries and mortality.
>
> For the abolition of child labor.
>
> For such regulation of the conditions of toil for women as shall safeguard the physical and moral health of the community.

For the suppression of the "sweating system."

For the gradual and reasonable reduction of the hours of labor to the lowest practicable point, and for that degree of leisure for all which is a condition of the highest human life.

For a release from employment one day in seven.

For a living wage as a minimum in every industry, and for the highest wage that each industry can afford.

For the most equitable division of the products of industry that can ultimately be devised.

For suitable provision for the old age of the workers and for those incapacitated by injury.

For the abatement of poverty.

Whatever the merits of these reforms, they were a long way from the Trinitarian affirmations of the Apostles' Creed. But that was precisely the point. The older creedal statements, whether Roman Catholic or Protestant, were incapable of underwriting a program of social justice or legislative reform because their subject was mainly doctrinal and ecclesiastical. They apparently left the affairs of state or economic life to rulers, without guidance from or accountability to a higher power. The theology of the kingdom of God was crucial, then, not simply for allowing Protestant church leaders to play a role in the important political debates of their day. It also removed the apparent remoteness of divine matters from politics by making God sovereign over all aspects of life, both secular and religious. Politics was no longer independent of faith but was in fact charged with spiritual significance. In turn, the expansive view of the divine kingdom brought polities like the United States directly under God by blurring any important distinction between church and state. If God were truly ruler of all, his will became the norm for the affairs of the United States as much as for those of Lutherans, Presbyterians, or Baptists. This idea of the kingdom may have upended the typical divisions between church and state that had been crucial to the American founding. But in the estimate of many Protestants who bothered to consider this difficulty, the afflictions threatening the United States in the decades after the Civil War were so grave that placing the nation's affairs under God's direct rule was either a proper corrective to the Founding Fathers' misunderstanding of religion or simply what they had in mind before Jefferson erected the artificial wall between church and state.

## The Rule of Christ

If, as the adage has it, God is in the details, the kingdom-of-God theology that developed within American Protestantism between the Civil War and World War I was fundamentally flawed. As much as it imbued all aspects of human life, especially social and political matters, with spiritual significance by making divine will the norm, it left unresolved which authorities were responsible for implementing divine rule. That the Federal Council of Churches could produce a platform for reforming the plight of American workers—aside from the very real consideration of expertise—was one example of the avenues now open to churches. And if churches could take on the functions of legislators, why couldn't government officials, now under divine rule, also add ecclesiastical duties to their set of responsibilities? In other words, the bloated view of the divine kingdom emerging in this period not only garbled the distinction between church and state but was also inefficient. It was a recipe for redundancy between political and religious authorities.

For some Protestants, however, the problems inherent in the theology of the kingdom of God were untroubling because of their different conception of the kingdom. In this scheme the kingdom of God was a generic affirmation of divine sovereignty over all affairs but lacked a blueprint for ushering in the kingdom within existing political realities. Thus the United States was under divine rule, but no more so than England, Canada, or China. According to this view, the will of God prevailed in all places and at all times, not because men and women actively sought to follow it but because, as the apostle Paul had taught in his letter to the Romans, God had ordained all the authorities in power and was carrying out his purposes through them. In turn, the site of religious exceptionalism, according to this generic view of the kingdom, was not in the state but in the church. Here some American Protestants distinguished—in a subtlety too fine for others—between the kingdom of God and the kingdom of Christ. That such a distinction could even be made indicated its elusiveness to the general tenor of American Protestantism, which nurtured adherents to look for direct implementation of divine will here and now as signs of the coming of the kingdom.

One Protestant responsible for this alternative construction of the kingdom was Stuart Robinson (1814–1881), a Kentucky Presbyterian who for different parts of his career taught at Danville Seminary and preached at a Louisville congregation. Just before the outbreak of the Civil War, Robinson wrote *The Church of God as an Essential Element of the Gospel* (1858), a book that despite its devotional title addressed implicitly the impending sectional crisis and the religious doctrines that were driving it, both North (antislavery) and South (pro-slavery). Like his own political commitments, Robinson's book was border-state and neutral. It essentially argued that the kingdom of Christ was fundamentally and categorically different from the kingdom of God, and so Christianity transcended the politics dividing North and South.

The key to this alternative idea of God's kingdom was a passage in Robinson's book in which he distinguished carefully between the nature and authority of civil and ecclesiastical powers in ways that were remarkably similar to a Jeffersonian reading of church and state. The Kentucky Presbyterian employed a set of seven contrasts to show that being under God's divine rule was different from being in Christ's kingdom. The state or civil authority, according to this scheme, derived its authority from the created order and its rule from the "light of nature." It governed physical and temporal affairs, used physical means of coercion (i.e., the sword), and could take a variety of forms (monarchical, republican, etc.). Ecclesiastical authority, in contrast, gained its authority for divine salvation through Christ, ruled according to Scripture, regulated only the "unseen" and spiritual sphere, executed its rule through the "keys of the kingdom" (i.e., preaching and church discipline), and took shape in the deliberations of "tribunals," Robinson's code word for a presbyterian form of church government as opposed to episcopal or congregational. In sum, the state and the church had different ends. The state's was to restrain evil and cultivate social order; the church's was to save a remnant of the human race for the world to come. According to Robinson, to ignore these essential differences between the ecclesiastical and civil realms was "destructive of the church." In fact, any degree of confusing church and state was "proportionally dangerous and corrupting." The history of Christianity testified that Christians "must render to Caesar the things that are Caesar's, as distinct from rendering to God the thing's that are God's."

In Robinson's mind, advancing the kingdom of Christ did not call for saturating public life with religious ideals, persuading church leaders to take stands on questions of political moment, or looking to the Bible for the most equitable distribution of wealth. The kindgom was narrowly religious, located ordinarily within the affairs and ministry of the church, the place where it was appropriate for citizens of the divine kingdom to confess that "Jesus Christ is Lord." The civil realm, as such, was not a site of Christian activity and should not be. It was a sphere "under God." But Robinson demonstrated no interest in American exceptionalism on this score. The United States might be under God, but so was every other nation on the planet, which meant that they all had equal access to the laws and norms of the created order and to human reason to try to figure out the best means for restraining wickedness and protecting the welfare of citizens. In so arguing, Robinson demonstrated an important axiom in Protestant experience with American politics: the higher (i.e., more religious or spiritual) one's view of the ministry of the church, the more realistic one's assessment of the possibilities of politics; conversely, the higher (i.e., more religious or spiritual) one's view of the state, the less unique the nature and purpose of the church.

Robinson's argument was so consistent that he drew criticism from fellow Southerners when he would not endorse the Confederacy and from Union soldiers when he questioned their tactics of preserving the Union. For his consistency, Robinson needed to go into exile during the war and lived in Canada until it was safe for him to return to Louisville.

Robinson's views were a minority position not only within American Protestantism but within his own Presbyterian denomination. Still, they revealed that construing the kingdom of God as motivation for Christianizing the United States was not the only option. Indeed, Robinson's reason for questioning the religiously inspired social reforms of the nineteenth century was that the confusion of civil and ecclesiastical realms was harming faith, not making it more important, as so many Protestants believed. For by appealing to the second person of the Trinity to justify better conditions for factory workers, Protestant activists were trivializing the much grander and glorious aim of Christianity. This did not mean that factory conditions were insignificant or unworthy of individual Christians' concerns as citizens, employers, or government officials. It did mean that the church had a different and, from a minister's perspective, more profound calling which would be neglected if ecclesiastical bodies began to take on the work of civil authorities.

## Under Caesar

When the U.S. Court of Appeals for the Ninth Circuit in 2002 found that the phrase "under God" in the Pledge of Allegiance was unconstitutional, American conservatives reacted in two different ways. Writing for the *Weekly Standard*, James Piereson argued that the words, despite their contested history and the changes in the United States since the 1950s and even Abraham Lincoln's invocation of it, served to remind Americans "of their heritage of liberty, and the price that was paid to maintain it." This was essentially a political argument, or at least one involving a political religion in which divine reference was essentially part of the American political order. The other reaction was theological more than political. Richard John Neuhaus observed that "under God" was a "statement of theological fact and of moral aspiration." He admitted that such affirmations were capable of political abuse and hypocrisy. But to say "that we are a nation under God means, first of all, that we are under Divine judgment," and the phrase also functioned as a prayer "that we may be under Providential care."

The idea that America, as a nation under God, may be under divine judgment is actually a notion with appeal beyond conservatives. In his recent book *God's Politics*, Jim Wallis, a fairly lonely voice for the evangelical left, also argues that the United States has an obligation to follow divine law. He does not address the question of the Pledge of Allegiance and would likely view it as window dressing on much more substantial ways of being under God. Wallis would also be critical of conservatives like Neuhaus, not simply on the Pledge but on the ways in which the Roman Catholic editor applies Christian conviction and morality to American politics (Wallis is generally supportive of the Democrats while Neuhaus has written favorably about and defended any number of Republican presidents and policies). Still, when Wallis asserts that the question "What would Jesus do?" crystallizes any number of public policy debating points, from war to welfare, he is not far from Neuhaus's understanding that the United States exists under divine judgment. When Wallis writes that "The Lord Jesus Christ is either authoritative for Christians, or he is not," and adds that "No nation-state may usurp the place of God," the religious left's calculation of being under God sounds a lot more threatening than the religious right's, especially since Wallis adds that the purpose of biblical faith is to "transform the world." Someone who believed in limited government might at least show restraint in applying the politics of the divine kingdom to the entire scope of American politics.

The problem for Christians on both the left and the right is that being under God needs qualification. For instance, it rarely involves a divine-right theory of divine sovereignty. Consequently Wallis concedes that the Christian activist's plans for transforming the world must be conducted without violating respect for the common good, and with a commitment to democratic rule and religious liberty. In other words, America is under God but also under modern political theories, many of which have no direct support from the very premodern (if not anti-modern) book of holy writ. A similar dilemma afflicts Neuhaus's construction of under-Godness. His several positive references to Abraham Lincoln's line about Americans being God's "almost chosen people" suggests a much more favorable understanding of the United States and its religious heritage. While for Wallis divine oversight threatens the United States with penalties for its record of racism, exploitation, and violence, for Neuhaus the record is one in which America has been and continues to be a source of blessing to the nations. According to Neuhaus, for America to retain its providential role in human history the country needs to maintain and acknowledge its dependence upon God. He adds that the concerns of the religious right do not constitute a religious agenda but stem from a "set of directions oriented to the common good and discussable on the basis of public reason." Nevertheless, neither believers on the right nor on the left are willing to stand directly under divine norms. Instead they prefer to have God's governance mediated by modern liberal political ideals, much in the way that the revision to the Pledge of Allegiance inserted "under God" within a string of affirmations, not readily evident in Jesus' teaching, the Old Testament, or the instruction of the apostles, such as the indestructibility of nation-states and the West's ideals of justice and liberty. At some point the Christian right and left may wish to answer the question of whether in fact God or liberal democracy is Lord. Settling this question might help explain why appeals to religion in politics invariably solve little and function as a divine benediction to one's own political ideals or preferences.

But for Christians like Stuart Robinson, for whom the spheres of religion and politics are distinct, trying to reconcile the God of the Bible with the goods of modern politics is not nearly so easy— but thankfully not very pressing either. The reason is that religion and politics, at least by the light of one strand of Christianity, have different standards and scope. The state's purpose is justice and, according to any number of New Testament writers, the magistrate is well equipped with physical penalties to accomplish it. The church's purpose is mercy, and it is similarly furnished with such means as preaching and the sacraments to pursue its redemptive tasks. To confuse the two is to misconstrue the bad cop (the state) and the good cop (the church). The difference is really not that hard to grasp, except perhaps for those believers who would like the church to have the trappings of the state and for citizens who would like politics to fill a spiritual void. Even run of the mill ex-cons, like Ulysses Everett McGill, the scheming ringleader of the three escaped prisoners in the movie *O Brother, Where Art Thou?*, could see that his colleagues' conversion would have no effect on their legal predicament as fugitives. When Pete and Delmar both appealed to their recent baptism in a muddy river as the basis for a general absolution of forgiveness for past and present violations of the law, Everett responded, "That's not the issue. . . . Even if it did put you square with the Lord, the State of Mississippi is more hardnosed." That remarkable insight into the ways of the Lord and his delegated authorities goes a long way toward explaining why the phrase "under God" raises more questions than it apparently answers.

# CHAPTER FIVE

# The People's Faith

Woodrow Wilson justly earned the title of "moralizer of American life." As the only American president with a Ph.D. (in history), Wilson was an earnest statesman who combined rigorous intellect with moral seriousness to infuse American politics with a sense of duty and higher purpose. From his acceptance speech as the Democratic candidate for governor of New Jersey, to his famous words before Congress that ushered the United States into the First World War, Wilson could not escape the Presbyterian upbringing that informed his understanding of politics and public service. In his first speech as governor, he told supporters in New Jersey, "We shall serve justice and candor and all things that make for the right" by making the Democratic party "the instrument of righteousness for the State and for the Nation." Seven years later, in declaring war on Germany, the twenty-seventh president was no less committed to the politics of righteousness. Wilson asserted:

> The world must be made safe for democracy. Its peace must be planted upon the tested foundations of political liberty. We have no selfish ends to serve. We desire no conquest, no dominion. We seek no indemnities for ourselves, no material compensation for

the sacrifices we shall freely make. We are but one of the champions of the rights of mankind. We shall be satisfied when those rights have been made as secure as the faith and the freedom of nations can make them.

By insisting that the nation's interests be selfless and universal, Wilson blended moral idealism with the kind of statesmanship that many American Protestants believed should characterize good government.

The lead sentence of that excerpt from Wilson's speech, the one about making the world safe for democracy, is the line for which Wilson is best remembered. It qualifies him as not only a moralizer of American life but also a crusader for democratic rule. As president of Princeton University, Wilson had already demonstrated his democratic ideals. He had participated in a prolonged struggle with alumni, faculty, and administrators over his desire to see social life for undergraduates at Princeton shift from its elitist trappings in a variety of eating clubs to the more egalitarian arrangement of residential colleges in which students lived and dined together. But Wilson was no common man, a voice of the people as, say, a William Jennings Bryan was. The model for the Princeton president's plan for residential life, after all, was the pattern at Oxford and Cambridge universities, not exactly bastions of populism. Wilson's idea of democracy drew more upon ideals of service, self-denial, and the common good rather than upon a drive for parity between elites and nonelites. Democracy for Wilson was always a means, the best to be sure, but a means to the supremacy of moral ideals in the life of any social arrangement, whether a university or a nation.

This conception of democracy was also the one behind Wilson's most ambitious moralizing experiment, namely, the postwar establishment of the League of Nations. This effort to construct an international body that would preserve peace tapped the Wilsonian drive, in the words of John Mulder, "to make social life predictable and orderly." As a Presbyterian who thrived upon the sense of decency and order for which John Calvin's heirs became legendary, Wilson believed that democracy was crucial to well-ordered relations between the Western powers that he strived to bring together in the League of Nations. In an 1918 speech to an English audience, he even attributed his designs to his Presbyterian heritage. "I wish it were possible for us to do something like some of my very stern ancestors did," Wilson declared, "for among my ancestors are those very determined persons who were known as the Covenanters." His hope for the League was to do not only for Great Britain and the United States, but also for France, Italy, and even the rest of the world, what the Covenanters had done back in the sixteenth and seventeenth centuries. That was, according to Wilson, to "enter into a great league and covenant, declaring ourselves, first of all friends, of mankind and uniting ourselves together for the maintenance and the triumph of right."

Wilson's appeal to the Solemn League and Covenant was an odd one. It suggested that the president may have understood his Presbyterian past even less than his American constituents who resoundingly rejected the League of Nations. The 1643 Solemn League and Covenant was a statement, adopted by the Westminster Assembly—the same body to produce the Westminster Confession of Faith and Catechisms—that joined English Puritans, Scottish Presbyterians, and Parliament in a promise to restore the true (read: Protestant) faith within Scotland, Ireland, and England, and that bound these parties together against Charles I as long as he continued to flirt with Roman Catholicism. The Solemn League and Covenant was one of the treaties produced during the English Civil War and was in effect an omen of the peril that awaited the English monarch. As a statement that opposed certain royal policies, and as a vow that called upon the people of England and Scotland to follow the Presbyterian faith, the Solemn League and Covenant could very loosely be described as democratic. And as part of the broader movement to unite the kingdoms of England, Scotland, and Ireland, the Covenant's oath did in some sense adumbrate the League of Nations. But since the Solemn League and Covenant was part of a political process that for starters led to regicide, the rule of a tyrannical Puritan, the slaughter of Scottish Presbyterian ministers, and a heightened animosity between the English and Irish, Wilson's appeal to it as the basis for international peace, friendship, or even "the triumph of right" sounded amazingly anachronistic and naive.

Still, this moralistic Presbyterian president was so committed to democratic ideals that he could turn one of the most provocative political documents in seventeenth-century British history into a platform for stablizing a world made safe for democracy. Wilson was not exceptional in his embrace of democracy, even though his appeal to a Presbyterian past may have been. For at least a century, American Protestants had baptized the American political order not simply in its republican features but also in its affirmation of popular sovereignty. In the early nineteenth century the democratization of American Christianity had unloosed various radical urges among Protestants. But by Wilson's day democracy was a shibboleth as honorable and holy as the three Christian virtues of faith, hope, and love. Less certain, however, was whether the harmony between democracy and Christianity was a legitimate consequence of Christian teaching or an attempt by the democratically inclined to acquire sanctity for their cause.

## *Democracy Christianized*

From the outset of the United States' relatively novel form of government, Protestants seemed to have little trouble adjusting to the new political arrangements. An important reason was that these Christians were not in fellowship with the Bishop of Rome (the pope), which was an office in the Roman Catholic church that provided real hurdles to anyone seeking to reconcile representative democracy with fidelity to Roman Catholicism. Without those objections or the hierarchical implications of episcopal church government, Protestants were apparently freer to welcome the principles of self-rule and popular sovereignty than Christians such as Roman Catholics. But in fact not every Protestant was pleased by America's political principles. Those ideals could threaten certain forms of Protestantism as much as Roman Catholicism.

The separation of church and state, no matter how objectionable to some Christians in the era following *Roe v. Wade*, was a boon to religion in America, especially to those Christians who would become known as evangelicals, that is, Protestants who would emphasize conversion and holy living. In the early nineteenth century these Protestants were more likely to be called by their denominational names, such as Baptists, Methodists, or Disciples of Christ. But these groups shared a similar commitment to and employment of revivalism as a means to grow their ranks and to Christianize the new nation. Revivalist techniques included itinerant preaching—ministers or circuit riders traveling from town to town in search of lost souls, preaching outdoors before large audiences, using various forms of publicity to attract these listeners, and delivering a simple message that would not lose those in attendance in the abstractions of the prayer book or the denomination's creed. Above all these were men who were generally young, ambitious, zealous, and usually wore their learning lightly. Evangelists later in the nineteenth century, such as Dwight L. Moody, would tinker with these features to make them work in urban centers. But the basic ingredients for the mega-revivalism of crusades such as those conducted by Billy Graham were all fairly well established by the first decades of the nineteenth century.

The success of revivalism was bound up with religious liberty (or the separation of church and state) because the disestablishment of churches in the United States placed all faiths on a voluntary footing (with the short-term exception of those states like Massachusetts that retained an ecclesiastical establishment until as late as 1833). Instead of depending on the state for tax support and for the licensing of appropriately trained clergy, with disestablishment all churches needed to go directly to the people for affirmation and support. This environment was remarkably conducive to revivalists who were already accustomed to taking their message directly to the people, and who were also used to sending out evangelists unencumbered by the refinements of learning or culture that public officials found agreeable. As a result, the churches that made the most use of revivals were the ones that grew the fastest and the largest. In 1776, for example, the largest denominations in America were the Congregationalists (20 percent), Presbyterians (19 percent), Baptists (17 percent), Episcopalians (16 percent), and Methodists (3 percent). By 1850 that list of top-five denominations was unrecognizable: Methodists (34 percent), Baptists (21 percent), Roman Catholics (14 percent), Presbyterians (12 percent), and Congregationalists (4 percent). (The strong showing of Roman Catholics was not owing to the use of revivalism but to the arrival of large numbers of European immigrants. In contrast, Presbyterians did not keep pace with Baptists, for instance, but did stay in the hunt because they generally adopted the techniques of revivals.)

With the advance of revivalism came a democratic form of Christianity that was unparalleled in the history of the faith. As Nathan O. Hatch argued in a pathbreaking book on antebellum Christianity, *The Democratization of American Christianity* (1989), the political and cultural changes wrought by the American Revolution provided a setting that revealed both the enthusiastic and licentious sides of the Protestant soul once freed from the restraints of state-controlled churches and universities. In this new environment, evangelical Protestants inverted "the traditional modes of religious authority." Rather than "revering tradition, learning, solemnity, and decorum," as Congregationalist, Presbyterian, Reformed, and Episcopalian clergy did, according to Hatch, "a diverse array of populist preachers exalted youth, free expression, and religious ecstasy." In so doing these proponents of revivalism assumed that "divine insight was reserved for the poor and humble rather than the proud and learned."

This religious version of popular sovereignty included three convictions that substantially changed the historic features of Christianity, whether Roman Catholic or Protestant. The first was an anti-creedal impulse that repudiated all theological formulations, whether historic or recent, as devices designed to keep the theologically illiterate in their place. Since Calvinism was the primary theological system available to English-speaking Protestants in the United States, Baptists and Methodists took aim at Reformed theology because it made God active and people passive in the process of salvation. Still, hostility to Calvinism also tapped an anti-intellectual contempt for all traces of systematic thought, whatever the shade of theology. As one Kentucky pastor put it, "We are not personally acquainted with the writings of John Calvin, nor are we certain how nearly we agree with his views of divine truth; neither do we care."

Closely connected to anti-creedalism was the second conviction, anti-clericalism. This was simply the extension of intellectual egalitarianism (i.e., the equality of all opinions) to all church members. Thus the clergy and any expertise they might possess, let alone the religious significance of ordination, were of no greater consequence than the average church member. Both anti-creedalism and anti-clericalism implicitly and explicitly threatened all attempts to discriminate between better or worse forms of religious devotion or reflection. According to another Kentucky Protestant, "[T]he preaching manufactories of the east appear to be engaged in sending hirelings to the west, and should any of those *man-made, devil sent*, place-hunting gentry come into our country, and read in our places, we shall likely raise against *them* seven shepards [*sic*], and eight principle [*sic*] men."

The only words and people exempt from these democratic instincts were Jesus and the prophets and apostles who wrote the Bible. This is another way of saying that anti-clericalism and anti-creedalism were simply different ways of expressing the third prong of religious popular sovereignty, namely, a bastardized understanding of the Protestant doctrine of *sola scriptura* (that is, the idea that the Bible is the final authority in determining religious controversies because it is the only infallible source of religious truth). What made the Bible different and turned these democratic Protestants into Bible-only advocates was the book's divine origin thanks to the inspiration of the Holy Spirit. This left populist Protestants with a wooden philosophy that determined everything of divine origin to be good and reliable, and anything of human derivation to be tyrannical and worthy of suspicion. Consequently Bible-onlyism leveled all earthly authorities and turned the individual into a sovereign. So deep was the conviction that free men should not submit to any human authority that many revivalists promoted the reading and distribution of a book as old and as undemocratic as the Bible as though it were as easy to interpret and decipher as the news contained in the penny press.

These dynamics, as church membership figures above suggest, posed real problems for denominations like the Lutherans, Episcopalians, Presbyterians, and Congregationalists, that is, churches that valued learning in their clergy, had somewhat strict regulations for ordination, relied upon creeds to govern the consistency of preaching and teaching, and used liturgical forms that restrained personal expression in worship. These older Protestant communions experienced what for lack of a better term might be called *Americanist* controversies, in which leading figures, either in important congregations or at seminaries, advocated measures to update traditional beliefs and practices according to the democratic and egalitarian sentiments of the United States. The result of these controversies was often polarization between high-church Protestants who denounced the democratization of their denominations and low-church evangelicals who tried to harmonize the techniques and devotional mood of revivalism with accepted forms and teachings. None of the historic Protestant denominations split over this tension. The emerging debates over slavery and the regional politics that accompanied them were sufficient to overshadow the conflict between high- and low-church parties. But even while high-church Protestants retained a standing within their respective denominations, they were becoming increasingly marginal because of the need for churches to attract followers who were committed to democratic ideals as much as they were faithful to a Lord named Jesus Christ.

An important factor in the triumph of democratic Protestantism over the more hierarchical or elitist arrangements of Lutheranism, Anglicanism, and Reformed Protestantism was the growing prominence of Roman Catholics in American life. In 1789, at the time of the ordination of their first bishop in the United States, Roman Catholics numbered 35,000 members, with 60 percent of these adherents in Maryland, the British colony in North America that had been the friendliest to Roman Catholicism. By 1830 the number of Roman Catholics had grown to 300,000. Within the next three decades, from 1830 to 1860, Roman Catholics expanded another tenfold, accounting for 3.1 million church members. In the 1840s alone some 800,000 Irish emigrated to the United States. Although the American population likewise was growing during the middle decades of the nineteenth century, it did so at a rate of only two and a half times, increasing from 13 to 31.5 million. The seemingly dramatic increase of a minority group that was clearly at odds with America's Protestant and democratic ideals was in large measure responsible for the nativist backlash that took expression in such new political parties as the Americans or the Know-Nothings. In 1856, with Millard Fillmore as their candidate, the Americans drew 21 percent of the vote on a platform that opposed immigration and the consumption of alcohol, two planks clearly aimed at Roman Catholics who were moving to America and known for not being as abstemious or as devout and industrious as Protestants.

American Protestant opposition to Roman Catholicism shaped the existing convergence between Protestantism and democracy into a religious and political axiom. For instance, Samuel F. B. Morse, the devout Presbyterian who developed the electric telegraph, wrote in his 1835 book *Foreign Conspiracy against the Liberties of the United States*, that Roman Catholicism was as objectionable politically as it was theologically. "Popery is a political as well as a religious system," he declared. "In the Roman States the civil and ecclesiastical offices are blended together in the same individual," thus making the pope "the *King*." It was a fairly easy call for Morse, then, to deduce that Roman Catholicism was anti-American because it was undemocratic: "Popery is a *political system*, *despotic* in its organization, *anti-democractic* and *anti-republican*, and cannot therefore coexist with American republicanism." Lyman Beecher, the author of the previously cited *A Plea for the West* (1834), was less concerned about democracy than political liberty in his assessment of Roman Catholics' ways. Still, he was not oblivious to the havoc that Rome's hierchical arrangements and demand for unqualified loyalty to the church's instructions could inflict on American democracy. Protestant clergy, Beecher wrote, would not "dare to attempt to regulate the votes of their people as the Catholic priests do, who at their confessional learn all the private concerns of their people, and have almost unlimited power over the conscience as it respects the performance of every civil and social duty." At the close of the nineteenth century, when immigration again seemed to threaten Protestant hegemony, Josiah Strong would demonstrate that Protestant fears of Roman Catholics' undemocratic faith had not waned but were as vibrant as at mid-century. In *Our Country* (1891) he wrote, "We have seen the supreme sovereignty of the Pope opposed to the sovereignty of the people," and so it was "as inconsistent with our liberties for Americans to yield allegiance to the Pope as to the Czar."

The cumulative effect of democratized Protestantism in the form of revivalism and opposition to Rome's hierarchical forms of government and allegiance was to deprive mainstream American Protestantism of nuance in evaluating democracy's benefits. Politically, Protestants assumed that the American form of representative democracy was the outworking of their religion because the Reformation had opposed priestcraft, superstition, and church dogma. Religiously, this identification of democracy and Protestantism eroded those aspects of Protestantism that smacked of Romanism, such as the authority of clergy, the binding address of creeds or confessions, and the sense of mystery in liturgical forms and ceremonies. To defend the Protestant faith as a system to which the laity needed to conform or give their unreserved assent was to engage in the abuses of Rome.

The stance of the Vatican throughout the nineteenth century and into the twentieth did not help Roman Catholicism's image among American Protestants. Over the course of the nineteenth century the papacy was staunchly opposed to democracy. It was viewed as one piece of the constellation of modernist ideas trickling down from the Enlightenment that included rationalism (human reason might discover truth independently from divine revelation), the social contract (rulers received their authority to govern through the consent of the governed), and laissez-faire economics (wealth grows most when unregulated by government). In many respects the reaction of the papacy to nineteenth-century liberal developments was only natural, given the brutal treatment that Roman Catholic clergy received at the hands first of the

French revolutionaries and then from Napoleon when the Roman Catholic church was stripped of its authority in France and had its powers in Italy substantially reduced. To retain the authority of the church, and specifically the papacy, many European Roman Catholics reacted sharply against policies that either secularized the state or set the church on a par with other religions. So, for instance, in two encyclicals Gregory XVI (1831–1846) condemned the views of the French theologian F. R. De Lamennais for urging that the church back away from its support for absolute monarchy and begin to support such reforms as freedom of the press and the separation of church and state in order to limit the abuses of the old political order. Gregory also opposed democratically minded reformers closer to home in the form of the Carbonari, an Italian faction that advocated the unification of Italy on the basis of divine will as well as the will of the people. When the democractic revolutions of 1848 broke out, Gregory's successor, Pius IX, was forced into exile by revolutionary Italian nationalists who saw the papacy as an enemy of Italian unification. This pope had initially favored moderation on liberal political developments but hardened as an opponent of democratic reforms.

The culmination of Rome's conservatism, which involved outright opposition to the building blocks of political liberalism, came during Pius's tenure. In 1864 he issued the *Syllabus of Errors*, which included a section on the powers of the state in relation to the church and blanket condemnations of "Modern Liberalism." Most of the assertions in the section on politics were sensible in that they argued for the rights of the church to rule in its own sphere. But because Roman Catholics were both citizens of a state and members of the church, questions of jurisdiction were intricate. Where in dispute, Pius would not give ground to the state. Consequently thesis Thirty-nine condemned the proposition "The State, as being the origin and source of all rights, is endowed with a certain right not circumscribed by any limits," an assertion that indicated how the papacy was interpreting the new powers granted to the state freed from ecclesiastical restraint. Likewise, thesis Fifty-five denounced the idea that "The Church ought to be separated from the State, and the State from the Church." As far as the general heading of "Modern Liberalism," thesis Eighty, the last on the list of errors, was sweeping. It rejected the notion that "The Roman Pontiff can, and ought to, reconcile himself, and come to terms with progress, liberalism, and modern civilization." Five years later, at the First Vatican Council (1869–1870), where Rome first articulated the doctrine of the infallibility of the pope, it also declared that clergy throughout the world were bound "to submit to this power by the duty of hierarchical subordination and true obedience, and this not only in matters concerning faith and morals, but also in those which regard the discipline and government of the church throughout the world." At the same time the First Vatican Council rejected and condemned any conception that papal power "should be dependent on the civil power," or that "what is determined by the apostolic see or by its authority concerning the government of the church, has no force or effect unless it is confirmed by the agreement of the civil authority." Instead of capitulating to the democratic spirit of the age, Rome was digging in its heels.

For some Roman Catholics in the United States, papal authority and infallibility was obviously difficult to square with the realities of the American political order, whether in the form of the separation of church and state or in the ideal of popular sovereignty. In the 1890s a controversy developed among American Roman Catholics between those more optimistic about the fortunes of Catholicism in liberal democracies like the United States, and those who shared Rome's generally conservative disposition. After a series of local disputes, which also played out in Europe when the American archbishop John Ireland spoke favorably about democratic rule during a tour of France, Pope Leo XIII issued the en-

cyclical *Testem Benevolentiae* (1899), which condemned Americanism as a breach of Roman Catholic faith and practice. In this encyclical, Leo attributed much of the dispute to "new opinions"
which held that "to more easily attract those who differ from her,
the Church should shape her teachings more in accord with the
spirit of the age and relax some of her ancient severity and make
some concessions to new opinions." To these opinions he responded that "The rule of life laid down for Catholics is of such a
nature that it cannot accommodate itself to the exigencies of various times and places."

Leo was particularly concerned about the argument of some
Americans that the liberties enjoyed in secular states like the United
States should find a counterpart in the church. Here the difference
between the church, "which is a divine society, and all other social
human organizations which depend simply on free will and choice
of men," was imperative. The danger of granting greater freedom
of opinion in the church, and more room for the voice of the people, was to confound "license with liberty." In fact "the passion for
discussing and pouring contempt upon any possible subject, the assumed right to hold whatever opinions one pleases upon any subject and to set them forth in print to the world," the encyclical asserted, "have so wrapped minds in darkness that there is now a
greater need of the Church's teaching office than ever before, lest
people become unmindful both of conscience and of duty." So
while the condemnation of Americanism granted the apparent legitimacy of human organizations that depended "simply on free will
and choices of men," the encyclical did not leave much room for
Roman Catholics to participate fully in democratic societies without giving up their duties of loyalty and submission to Rome.

The papacy's reactions to democratic government, consequently, confirmed American Protestants' commitments to popular sovereignty and democratized Christianity as two sides of the
same coin. Although two world wars and a cold war gave American

Protestants plenty of anti-democratic targets other than Rome during the first half of the twentieth century, anti-Catholicism remained strong among Protestants, and democratic convictions continued to be a source of antagonism. A classic statement of twentieth-century anti-Catholicism by liberally minded American Protestants was Paul Blanshard's *American Freedom and Catholic Power* (1949). This no-holds-bar condemnation of Roman Catholicism was breathtaking both for its scope and acerbity. In his personal prologue, Blanshard tried to explain why after eighty years since the *Syllabus of Errors*, and after a world war that saw the vindication of liberal democracy, Rome remained an object of fear if not loathing. He wrote:

> There is no doubt that the American Catholic hierarchy has entered the political arena, and that it is becoming more and more aggressive in extending the frontiers of Catholic authority into the fields of medicine, education and foreign policy. In the name of religion, the hierarchy fights birth control and divorce laws in all states. It tells Catholic doctors, nurses, judges, teachers and legislators what they can and cannot do in many of the controversial phases of their professional conduct. It segregates Catholic children from the rest of the community in a separate school system, and censors the cultural diet of these children. It uses the political power of some twenty-six million official American Catholics to bring American foreign policy into line with Vatican temporal interests.

That leap from the concrete instance of parochial schooling to the abstract claim about foreign policy is what would eventually make Blanshard's book appear dated, bloated, and paranoid. But at the time of its publication it was by no means an isolated case of one Protestant's vituperation. *American Freedom and Catholic Power* started as a series in the *Nation*, was a recommended title of the Book-of-the-Month Club, and was a national best-seller, enticing forty thousand buyers within the book's first three months of publication. As one Harvard faculty member recalled, at every Cambridge social event during the winter of 1949 "discussion centered on either Blanshard's 'American Freedom and Catholic Power' or on T. S. Eliot's 'The Cocktail Party.'"

Blanshard was by no means a poster boy for mainline Protestantism of the era. Having studied divinity at Harvard before pursuing ordination in the Congregationalist church, he eventually left the ministry and his faith after having read the New Testament "carefully" for the very first time. After working for the government in New York City and at the State Department, Blanshard decided to retire and write books. *Catholic Power and American Freedom* was an amazing start to his literary career.

Blanshard's objections to Roman Catholicism were in fact no different from what most American Protestants had thought since the founding of the nation. The heart of the book was a string of chapters exposing the un-American habits and ways of American Roman Catholics in the realms of education, science, medicine, sex and reproduction, labor, and tolerance. In the one chapter that Blanshard devoted to democratic theory, he quoted a number of Roman Catholic officials and publications that claimed the church was simply indifferent to forms of government. Absolute monarchy or democracy were essentially equal since they were versions of rule distinct from the church. According to Blanshard, "Under the theory of two powers, divine and civil, democracy is simply one of a number of acceptable types of civil government which may exist side by side with the divine kingdom of the Church." But rather than taking comfort from this apparent political neutrality, Blanshard regarded it as insufficiently supportive of democracy, and so essentially hostile to American ideals. Of course the real problem in Blanshard's estimation was the unreserved loyalty and obedience that the church demanded of its members, a submission that trumped their duties as citizens. This was hierarchy pure and simple, and a direct violation of freedom properly understood.

Still, Blanshard believed he detected in Rome's polity a basic theory about civil society and the power of the state. Aside from its theories about the relation between church and state, or about the delegation of authority to the two powers, Roman Catholicism's fundamental assumption inevitably contradicted democracy. "The state is something *over against* the people," Blanshard wrote. "It is not the people themselves and it does not express the genuine aspirations of the people as well as the Church does." The reason for Rome's political philosophy was not intellectual but historical. The church's theory had developed "when governments consisted of minority groups of nobles, warriors and gentry," and when the church was "one of the privileged classes ruling over the people. . . ." In effect, Rome was still acting like a medieval lord in its dealings with American Roman Catholics, protecting them "from their own government," when in fact the church was simply "one agency within the state, and . . . the state expresses the will of the people as a whole."

Blanshard's hostility to Rome may have summarized the thoughts of many liberal Protestants, but it was also not far removed from those of evangelical Protestants who had emerged as a Protestant subgroup since the 1920s. Only thirteen years after Blanshard's book appeared, Lorraine Boettner, a writer better known for defending the mysteries—or what H. L. Mencken called the horrors—of Calvinism, produced another anti-Catholic diatribe, *Roman Catholicism* (1962), a book that went through twenty-seven printings and sold close to 150,000 copies. As William Shea recently wrote, along with Blanshard, Boettner's book represents the "high point" of twentieth-century anti-Catholicism.

Boettner's book was, as one would expect from a conservative Protestant, more explicitly religious than Blanshard's, but it nonetheless used politics to bolster the argument. Instead of devoting individual chapters to education or science, Boettner examined in detail Roman Catholic teachings and practices that Protestants had historically found objectionable, such as the Virgin Mary, purgatory, and tradition. Still, his reasons for writing turned out to have less to do with efforts to observe the Mass in Boettner's own denomination, the Orthodox Presbyterian Church, than with the threat of two "totalitarian" systems to "our American freedoms," namely, communism and Roman Catholicism. Of the two, communism was the greater threat and Boettner was an inveterate anti-Communist. Yet Roman Catholicism was a poor weapon in America's opposition to communism because it was a totalitarian church from which it was "only a short step" to a totalitarian state, "since people have been trained to accept authority as it is imposed upon them rather than to think for themselves and to manage their own affairs." For this reason, and undoubtedly with John F. Kennedy's recent electoral success in mind, Boettner believed he needed to expose Roman Catholicism's true state of affairs. The Catholic church in America was not the genuine article but rather "a modified and compromised form that has adjusted itself to life with a Protestant majority." Where Boettner differed from Blanshard, aside from doctrine, was over the appeal of democracy. For the lapsed Protestant, Roman Catholicism opposed liberty *and* popular sovereignty; for the Calvinist, Rome was a threat to religious freedom from which the rest of America's political ideals flowed.

As popular as Blanshard and Boettner's books may have been, they were as long on Rome's abuses as they were short on the actual Christian teachings that showed liberal democracy to be divinely revealed or even more compatible with the Christian religion than other forms of government. One of the mid-twentieth-century Protestants who tried to provide a bit of religio-political theory was James Hastings Nichols, a church historian at the University of Chicago, who wrote *Democracy and the Churches* (1951). Like the other two authors, Nichols had one eye on the illiberal and undemocratic character of Roman Catholicism. His chief task was to unearth the religious origins of American democracy. But the most that Nichols could muster was a historical as opposed to a theological or philosophical basis for American political ideals. Calvinism had contributed to the idea of limited government, and Puritanism had undergirded certain democractic practices. Nevertheless the political consequences of Protestantism were almost exclusively the by-product of church rather than political reforms. Had some of these changes to church polity not occurred within a state-church environment, they may have had no direct bearing on affairs of state. As Nichols himself conceded through the words of another church historian, Hans Baron, "the *primum mobile*" of the Protestant Reformation "was religious." In fact, "Civil rights are secondary, a means to an end, never successfully preserved either among Protestants or Catholics except where dangers to religious belief sharpen the determination to resist by a higher utilitarian motive."

Without a clear intellectual tie between Christian doctrine and modern political theory, American Protestant anti-Catholicism became anachronistic shortly after Boettner's book appeared. At its Second Vatican Council, Rome embraced modernity and the political structures that defined it. To be sure, Vatican II affirmed religious liberty and had almost nothing to say about democracy. But its two declarations on religious freedom, combined with a self-professed openness to the modern world, offered not only a stark contrast with Vatican I's conservatism but also pulled the plug on one of the principle generators for Protestant opposition to Rome. Even so, if anti-Catholicism waned in the decades after Vatican II, the reasons stemmed less from Protestants reconsidering their belief in popular sovereignty than from Rome's substantial endorsement of liberal democracy, at least in the civil realm.

## *Democracy's Christian Schoolhouse*

American Protestants were not the only ones to detect a close relationship between their faith and the political order of the United

States. The most perceptive and theoretical understanding of American Protestantism's democratic character perhaps came from Alexis de Tocqueville. In his immensely popular and influential *Democracy in America*, Tocqueville gave political scientists a research agenda and American Protestants vindication for their public involvements when he wrote, "Religion, which, among Americans, never mixes directly in the government of society, should therefore be considered as the first of their political institutions; for it does not give them the taste for freedom, it singularly facilitates their use of it." By this Tocqueville had a variety of aspects of civil society in mind, from the inherent egalitarianism involved in democratic rule to faith's restraint of the license that often accompanies political freedom. But he also had in mind an important point about the nature of civil society, namely, that religious voluntary associations, which abounded in the United States during Tocqueville's 1831 tour of the country, supplied lessons in self-governance and social responsibility that enabled democracy to flourish in America, rather than degenerating into the revolutionary chaos that had turned the French Revolution into an excuse for tyranny, and that threatened the European order with the democratic uprisings of 1848. Most recently, political scientists such as Robert Putnam, in his often-cited book *Bowling Alone* (2000), have observed that American democracy has suffered since World War II precisely because Americans are detached from community and civic organizations, even to the point of abandoning bowling leagues. For proponents of Christianity's political blessings, participation in churches and other religious organizations provides some of the most valuable social capital on which democracy depends. As another political philosopher, Jean Bethke Elshtain, has written, through "churches, schools, and solidaristic organizations, such as mothers' associations, American society was honeycombed by a vast network that offered a densely textured social ecology for the growing citizen."

Yet anyone familiar with the history of Christianity may wonder if churches are truly the schoolhouse of democracy that some political theorists imagine. The early church lacked an elaborate structure of authority, and Christ and the apostles' call for love and humility nurtured a sense of equality that may have actually embodied a democratic spirit. But after the conversion of Constantine and recognition from the state, the church in both the East and the West quickly adopted the political forms and hierarchy of the imperial state. So too, when the Constantinian order of state churches collapsed with the American and French revolutions, Christianity again easily adapted to the new political reality. In the United States it embraced democratic forms of rule as essentially Christian. To say that the churches were chameleonlike in their relation to the surrounding political environment may be an overstatement. But the lack of resolve may also be indicative of the point that H. Richard Niebuhr, the lesser-known brother of Reinhold, made in his widely cited book on Christianity's relationship to Western culture, *Christ and Culture* (1951), that Christ was almost entirely silent about politics.

Sometimes the ties between Christianity and a certain political order were so thin that a church might say one thing about democracy and do precisely the other. The case of J. Gresham Machen and his difficulties with the Northern Presbyterian church during the 1920s and 1930s is one to suggest such fickleness. Presbyterians were of course freedom and democracy lovers from the beginning of the republic. That political outlook always placed a measure of strain on the church's Calvinistic theology, which through the doctrine of predestination encouraged much more of a divine-right outlook than a democratic one. The Cumberland Presbyterian church, which came into existence during the 1810s as an outgrowth of the mainline Presbyterian church, was a case in point. The Presbyterians in Tennessee and Kentucky who flocked to the Cumberland churches were so uncertain about the harmony between Calvinism and popular sovereignty that they gutted the Westminster Confession of its predestinarian teaching and became a separate denomination. After the Civil War and through World War I, Northern Presbyterians continued to give undying support to the United States and its political ideals, all the while acquiring new methods to reduce the tension between Calvinism and democracy. The new techniques for studying the Bible (known as higher criticism), with their historicist assumptions about doctrinal truth being a creature of time and place, gave theologically liberal Presbyterians a way to take vows of creedal subscription while also holding substantial reservations—without seeming to be inconsistent or deceitful. They could claim to retain traditional Presbyterian beliefs while also understanding that those beliefs were no longer relevant for modern democratic men and women. They were Presbyterians in spirit, modern Americans in body.

J. Gresham Machen (1881–1937), who taught the New Testament at the Princeton Seminary, believed that this inconsistency was to blame for American Presbyterianism's infidelity. He set out to expose the triumph of Americanism over Calvinism in his denomination, the Presbyterian Church U.S.A., the Northern church. An accomplished scholar from Baltimore, Machen wrote two books, *Christianity and Liberalism* (1923) and *What Is Faith?* (1925), that were highly critical of liberal Protestantism, first for denying the basic affirmations of Christianity in its effort to modernize the faith, and second for undertaking a process of revision that was essentially anti-intellectual. Machen's arguments gained a following among the Presbyterian laity but displeased denominational officials. As even H. L. Mencken would later concede at the time of Machen's death, although the Princeton professor had tried to prevent church reformers from converting the Presbyterian Church "into a kind of literary and social club, devoted vaguely to good works," he was "undoubtedly right." At a series of General Assemblies during the mid-1920s, the Presbyterian Church ruled in effect that conservative arguments like Machen's were mean-spirited and therefore out of accord with Christian love and fraternity. Aside from this, Machen was clearly an embarrassment because his conservative Presbyterianism was apparently at odds with modern notions of science and politics. The denomination even reorganized the administration of Princeton Seminary, the church's oldest and most reputable school, to ensure that conservatives were in the minority and firmly under the thumb of theological moderates and liberals. In 1929, Machen defied the Presbyterian establishment and helped found a rival to Princeton in Philadelphia, Westminster Seminary.

Machen's final comeuppance from his democratic-defending Presbyterian peers came during a trial in 1935 that looked more like a textbook lesson in tyranny than in the nation's beloved political ideals. In 1933, after being rebuffed in his efforts to reform the Board of Foreign Missions, an agency that had recently gained publicity for aiding and abetting liberalism, Machen began an independent missions agency that was both defiant and small; it had fewer than ten missionaries on its rolls. This was a form of Tocquevillian voluntary association that was fairly simple if not so pure. Despite its size, Presbyterian officials went after the new institution with all the clumsiness of an armored tank trying to rid a picnic of ants. The church declared in 1934 that the new missions board was illegal, a verdict that would ordinarily be delivered through an appeal process in Presbyterian courts. It also ordered its presbyteries, the local bodies that credentialed ministers, to bring all the missions agency's board members to trial on the basis of violating the recent ruling. This was the sort of decision usually reserved for bishops, not delegated committees. Machen tried to avoid a trial by transferring his credentials to the Presbytery of Philadelphia, a much more conservative body that would either have not brought him to trial or acquitted him. But despite being received by Philadelphia, the paperwork had not been properly filed, and Machen found himself in 1935 having to defend his actions before his former presbytery in New Jersey.

In opening skirmishes at the trial, Machen succeeded in having the proceedings opened to the public (Presbyterian officials were as embarrassed by the bad publicity of a church trial as they were of Machen), and failed in arguing that Philadelphia was the proper court of jurisdiction and that the judicial committee was partisanly packed with theological liberals. The affair then finally turned to the actual charges. They were six in number, all very serious, and all variations on the theme of defying ordination vows that required subjection to the church and protection of its peace. At the heart of Machen's defense was the question of the legality of the 1934 ruling that declared his missions agency illegal. Outside the trial he told reporters that the church had declared him guilty before ever hearing his case. Indeed, at the point in the trial when his ecclesiastical counsel was prepared to make its opening arguments, the judicial commission ruled that it could hear no arguments questioning the constitutionality of the 1934 decision. As Machen later told reporters after the proceedings had adjourned, the Presbyterian Church did exactly in his trial what it had done by changing church law unconstitutionally—it convicted him without due process. It was a remarkable show of force and a significant breach of Presbyterian order and decorum not to allow Machen even the opportunity for defense. Scarcely anyone had wondered if he would be successful in persuading the judicial committee, which was, as Machen observed, weighted with modernists who would have been just as glad to be rid of this Presbyterian nuisance. The committee could have gone through the motions of a fair trial and still had the same outcome without the bad press of Machen's comments, which were headlines in most East Coast papers.

Even more clever would have been a democratic and liberal response to the critic of liberalism. Instead, in order to prevent the denomination from being held back by theological conservatism, the Presbyterian Church ran roughshod not only over its own procedures for disciplining its own ministers and for revising church law, but even over American norms for free and fair trials. The modernist agenda of adapting Christianity to liberal and democratic ideals turned out to be a lot more complicated than many had imagined. Of course, the Presbyterian Church was not wrong to bring Machen to trial. Holding trials for heresy, sinful conduct, and abuse of power, among other misdeeds, is what churches do. What went wrong in the Machen episode was a denominational establishment trying to adapt an old world institution to the demands of the new world, all the while engaging in the sort of ecclesiastical tyranny that Protestants associated with Roman pontiffs.

This episode also suggests that looking to churches and religious organizations as classrooms of democracy may be a form of schooling always in need of remedial education. If the Northern Presbyterian Church, a denomination that boasted such political statesmen as John Witherspoon, Andrew Jackson, William Jennings Bryan, John Foster Dulles, and Dwight D. Eisenhower, could not trust democracy to settle its own affairs, how could churches become sites for lessons in civil society under democratic rule? Maybe the church and society are different, with varying norms governing each sphere. Granted, the Machen trial was only one case. But it was in fact part of a larger bureaucratization of American Protestantism, in which religious dissenters like Machen became a public relations problem in need of fairly arbitrary and undemocratic solutions. More important, however, was the Presbyterian Church's claim to be a denomination of the church of Jesus Christ whose domain was a kingdom, not a democracy. The much more important lesson to be learned from being a Presbyterian or any Christian for that matter, was not how Robert's Rules, deadlines for filing paperwork, or the value of deliberative assemblies might contribute to the nation's social capital but whether the church was duly submitting to the rule of king Jesus. That aspect of church government, though invariably ignored by social scientists, is the one that counts if the church is to be a Christian as opposed to an American institution.

## *Democratic Doubts*

What was once assumed to be the harmonious relationship between Christianity and democracy, at least by Protestants, has fallen on discordant times since the 1960s, when the complaints of African Americans, women, and other minority groups revealed the limits of American democracy and the complacency of the Protestant churches. So troubled has the relationship become that Jeffrey Stout attempted to address it and clear a path for a renewed consensus of democratic and religious ideals. In *Democracy and Tradition* (2004), Stout is particularly concerned to counter the backlash from religious traditionalists against "contractarian liberalism." In the former category he placed the Duke University ethicist Stanley Hauerwas, who has for almost two decades been pointing out the destructive consequences of the church's embrace of liberal democracy. For Hauerwas, according to Stout, liberalism "is a secularist ideology that masks a discriminatory program for policing what religious people can say in public." Hauerwas considers liberty and democracy to be "bad ideas" best repudiated by the church. Although Stout is troubled by Hauerwas's separatist attitude toward democratic culture, he recognizes that the Duke University professor has a point. For contractarian liberalism as explained by the likes of a John Rawls or a Richard Rorty has left no room in democratic theory for religious voices or arguments. In an effort to protect democracy from the harmful influences of authoritarian traditions or coercive impulses, Rawls, for instance, so narrowed the range of reason that even the speeches of a Martin Luther King, Jr., or an Abraham Lincoln became illegitimate.

What Stout offers as a *modus vivendi* is a form of democratic pluralism that allows "citizens with strong religious commitments" to participate fully in public life "without fudging on [their] own premises." This pluralism involves the discussion essential to democratic culture, a commitment "to talk things through with citizens unlike themselves."

Stout's attempt to avoid privileging religion over politics or vice versa is laudable, but the order of the words in the title of his book is significant. "Democracy" comes before "tradition," and the reason stems from Stout's prior commitment to defending the political ideals that have defined the West for centuries. If the order were reversed, if religion set the terms for democracy rather than the other way round, what would the relationship look like? Seldom have American Christians or religious sympathizers put the question in just that way. The reason, according to Robert Kraynak, is that such people are engaged in a form of "wishful thinking." So much do they feel the need to clothe democratic politics in the robe of religious dignity that they mistakenly fuse two worthy ideals, democracy and Christianity. In effect the modern attempt to harmonize democracy and Christianity has produced a "grand convergence theory" that for Kraynak is as improbable as it is wrong: "It sounds too sweeping to say that Judaism and the Hebrew prophets, Christianity in its Catholic, Orthodox, and Protestant forms, as well as the American and French Revolutions are all converging toward a common conception of freedom and dignity." But this is what happens when democracy assumes the lead position in relating Christianity with modern forms of politics.

Kraynak posits another theory for understanding this relationship: it is one of antagonism rather than compatibility. Historically, he argues, Christianity supported kingships and hierarchical institutions. This was not merely a function of cultural conditioning but also the product of biblical and church teaching. Although Christ and the apostles spoke of a preference for the poor and humble over the rich and poweful, they did not apply this to the political realm where the clear message was to obey the established powers. Theologians and church officers in turn interpreted the words of the New Testament to favor in some cases monarchy, emperors, or constitutional monarchies, but never democracy. According to the New England Puritan minister John Cotton, whom Kraynak quotes, "Democracy, I do not conceive that God ever did ordain as a fit government for church or for commonwealth."

On the basis of his reading of the Christian tradition, Kraynak concludes that "Today's condition, where most Christian theologians and churches accept democratic politics, is a historical anomaly, a peculiarity of modern times." The chief culprit in Kraynak's analysis is Immanuel Kant's philosophy of freedom, which offered the most influential modern account of human dignity. The German philosopher's insistence on the infinite and absolute worth of every person fundamentally altered Christian political outlooks. Whereas traditional Christians regarded democracy and other political structures as a prudential matter, modern Christians tend to see democracy as a "categorical imperative" that demands the support of faith. Kraynak explains that for older forms of Christianity, "the command to love one's neighbor, especially the poorest among us, required acts of charity; but it did not necessarily contain an imperative to set up a democracy in which the poor ruled or to establish a social welfare state; nor did it mean that one automatically had to abolish all class distinctions or social inequalities." For most modern Christians, however, the duty to love one's neighbor "requires one and only one legitimate political regime in all circumstances, namely, a democratic form of government based on human rights." Ironically the modern Christian assumption fuses the political and religious realms that traditional Christianity kept separate. The convergence of democracy and Christianity through Kant "makes political choices a direct deduction from the first principles of the spiritual realm." Nevertheless Kraynak's concern has less to do with pointing out the discrepancy between the secular flexibility of Christian hierarchy and the religious intolerance of Christian democracy. Instead his chief aim is to show that by using Christianity to underwrite democracy, the modern church has misunderstood both its own faith and political theory. "When Christianity associates its spiritual and ethical teachings so closely with democratic politics," Kraynak warns, "the Christian faith eventually turns into a mirror image of modern political ideologies, such as liberalism or socialism, that sap its spiritual energy and eventually undercut even the political utility of religion."

Given the history of Roman Catholicism's suspicions of modern politics, Kraynak's views may be more understandable as a reflection of the serious and critical attention that members of that tradition have devoted to democratic forms of government. But if Protestants are supposed to be such careful students of the Bible, as opposed to Rome's higher estimate of church tradition, it is a wonder that the American descendants of the Reformation fail to see what Kraynak observes, namely, that Scripture's teaching on human dignity is fundamentally different from the premise assumed by modern democratic theory. Whether or not Kraynak is right about Christianity's incompatibility with modern democracy, his point about the damaging effects of insisting upon harmony between Christianity and democracy is worth pondering. Rather than learning about democracy from Christianity, more often than not American Protestants have felt compelled to defend democracy under a veneer of Christian devotion. For their churches it meant an enforcement of political orthodoxy that had slim or at least contested foundation in Christian teaching. For their nation it involved a semi-establishment of religion that was at odds with the American founding. This mixture, as opposed to the separation of religion and politics, has compromised the integrity of both the American church and the American state.

# CHAPTER SIX

# Impersonal Politics

John F. Kennedy was the second Roman Catholic to run for the presidency of the United States. The first was Al Smith, the governor of New York who in 1928 ran against Herbert Hoover. In both contests religion was a significant factor. In Smith's case it was decisive. Although as the Democratic nominee he might have expected to win the South, the overwhelmingly Protestant voters in Dixie who were loathe to vote for the party of Lincoln were even more reluctant to vote for a papist. As a result, the Quaker Hoover won handily. In 1960, some three decades removed from the religious antagonisms of the 1920s, Democratic party officials might have hoped that Kennedy would face a different situation. But despite his nominal religious practice, the issue of Kennedy's Catholicism would not go away. So with eight weeks left in the campaign against Richard Nixon, Kennedy decided to address the question of his faith directly. He did so on September 12, 1960, in what might have appeared to be the American equivalent for Roman Catholics of Daniel's lion's den—the Greater Houston Ministerial Association, a body dominated by Southern Baptists, a denomination steeped in the logic and animus of anti-Catholicism.

The typical objection to a Roman Catholic holding public office, but especially the presidency, was that an oath of allegiance to the U.S. Constitution would directly contravene a prior vow of obedience to the teaching and authority of the pope. American Protestants seldom saw that they might be caught in the web of this logic, that their own submission to the teachings of the Bible might also pose an obstacle to their loyalty to the Constitution. Kennedy astutely implied as much when about a quarter of the way into his short statement he asserted:

> I believe in an America that is officially neither Catholic, Protestant nor Jewish—where no public official either requests or accepts instructions on public policy from the Pope, the National Council of Churches or any other ecclesiastical source—where no religious body seeks to impose its will directly or indirectly upon the general populace or the public acts of its officials—and where religious liberty is so indivisible that an act against one church is treated as an act against all.

Kennedy's appeal to religious liberty was standard fare for Roman Catholics, but when he added that someday Baptists themselves might be suspected of being unsuitable for public office he was as smart as he would prove to be prophetic. "While this year it may be a Catholic against whom the finger of suspicion is pointed, in other years it has been, and may someday be again, a Jew—or a Quaker—or a Unitarian—or a Baptist." Here Kennedy observed that Jefferson's statute of religious liberty was designed to protect Baptist ministers in Virginia. "Today I may be the victim," he explained, "but tomorrow it may be you—until the whole fabric of our harmonious society is ripped apart at a time of great national peril."

But as predictable as Kennedy's appeal to religious liberty may have been, his account of the way his own faith would inform his policies and decisions was, by the standards of contemporary faith-informed politics, unusual. First, he remarked, "I want a chief executive whose public acts are responsible to all and obligated to none—who can attend any ceremony, service or dinner his office may appropriately require him to fulfill—and whose fulfillment of his Presidential office is not limited or conditioned by any religious oath, ritual or obligation." Texas Baptists, in other words, did not need to worry that Kennedy would import Roman Catholic liturgical forms into state events. Second, he explained why he could keep his political and religious responsibilities distinct. "I am not the Catholic candidate for President [but the candidate] who happens also to be a Catholic," he said, "I do not speak for my church on public matters—and the church does not speak for me." If elected, no matter what the issue—"birth control, divorce, censorship, gambling,"—Kennedy pledged that the he would base his decision on "what my conscience tells me to be in the national interest, and without regard to outside religious pressure or dictate." If any circumstance prompted a conflict between Kennedy's conscience and national interest, he would resign. For this reason, he concluded, he could confidently take the oath of office, to swear solemnly "that I will faithfully execute the office of President of the United States and will preserve, protect, and defend the Constitution so help me God."

Whether Kennedy's speech was responsible for his victory later that year, his explanation of the relationship between his personal beliefs and public responsibilities would eventually prove unsatisfactory. Since the 1976 election of Jimmy Carter, the first outspokenly born-again Protestant to run for president, religion has returned to the naked public square with sufficient vigor to make Kennedy's distinction between the private and the public sound naive. Some contend that Kennedy's secular logic hurts public life by denying the valuable contribution religion can make to politics and civil society. Others argue that such a separation of faith from professional responsibilities is impossible because religion is so essential to personal identity that it cannot help but affect one's outlook and decisions. The question here may have less to do with the difficult relations between religion and politics than with the forty-year-old assumption that the "personal is political." Well before the Protestant right began to poke its collective nose under the tent of America's secular politics, civil rights activists and especially feminists had been arguing that political affairs could not be settled abstractly without significant attention to questions of personal identity such as race and gender. That religion became another item on the list of personal characteristics was inevitable. But whether Christianity itself justifies the addition of religion to race, class, gender, and sexual orientation is another question altogether. In point of fact, Kennedy in his clumsy way may have been groping for a genuinely Christian conception of the self in his remarks before Houston's ministers, a construct that has much to say to contemporary disputes about religion and politics.

## *Religious Test for Office*

André Siefried's book *America Comes of Age*, published in 1927, was yet another of those accounts, written by Europeans during visits to the United States, that yielded if not an objective perspective at least a somewhat cosmopolitan view of American society. Martin E. Marty has observed that Siefried, a French economist and journalist, was not the font of wisdom or source of quotations that his forerunner Alexis de Tocqueville had been, but Siefried did have "an instinct for discerning and elaborating the central plot of American spiritual life." Siefried's significant insight into 1920s America, as the book's title suggests, was the nation's emerging maturity as a society. It had been dominated by "the Anglo-Saxon and Puritan stock" and was then reckoning with several decades of immigration which added a great many Americans without cultural or ethnic ties to Anglo-American culture. The burning question that Siefried put to American readers was, "Will America remain Protestant and Anglo-Saxon?" This query, according to Marty, made Siefried's book and visits to the United States, taken together, "an important event of the decade."

Siefried's wise question about the longevity of Protestant cultural hegemony also established the terms for the presidential election of 1928. As he saw it, "No one can possibly understand the United States without a profound, almost innate appreciation of their Puritanism." Siefried even went so far as to observe that Protestantism was "the only national religion, and to ignore that fact is to view the country from a false angle." Obviously this did not bode well for the Roman Catholic governor of New York who in 1928 gained the Democratic party's nomination for president. According to Siefried, "The Catholic Church is . . . a thing apart in the heart of the American body politic." That Smith backed repeal of Prohibition also did not endear him to those original-stock Protestants whose dryness could be correlated directly to their membership in any of the historically English-speaking denominations. But if original stock Protestants were feeling threatened by what Siefried called the "heterogeneous elements" of American society, the Democrats' choice of a Roman Catholic wet was certainly ill-timed.

Evidence of that poor timing came before Smith's nomination, in the pages of the *Atlantic Monthly*. In the May 1927 issue a well-respected Episcopalian attorney, Charles C. Marshall, wrote an open letter to the New York governor in which he challenged Smith to address the apparent conflict between his Catholic identity and his ability, if elected president, to uphold the Constitution of the United States. Marshall's lengthy communication addressed fairly typical Protestant concerns about Roman Catholicism, all of which stemmed from the supremacy and authority of the pope— religious liberty, disputes between church and state, education, and marriage. Marshall also mentioned constitutional developments in Mexico in which the Catholic church was, in his estimate, exerting too much influence. Perhaps he showed a bit of condescension in

allowing that he had little doubt that a Roman Catholic would execute his political duties with great moral integrity. But Marshall's
concern was not with Catholic licentiousness. The problem was
that Roman Catholics had a different morality from Protestants,
one that granted the papacy authority to rule over the religious
sphere. "Is not the time ripe and the occasion opportune for a declaration," Marshall asked Smith, "if it can be made that shall clear
away all doubt as to the reconcilability of her status and her claims
with American constitutional principles?" Such a statement would
obviously quell doubts about Smith's "proud eligibility to the Presidential office" and resolve the matters in the governor's "favor."

Smith's initial response to the criticisms of Protestants was one
of astonishment—"I never heard of these bulls and encyclicals and
books"—an indication perhaps more of Smith's religious devotion
than of the relationship between Roman Catholicism and the
United States government. But in a more measured rejoinder, Smith
took on Marshall's challenge to relate his own obligations as a Roman Catholic to his duties in upholding American constitutional
principles. First, as governor of New York, Smith claimed to have already taken an oath to uphold the U.S. Constitution, not once but
nineteen times, an act that never once gave him pause about either
his citizenship or church membership. Clearly the citizens of New
York saw no conflict. As Smith explained, "All of this represents a
period of public service in elective office almost continuous since
1903." The people of his state in fact "testified to my devotion to
public duty by electing me to the highest office within their active
gift four times." Popularity with the voters of New York allowed
Smith to list his many accomplishments as governor, thus proving
that his faith was no obstacle to serving a religiously diverse public.

Second, and for good effect, Smith responded to Marshall by
noting that the Thirty-nine Articles of the Episcopal church recognized a similar division between the authority of the church
(spiritual) and the state (physical). "Your Church, just as mine,"

Smith observed, "is voicing the injunction of our common Saviour to render unto Caesar the things that are Caesar's and unto God the things that are God's." If members of the Episcopal church could serve in the United States government in good conscience, so could Roman Catholics, according to Smith.

The third point that Smith made in his reply was not so much a parry to Marshall's thrust as simply an affirmation of his "creed as an American Catholic."

> I believe in the worship of God according to the faith and practice of the Roman Catholic Church. I recognize no power in the institutions of my Church to interfere with the operations of the Constitution of the United States or the enforcement of the law of the land. I believe in absolute freedom of conscience for all men and in equality of all churches, all sects, and all beliefs before the law as a matter of right and not as a matter of favor. I believe in the absolute separation of Church and State and in the strict enforcement of the provisions of the Constitution that Congress shall make no law respecting an establishment of religion or prohibiting the free exercise thereof. I believe that no tribunal of any church has any power to make any decree of any force in the law of the land, other than to establish the status of its own communicants within its own church. I believe in the support of the public school as one of the cornerstones of American liberty. I believe in the right of every parent to choose whether his child shall be educated in the public school or in a religious school supported by those of his own faith. I believe in the principled noninterference by this country in the internal affairs of other nations and that we should stand steadfastly against any such interference by whomsoever it may be urged. And I believe in the common brotherhood of man under the common fatherhood of God.
>
> In this spirit I join with fellow Americans of all creeds in a fervent prayer that never again in this land will any public servant be

challenged because of the faith in which he has tried to walk humbly with his God.

Smith's response did nothing to change the outcome of the 1928 election. He lost decisively to Hoover, picking up only 87 of the 531 votes in the electoral college. But his defense of his faith did plant seeds that John F. Kennedy would harvest almost three decades later. And it is no wonder. Kennedy's Catholicism had kept him from running as vice president in 1956 with Adlai Stevenson at the top of the Democratic ticket. Despite vigorous efforts by Kennedy supporters to show that Smith had lost in 1928 not because of anti-Catholicism but on the basis of a variety of other factors, the Democratic leadership could not ignore a widespread perception that Kennedy's faith would add even greater doubts about the party's nominees. In 1960, when Kennedy entered the primary contests, the religion issue continued to dog him. It was decisive in the early primaries in Wisconsin and West Virginia, accounting for more newspaper coverage than the issues of labor and agriculture. When Kennedy exceeded expectations in his victory in Wisconsin, the consensus explanation was that his religious identity had galvanized the state's Roman Catholics to turn out in greater numbers than pollsters had predicted. In July, when Kennedy won decisively in West Virginia, an outcome that forced Hubert Humphrey to withdraw from the race, the Massachusetts senator declared that the issue of religion had been "buried."

Obviously Kennedy's late-summer address before Houston's ministers demonstrated that the question of his Roman Catholicism had not gone away. By the time of his campaign against Nixon, the Democratic nominee still needed to answer the lingering American Protestant fear that a Roman Catholic's faith required a form of religious devotion that would precede his obligation to uphold the Constitution and act solely on the basis of what was good for the United States, not for the holy Catholic church.

If anyone or anything buried religion in the 1960 presidential contest, it was Kennedy who followed Smith's lead in appealing to his own past experience, even while a Roman Catholic, in following and maintaining the laws of the land, and in acknowledging that the duties of a public official were to act out of public rather than private or religious interest. Like Smith before him, Kennedy made clear that the issues before the American public in the 1960 presidential race were precisely that—public, not private. Neither the voters themselves should have been deciding their votes on the basis of their religious convictions, nor should the religious views of the candidates make a difference in their ability to govern a religiously mixed society in which church membership was not required for holding public office. Kennedy summarized this logic well when he told the Houston ministers, "If this election is decided on the basis that 40,000,000 Americans lost their chance of being President on the day they were baptized, then it is the whole nation that will be the loser in the eyes of Catholics and non-Catholics around the world, in the eyes of history, and in the eyes of our own people." Even more forceful was Kennedy's epigrammatic assertion, "I do not speak for my church on public matters—and the church does not speak for me." As one religious historian has argued, Kennedy's secular vision of American politics was "the most private model of piety's place in public life ever advanced by a presidential candidate until Michael Dukakis."

If Kennedy and Smith's understanding of politics relegated religion to the private sphere, it also recognized the flip side, which is the public nature of government in a liberal democracy. The nature of politics required public officials to act in the national or public interest, not on the basis of their personal or private convictions. Despite the prominence of religion throughout the history of American politics, the national or public character of government decisions has generally been the accepted norm. The public was political; politics was a public activity. And even if religion entered the picture, it did so only as it contributed to public or national life. With the rise of the Protestant right, however, during the 1970s, the public nature of politics took a back seat to the notion popularized by feminists and civil rights advocates that the personal is political. In turn, religion changed from a matter bounded by national interest into an essential ingredient of a candidate's character, thus predicting his or her ability to govern well. The Kennedy and Smith era of religion and politics came to an abrupt end in the so-called year of the evangelical, that is, 1976, the year that saw the first openly born-again Protestant, Jimmy Carter, elected president.

Nineteen seventy-six turned out to be quite a year for evangelicals since both candidates, Carter, the Democratic nominee, and the Republican incumbent, Gerald Ford, each claimed to be evangelical. The idea of placing a man of character in the White House had obvious appeal to a nation still reeling from the perceived immorality of the Vietnam War and from the stunning embarrassment of Nixon's moral failings in the Watergate imbroglio. Despite Ford's attempt to present himself as a devout man, Carter did not carry the baggage of having pardoned Nixon. He came across as a simple man of resolute convictions, among which his evangelical faith was a genuine part. According to his press secretary, Jody Powell, "for a lot of people, the idea that this was a man of religious faith gave them some measure of hope that he meant what he said, that he would do what he said, that he would abide by the law, that he would behave in a way that was moral and decent and just." Powell added, in a line that would prove prophetic of the religiously inspired politics to come, "That is one of the things religion is supposed to do for us."

Carter had only in passing mentioned to a *New York Times* reporter that he was a born-again Christian. The reference caught most in the press by surprise, many of whom knew nothing about evangelical Protestantism. But for evangelicals themselves, Carter's description of his religious identity signaled a candidate who shared their faith and its implications for public life. Throughout the campaign the Georgia governor indicated that religion was important to his own understanding of himself and of his duties as a public official. The 1976 Democratic convention, according to several reports, resembled more a revival meeting than the culmination of a presidential primary season. Carter also campaigned not simply as a man of honesty who would work to return integrity to Washington but as a candidate who was genuinely concerned about the health of American families and who was himself a family man. His candidacy attracted a wide swath of Roman Catholic voters, many of whom admittedly were already registered Democrats, and also aroused the slumbering giant—evangelical Protestantism—which had not been a significant factor in contests between Democrats and Republicans since the 1920s. Instead of being a liability for a politician, Carter was finding faith to be an asset.

This is not to say that religion and politics were a natural fit. Carter's campaign exhibited some of the real difficulties that afflict a close identification of faith and the affairs of state. Abortion was one sign that Carter was not up to the juggling that mixing religion and politics required. He had no way of satisfying both religious conservatives who supported a ban on abortion and liberal Democrats who favored unlimited access for pregnant women. So he ended up advocating a position that steered clear of legal prohibition and withdrew federal funding for abortion, adding that the instances of sexual promiscuity that led to unwanted pregnancy were "not acceptable on any sort of measurement of moral standard." Then, about a month before the general election, *Playboy* magazine published its interview with Carter in which the Georgia governor admitted that he had committed adultery by lusting after women "in his heart." This was a clear reference to Christ's teaching in the Sermon on the Mount that showed the candidate's familiarity with Scripture and its requirement that believers not merely avoid looking at magazines like *Playboy* but also staring for too long at beautiful women who kept their clothes on. But it also indicated that Carter had no feel for some evangelicals whose demands for upright conduct rarely countenanced public admission of sin or even weak will, let alone giving interviews to publishers of men's magazines. According to Jerry Falwell, whose fame as the organizer of the Moral Majority was still three years away, "Like many others, I am quite disillusioned. Four months ago the majority of the people I knew were pro-Carter. Today that has totally reversed."

These problems foreshadowed difficulties that would follow during Carter's presidency and prompt the Protestant right to look for a president more attuned to their convictions. The biggest stumbling block for Carter proved to be the family, an issue that also involved women's roles and rights. The president had tried to address matters that were clearly important to him because of his religious beliefs; but, as was the case with abortion, finding a middle position that could satisfy liberal Democrats who regarded the family as an important site of women's oppression and conservative evangelicals who believed the traditional nuclear family was under siege was virtually impossible. As Tim LaHaye, then a popular Southern California pastor, put it, "We had a man in the White House who professed to be a Christian, but didn't understand how un-Christian his administration was." He added that he remembers having prayed this prayer, "God, we have got to get this man out of the White House and get someone in here who will be aggressive about bringing back traditional moral values." Had a Roman Catholic priest ever admitted to offering up such a prayer during Kennedy's administration, evangelical and mainline Protestants would have trotted out the familiar national postulates regarding the separation of church and state.

Carter's candidacy, presidency, and equivocation whetted the appetite of evangelicals for a man who would restore moral order to America. Key to this effort was a candidate who was religious like they were, not someone who merely believed in the family and traditional values in abstract terms. Ronald Reagan, a Republican with no overt ties to evangelicalism, emerged as that man the year before the 1980 campaign, in a surprisingly low-key manner. During a precampaign session with potential supporters, Reagan had the following question put to him by an evangelical pastor: "If you were to die tomorrow, and you wanted to go to heaven, what reason would you give God for letting you in?" According to one version of the incident, "Reagan dropped his eyes, looked at his feet, and said, 'I wouldn't give God any reason for letting me in. I'd just ask for mercy, because of what Jesus Christ did for me at Calvary.'" For many evangelicals this was the moment that demonstrated Reagan was one of them. It was also a time when presidential candidates talking openly of their faith began to be not simply acceptable but necessary to attract the "God vote."

The 2004 presidential election was yet one more instance of this demand for candidates to divulge their religious identity and its implications for policy. George W. Bush had already claimed in 2000 that his favorite political philosopher was Jesus Christ, and in 2004 he continued to identify himself as a born-again Christian whose character and integrity tapped genuine religious conviction. No less striking was the candidacy of John F. Kerry, the Democrat who was faulted, unlike his Roman Catholic Democratic predecessors, for *not* being too devout and so under the sway of a foreign power. A story in the *Washington Post* during the summer of the 2004 race described the Democratic nominee in the following manner: "On the road, Kerry carries a rosary, a prayer book and a medal with the image of St. Christopher, patron saint of travelers. . . . Kerry prays, sometimes with friends, including in 1999 when he helped former Vietnam crewmate Del Sandusky through hard times." In 1928 or 1960 such displays of piety would have spooked Protestant voters. But by 2004 Kerry's defect, as the voting results seemed to indicate, was that he was not sufficiently devout but waffled on Rome's teaching about abortion and gay marriage. Different perceptions of the religion of each candidate help account for the disparity between voters who attended church frequently and supported Bush, and those who were either spare in their religious observance or irreligious and voted for Kerry. This difference has entered the American electoral lexicon as the basic difference between the so-called red and blue states, between the God-fearers who vote Republican and the skeptics who vote Democrat.

In fewer than forty years religion went from an uncomfortable subject in electoral politics to a topic as readily discussed as a candidate's views on energy policy or tax relief for the middle class, maybe more so. To be sure, the American electorate has always used religion, especially in the form of ethno-cultural politics, to determine its voting preferences. In this respect the recent visibility of evangelical Protestants in national elections is not new. What is unusual, however, is the demand for political candidates to comment publicly on their own faith, as if Article Six of the Constitution, which requires no religious test for office, has been annulled. Here the evangelical factor in American politics is significant since born-again Protestantism blurs the distinction between the public and private. Because religion pervades all of life, and because true faith yields persons of character and integrity, religion has become a desirable attribute of anyone seeking public office. In contrast, the irreligious person, or the one uncomfortable discussing the intimate nature of his or her faith, is supected of not having an adequate moral basis upon which to decide questions of public moment. Aside from the constitutional problems inherent in such an outlook, the Christian difficulties with such a conflation of religious identity and public service may be even greater.

## *The Politics of Religious Identity*

To identity the evangelical right with the politics of multiculturalism would appear to be a stretch of muscle-tearing proportions.

Born-again Protestants—or at least the most politically visible ones—are, after all, white, middle class, and comfortable with some degree of male authority, if not in the church at least in the home. Their cultural interests generally reflect the older white Anglo-Saxon Protestant outlook that dominated American culture and politics until the 1960s, when dead white European men or their male descendants lost their privileged status. Thus the Protestant right is the lingering residue of American history and culture, seemingly oblivious to the multiculturalists' trinity of race, class, and gender. Add that evangelicals are also overwhelmingly heterosexual and opposed to gay marriage, and they come up even shorter on the voters' guide to identity politics that has in the last two decades been expanded to include sexual orientation.

This antagonism between the religious convictions of the Protestant right and the sensibilities of multiculturalism has not, however, prevented the former from taking a page from the political game plan of the latter. David A. Hollinger observes that the American nation-state and the national culture it has nurtured has come under attack by several groups claiming that the U.S. political order does not make room for their personal identities. One of these groups is evangelical Protestants who, according to Hollinger, have claimed the status and protection "now afforded to ethno-racial groups." They see themselves as "the newest minority in need of protection to guarantee their cultural equality and to facilitate their survival in the face of a secular intellectual establishment." The evangelical appeal to minority status, Hollinger explains, stems from the widespread appeal of ethnic as opposed to religious affiliation. Either intellectually or emotionally, religion does not have nearly the force that ethnicity does. Thus in the climate of multiculturalism, where various minorities seek equal protection from the state for the preservation of their personal identities, evangelicals have resorted to an argument that embraces cultural diversity, despite their own obvious physical differences from multiculturalists and despite their own monocultural program of social and political reform.

Amy Gutmann provides a useful explanation for evangelical Protestants' anamolous reliance upon the arguments of their political antagonists. She contends that liberal democracies since 1960 have experienced controversies over how to recognize "the identities of cultural and disadvantaged minorities." Political liberalism's basic difficulty is its egalitarian ideal. In trying to offer "equal representation" of all people, liberalism stumbles over the particularities of persons. The price that citizens of modern liberal democracies pay for such equal recognition is "the impersonality of public institutions . . . regardless of our particular ethnic, religious, racial or sexual identities." In effect, liberalism has sought to recognize all people as abstract persons—people who have common characteristics and traits as human beings. In the era of multiculturalism, however, many people have found this universal human self to be seriously impoverished. It did not (because it was not supposed to) account for the personal properties of kin, region, and creed, or of financial income and sexual preference. Gutmann writes, "Liberal democracies, *pace* Rousseau, cannot regard citizenship as a comprehensive universal identity because (1) people are unique, self-creating, and creative individuals . . . and (2) people are also 'culture-bearing,' and the cultures they bear differ depending on their past and present. . . ." Although she does not address religion per se, Gutmann's account of liberalism's limits makes complete sense of the Protestant right's multicultural turn. Liberalism may allow evangelicals into the public square and even grant them a seat at the proverbial table, but it does so by disregarding their personal faith. Political participation comes with a price tag that evangelical Protestants are unwilling to pay.

The cost of political participation for born-again Christians is particularly excessive because of the evangelical conception of true faith. Since the revivals of the so-called Great Awakening of the

1730s, evangelicals have pursued a faith aimed at authenticity and sincerity. The revivalists of that era and since, from Jonathan Edwards to Billy Graham, have insisted that the danger of Christianity is a cold or dead formal religion in which adherents only go through the motions. The forms and rites of Christianity before the eighteenth century, both Protestant and Roman Catholic, were not sufficiently rigorous. Revivalism was a way to address this, first by guiding converts through a soul-wrenching decision to follow Christ, and second by demanding that true believers lead holy and righteous lives. Evangelical Christian devotion, accordingly, is never halfway or something that can be bracketed from the rest of a person's life. It is a total reorientation to serve God and love neighbor. Liberalism's demand for abstract persons runs directly counter to evangelical devotion; it seeks from evangelicals a kind of adherent that cannot possibly exist if truly converted. After all, if the first great commandment as summarized by Christ is to love God with all one's heart, soul, and mind, how could such devotion make room for another loyalty or authority?

Hollinger proposes a way out of such a predicament: a postethnic perspective on the nature of personal identity. He writes that "most individuals live in many circles simultaneously," which involves "a shifting division of labor between the several 'we's' of which the individual is part." For instance, "how much weight at what particular moment is assigned to the fact that one is Pennsylvania Dutch or Navajo relative to the weight assigned to the fact that one is also an American, a lawyer, a woman, a Republican, a Baptist, and a resident of Minneapolis?" Sorting through these various claims upon the self distinguishes the postethnic outlook from both the "unreconstructed univeralist" of classical liberal theory or the "unreconstructed ethnocentrist" of multicultural logic. Rather than looking merely for identity and signficance in abstract conceptions of humanity (universalist) or in the "ostensibly primordial ties" of particular communities (multiculturalist),

Hollinger's notion of postethnicity calls for constant sorting through both the particular and universal claims upon the person. In his own words, postethnicity involves "sensitivity to the potentially overlapping character of various local communities" matched with "a recognition of the reality and influence of communities global in scale."

On the surface, Hollinger's prescription for resolving the politics of identity would appear to be a long way from Christian conceptions of the self. Not only has he been outspokenly critical of the Protestant right but his adjudication of the conflict between liberalism and multiculturalism is informed more by the arguments of secular intellectuals than Christian teaching. The chances of Christians following Hollinger's advice consequently seem farfetched. Still, the apparent remoteness of postethnicity to Christian identity is simply the result of a one-sided understanding of Christianity's teaching about the human person. Plenty of Christian instruction, from the Bible to sermons, can be read in ways to make faith all-encompassing for the individual believer. But on closer inspection, Christian views about the nature of religious identity are more complicated than commonly supposed.

Take, for instance, the apostle Paul's widely cited teaching about the relationship between Christian and human identities. In his epistle to the Galatians he wrote, "For as many of you as were baptized into Christ have put on Christ." Consequently "there is neither Jew nor Greek, there is neither slave nor free, there is neither male nor female; for you are all one in Christ" (Gal. 3:27, 28). These verses have been the basis for churches following liberalism's universalistic project of eradicating all particular identities and loyalties, at least within the church if not also within societies that might legitimately be called Christian. This involved eliminating the obvious enormity of slavery but also the divisions between capital and labor (class), between men and women especially concerning ordination (gender), and among ethnic groups (race).

In effect the water of baptism washes away those physical and inherited traits that separate people, uniting them instead in the common religion of Christ.

Obviously the defenders of male ordination, slavery, and capitalism have read this biblical passage in less egalitarian and universalistic ways. But aside from the merits of each side on these particular issues, Paul's instruction could not have meant that membership in the body of Christ rendered gender, legitimate authority, or ethnicity meaningless. If maleness and femaleness no longer mattered to Christians, why did the apostle still teach men and women about their respective duties in marriage and the responsibilities of procreation and child-rearing? Clearly "neither male nor female" went only so far. Similarly, if social status and political duties were inconsequential to Christians, why also instruct them to submit to the emperor or to pray for the peace and prosperity of the empire so they could enjoy tranquil lives? "Neither slave nor free" also had its limits. And if being a Greek or Jew did not matter to a Christian's identity, then why didn't Paul, the missionary to the Gentiles, write in his native tongue, Aramaic? In fact ethnic differences continued to matter to the church (and have since the first century) because Christians have used different languages for worship. (Roman Catholicism's use of Latin is one exception to this rule, though the development of national parishes according to ethnicity and language reflected the difficulty of obliterating all particularites within the bond of Christian fellowship.) Going back in the history of salvation to the story of the Tower of Babel, where the introduction of diverse languages was designed to prevent a one-world order, biblical religion has implicitly recognized and lived with cultural and ethnic differences that will become obsolete only in the new heavens and new earth. On this side of heaven, the church adapted its ministry to the variety of cultures it encountered. Christianity did not have its own language or culture but instead sometimes cooperated with and other times resisted the culture in which its members lived. Unlike Israel, where cult and culture were seamless, the church presented an arrangement whereby Christians were called to live hyphenated lives with multiple identities because cult and culture were in constant negotiation.

Paul's instruction, then, about Christian identity is actually more compatible with Hollinger's idea of postethnicity because the apostle recognized that Christians were more than church members. They were still members of families and communities, and still involved in work and activities beyond the fellowship of the saints. This is not to deny that some Christians have attempted to establish religious communes that would reflect Paul's teaching in his epistle to the Galatians and so disregard all physical differences. But the body of historic Christian teaching and example has looked askance at such utopian schemes precisely because the church acknowledged that Christians have multiple responsibilities that prevent a monoreligious identity. The apostle Paul himself provides an example of particular value for considering the politics of personal identity.

Paul had multiple identities—as Jew, Christian, and Roman citizen. He also attempted to live in compliance with those loyalties. Clearly, harmonizing his Jewishness and Christianity was a problem. Until his conversion to Christianity, Paul was one of the foremost persecutors of Christians because of their belief that Jesus was the Messiah. But after his conversion, Paul repeatedly claimed that his new faith was rightly understood in complete continuity with that of his upbringing. His efforts to find coherence in Christianity as the fulfillment of Judaism became the chief way for the church to hold on to both the Old and New Testaments. Even so, Paul's Christian teaching became the object of much controversy, especially during one of his trips later in life to Jerusalem where he ran into opposition from Jewish authorities. As part of the imperial arrangements, these Jewish leaders held the powers of local rule, which they used to imprison Paul and place him on trial for blasphemy, a capital offense. But Paul was also a citizen of the Roman Empire, not the most common of identities for Jews or Christians in Jerusalem. Consequently, during the course of his examination by Jewish and Roman authorities, Paul appealed to Rome's jurisdiction. As he explained to the Roman governor, Festus, "I am standing before Caesar's tribunal, where I ought to be tried; . . . If then I am a wrongdoer, and have committed anything for which I deserve to die, I do not seek to escape death; but if there is nothing in the charges against me, no one can give me up to them. I appeal to Caesar" (Acts 25: 10–12).

Paul's appeal to Rome was unusual on several levels. As it turned out, had he not issued it, he would have been freed in Jerusalem because the Roman governor, in consultation with King Agrippa, another Roman official familiar with Jewish customs, found Paul innocent. But instead of being emanicipated, Paul had to endure a long and precarious trip to Rome which resulted in further imprisonments and ultimately death. The import of his appeal to Roman law was that, unlike any of the other apostles, Paul could gain certain protections that his Christian colleagues could not. Ultimately his status as citizen did not spare him from a martyr's death, though it allowed him to be beheaded instead of crucified. Like most of the other apostles, Paul finally had to choose between the competing loyalties of obeying Christ's command to preach or the emperor's proscriptions against Christianity. Paul's Christian identity did take precedence over his Roman citizenship. But the nature of his Christian commitment did not keep him from appealing to Roman law to prolong his life. Short of having to forsake his duty to preach, Paul was willing to play by nonreligious rules. In other words, he thought of himself as more than a Christian; his identity was hyphenated—Roman citizen and Christian apostle.

Paul's example may help explain two apparently rival notions in Christian teaching. On the one hand, Christ spoke of the impossibility of his followers serving two lords. Luke 16:13 reads, "No servant can serve two masters; for either he will hate the one and love the other, or he will be devoted to the one and despise the other. You cannot serve God and mammon." On the other hand, Christ also informed his disciples to submit to temporal authority. Matthew 22:21 records him as saying, "Render therefore to Caesar the things that are Caesar's, and to God the things that are God's." Zealous believers have usually looked to the former of these texts for understanding the scope of faith's claim upon the person, leaving little room for negotiating the multiple identities that people possess simply by virtue of their various duties. In contrast, those looking for ways to accommodate the Christian's duties to both God and the state have emphasized the Matthew text. Perhaps the middle position lies in a conception of *serving* a master (God) who entertains guests (political rulers) for whom the servant (Christian) *renders* assistance and hospitality. Such a servant would not mistake his identity as consisting in loyalty to any master other than his. But neither would such identity regard rendering service to the master's guest as a betrayal of his ultimate loyalty. In other words, by serving Caesar, Christians may better serve Christ.

## *Keeping Religion to Yourself*

The idea of living a hyphenated existence—one part private and religious, the other part public and political—strikes many as oxymoronic, and not just evangelical Protestants. Jean Bethke Elshtain, for instance, took issue precisely with the idea that politics requires faith to be kept personal and private. For support she summarized a talk given in 1996 by Joseph Cardinal Bernardin at Georgetown University, where he remarked upon the incoherence within American society of showing respect for religion while "simultaneously insisting that people keep it to themselves." This is, according to Elshtain, "precisely what a devout person cannot do." Faith is not private but rather "constitutive of membership in a particular body—the church, the temple, the mosque, the synagogue." As such, religious adherents "cannot bracket their beliefs when they enter the public square." Elshtain adds that "a private religion . . . makes no sense. One must have public expression of a faith in order for it to be faith."

While Elshtain is keen to preserve the public and communal nature of faith, the philosophical theologian Nicholas Wolterstorff is equally intent on defending the capacity of religion's "inner voice" to express itself in the public arena. The Yale philosopher argued that the suppression of religious voices in public life was to silence "the most powerful force available to us for the cause of justice and human flourishing." Here he cited the number of humanitarian and civil rights causes that faith had motivated. But the question of religious voices finding a public outlet went even deeper. Wolterstorff pointed out that for many people "religion is the deepest aspect of their way of being in the world." To deny this basic aspect of human existence was to border on disrespect "for the individual." Or, as he put it in a book length debate on religion's role in public life with the political philosopher Robert Audi, the issue is one of personal integrity. Wolterstorff writes:

> It belongs to the *religious convictions* of a good many religious people in our society that *they ought to base* their decisions concerning fundamental issues of justice *on* their religious convictions. They do not view it as an option whether or not to do so. It is their convictions that they ought to allow the Word of God, the teachings of the Torah, the command and example of Jesus, or whatever, to shape their existence as a whole, including, then, their social and political existence. Their religion is not, for them, about *something other* than their social and political existence: it is *also* about their social and political existence.

Aside from the obvious difficulty of adjudicating the convictions of those religious citizens who might desire to follow the

Word of God but oppose efforts of other citizens to follow the Book of Mormon or the Koran or the Torah, Wolterstorff's appeal to the teachings of Jesus could meet with opposition from the instructions of Jesus himself. In the widely cited Sermon on the Mount, about midway through the discourse (as recorded by Matthew), Christ uttered a statement sure to take some wind out of arguments like those of Wolterstorff or Elshtain. Matthew 6:1 reads: "Beware of practising your piety before men in order to be seen by them; for then you will have no reward from your Father in heaven." Obviously the meaning of this statement was a warning against hypocrisy or wearing one's religion on one's sleeve in order to be seen as devout. At first blush, then, this comment would seem to have little to do with religion and public life.

But as the sermon unfolds, Christ gives instruction about prayer and almsgiving which reinforces a point about the personal and private nature of faith. "When you give alms, do not let your left hand know what your right hand is doing, so that your alms may be secret" (Matt. 6:3), and "when you pray, go into your room and shut your door and pray to your Father who is in secret" (Matt. 6:6). One of the implications of this set of instructions is not only to avoid the hypocrisy of sanctimoniousness. It also teaches that the nature of genuine religion is precisely private, personal, and not something for public display or consumption. In other words, Christ seemed to be saying that these hallmark properties of religion—prayer and generosity—should be characterized by privacy. Which invites the question: If it is possible to keep such essential aspects of faith as prayer and almsgiving private, even within the privacy of one's devotional life, why wouldn't it be possible for a serious believer to keep that faith bracketed once entering the public square or the voting booth? The very essence of faith, at least the Christian variety, might be that it is private, personal, and something to be kept distinct from expression in the public arena of politics (as opposed to the public arena of worship, often re-ferred to as "public worship"). If this is the case, the demand that liberalism makes of the religious person is not terribly burdensome or at odds with the demands of true faith. The point of Christian devotion could very well be to live a hyphenated existence, always juggling the public and the private, recognizing the significant dif-ference between those spheres because of the inherently private and personal nature of Christian devotion.

Martin Luther, following in the pattern of Augustinian notions about the City of Man and the City of God, clearly had a sense of the differences between private and public roles. In one of his ser-mons he wrote:

> In the outward life a Christian goes about like an unbelieving man: he builds, tills the ground, and ploughs like other men. He does not undertake any special task, neither as regards eating, drinking, sleeping, working, nor anything else. These two organs alone make a difference between Christians and non-Christians: that a Christian speaks and hears in a different manner and has a tongue which praises God's grace and preaches Christ, declaring that He alone can make men blessed. The world does not do that. It speaks of avarice and other vices, and preaches and praises its own pomp.

This construction of the self has all the marks of a hypenated ex-istence, one in which the Christian leads a double life. The public life is indistinguishable from those things he holds in common with neighbors and fellow citizens. The private life is different and can be perceived only through spiritual insight—all the more reason why it should be separated from the criteria that govern public settings. This doubleness does appear to be at odds with the modern self's quest for authenticity and integration. But in the end those notions of personal wholeness may be as much the product of liberal individualism as the same thinking that concocted the abstract individual of modern political theory. If so, the theorists of liberalism may have plenty of work to do, but Christians may wish to beware of taking their understanding of the self more from the demands of modern politics than from historic Christian teaching.

# CHAPTER SEVEN

# The Tie That Divides

On March 28, 1963, Martin Luther King, Jr., delivered perhaps the most rousing and memorable speech in American history, at least since Abraham Lincoln's Gettysburg Address a century earlier. The "I Have a Dream" speech was laced with rhetoric familiar to all Americans and to all Christians. King's initial rhetorical strategy was to employ the language of the Declaration of Independence to show that African Americans had not been guaranteed the "inalienable Rights" of "Life, Liberty, and the pursuit of Happiness." But not far from his appeal to the rights of citizenship was the language of universal brotherhood that he attached securely to Christian ideals in phrases like making justice a reality "for all God's children." The Christian overtones of King's speech were particularly forceful in the litany of "I have a dream" assertions that punctuated the conclusion of his address. This dream sequence began with the American version from the Declaration of Independence: "We hold these truths to be self-evident, that all men are created equal." It concluded with the messianic dream of the prophet Isaiah: "I have a dream that one day every valley shall be exalted, and every hill and mountain shall be made low; the rough places will be made plain, and the crooked places will be made straight; and the glory of the Lord shall be revealed, and all flesh shall see it together." The fulfillment of this prophecy would allow all "of God's children, black men and white men, Jews and Gentiles, Protestants and Catholics" to sing not just "My Country 'tis of Thee" but also the black spiritual "Free at Last!"

To complain that King's blending of American and biblical imagery now sounds hollow in the light of September 11, 2001, might involve both caricature and anachronism. The courageous civil rights leader could not have seen a time coming when the American Dream would be as much an object of scorn to some devout Muslims as it would continue to inspire white Americans. But he certainly was aware that Muslims, well before Osama bin Laden orchestrated a breathtaking attack on one of the architectural landmarks of the American Dream, were not entirely enthusiastic either about the American or Christian millennial versions of the dream King proposed before an enthralled nation in the shadow of the Lincoln Monument in Washington, D.C. For at least a decade, Malcolm X, the separatist rival to King for leadership among African Americans, especially in Northern cities, had been challenging whether the dreams of white Christian America could ever include blacks. Malcolm X made his objections clear in his "Message to the Grass Roots," which he delivered only ten weeks after King's "I Have a Dream" speech. Malcolm mocked the unifying character of Christianity and American political ideals:

> What you and I need to do is learn to forget our differences. When we come together, we don't come together as Baptists or Methodists. . . . You don't catch hell 'cause you're a Methodist or Baptist. You don't catch hell because you're a Democrat or a Republican. You don't catch hell because you're a Mason or an Elk. And you sure don't catch hell 'cause you're an American; 'cause if you was an American, you wouldn't catch no hell. You catch hell 'cause you're a black man. You catch hell, all of us catch hell, for the same reason.

Even though Malcolm's separatist program had no chance of succeeding short of armed revolution, his point about the inability of religion and politics to overcome the more fundamental racial divide in the United States was one that King's dream was loathe to concede.

In point of fact, Malcolm may have shared with King more than he thought on the unifying capacity of Christianity. King clearly expected the American Dream to be an expression of the kingdom of God prophesied by biblical writers. According to Kenneth L. Smith and Ira G. Zepp, Jr., King believed that the prophetic vision of justice associated in the Bible with the Messianic era was to be achieved within history, not in some otherworldly utopia at the end of time. Malcolm also seemed to acknowledge that Christianity should be a unifying force. He didn't object to the reality that little separated Methodists from Baptists on questions of heaven and hell; instead he objected that these versions of Protestantism were incapable of uniting blacks and whites. At some level, then, Malcolm and King ironically shared the idea that Christianity was a unifying force in America; the trouble, as Malcolm noted, was that religion could not overcome the nation's racial divide. In so doing they were simply following in paths well worn by white Protestants before them. Whether American Protestants came to that view honestly on the basis of religious conviction, or baptized the cause of political union with the holy water of Christian ecumenism, is an issue worth raising.

## *One World Under God*

November 29, 1950, was a banner day for mainline Protestants, and the banner specifically read "This Nation Under God." At a meeting in Cleveland, Ohio, of close to 5,000 delegates from various Protestant denominations, the National Council of the

Churches of Christ in the United States of America became a reality and superseded the old Federal Council of Churches. According to Robbins W. Barstow, who reported on the proceedings for the commemorative volume, to read the Council's own press was to understand the significance of the gathering. Ninety journalists "toiled over their clip sheets and typewriters"; radio programs that mentioned or gave extended coverage "exceeded 100 in number and totaled some 26½ hours of radio time"; seven television programs covered the Council's constitutional convention; the Voice of America carried news to Europe and other continents; "movie houses with 80,000,000 weekly customers showed newsreel shots of the Act of Constitution"; and even the weekly magazines *Life*, *Newsweek*, and *Time*, "with a total circulation of millions," took notice. With the hindsight of history, however, the proceedings in Cleveland during an early and difficult snowstorm looked much less newsworthy. Martin E. Marty was almost ho-hum in his evaluation: "In Cleveland, sixty delegates voted into existence a new National Council of Churches of Christ in the United States of America. The fledgling council was cumbersome and hardly ready to meet expectations." Somewhere between Barstow's enthusiastic hype and Marty's deadpan lay a realistic assessment. For starters, Marty was counting only voting delegates (and even rounded the figure down by two) while Barstow was counting anyone who had a role and attended the meetings. Still, what looked to Protestants like the dawning of a new day (Barstow's depiction) was simply one more hamstrung effort to achieve greater church unity (Marty's impression).

As lackluster as the mid-century Protestant effort at ecumenism may have turned out to be, it was nevertheless a window into the mind-set that fervently sought church unity. Here the banner over Cleveland's Public Auditorium, where the Protestant delegates met, as well as the name of the new organization were revealing. Several years before Congress added the phrase "under

God" to the Pledge of Allegiance, mainline Protestants had used the words as half the slogan that announced the National Council's purposes to all those journalists—"This Nation Under God." In case anyone missed the national significance of this religious organization, the name of the Council was a sure reminder that this coalition of denominations and religious organizations may have been more national than Christian. The *National* Council of the Churches of Christ in the *United States of America* gave more space to America than it did to the second person of the Trinity. Also reinforcing the church-in-service-of-the-nation theme was the correspondence between this constitutional assembly and Harry S. Truman, the chief executive of the nation these Protestants so hoped to assist. In the Council's letter to the president, its executive secretary concluded with a reminder and word of encouragement that "the responsibilities which are yours can be borne only with the aid that comes from God and to Him we commend you in our prayers." Truman's response was completely in synch with the ecumenism of the mainline Protestant denominations. "I am indeed grateful—more grateful than I can say—for the advice that I was kept in prayerful remembrance during the assembly in Cleveland," he wrote. "With true insight your thoughtful body perceives that the United Nations, under God, is the world's last, best hope for peace and for the welfare of the human race."

Truman's reference to the United Nations may have been a bit surprising to anyone who read with care the National Council's message to the American nation. Its self-proclaimed mandate avoided specific political realities and spoke in general terms of the social welfare that Christianity provided. When the Council began by describing its purpose as being "for the glory of God and the well-being of humanity," it clearly assumed a broad mission. But it narrowed and made more realistic this mandate when it claimed that it was designed to be an instrument for such ministries as evangelism, education, and relief "as are better achieved through Christian cooperation than by the labors of separated groups." The fine print of the Council's self-understanding revealed that its powers were negligible. The statement clarified that the Council was not a denomination or a "Church above the Churches," thus assuring the autonomy of each institutional member. The description of the Council's functions, while primarily religious and only implicitly political or social, also revealed that it was only as powerful as its member denominations would allow it to be. Its services included Bible translation and distribution, statistical surveys of the churches in the United States, aiding the churches "in undergirding and coordinating" home and foreign missions, lifting up a voice "in behalf of the Christian way of life in messages to the people of the country," coordinating for denominations—"if they wish"—the supply of chaplains to the U.S. military, arranging "a means of approach" to the government on matters of justice and goodwill, and producing Christian programs for television and radio. In general, the Council's function was to be an "organ of evangelism both specifically and broadly conceived, standing ready to serve the cause of Christ in every area as need arises, to the end that the entire country may be permeated by the blessings of His Gospel." But it did so only in the capacity of serving members, "bringing the experience of all to the service of each." As Marty explained, no matter what its boosters then may have said, the Council was a disappointment from the perspective of organic church unity, the hope of many Protestants since at least World War I, because "not one denomination ever surrendered any of its autonomy to this 'body.'"

Still, if the National Council could not supply mainline Protestantism with the unity for which Christ had prayed for his church, it might be able to shore up the ties that bound together the United States. In the section of its statement that described the Council's spirit, these Protestants issued a call to "our fellow citizens to Christian faith," which would defend them from "groundless social dreads and lift them to concerns worthy and productive." From here the statement abruptly turned to the political ideals for which the National Council stood, leaving readers to suppose that these were the worthy and productive concerns that Christianity nurtured. One of these, for which the Council stood as a "guardian," was democractic freedom, since "no person who knows that God as Father has given him all the rights of sonship is likely to remain content under a government which deprives him of basic human rights and fundamental freedoms." A second ideal was liberty understood "with the richest content," meaning a freedom for men and women "to be as the Lord God meant them to be." "The nation may expect from the National Council," the statement explained, "in the name of One who suffered death upon a cross, an unrelenting, open-eyed hostility, as studious as it is deeply passionate, to all of man's inhumanity to man." The third ideal for which the Council stood was opposition to materialism as well as "every political system that is nourshed on materialism, and of every way of living that follows from it." With these ideals in mind the Council could assert with confidence that its member churches "are in their true estate the soul of the nation." "The Church is not the religious phase of the civilization in which it finds itself," the Council explained, but "the living center out of which lasting civilizations take life and form." As such, the Council would function as an "animating, creative and unifying force within our national society."

Finally, the Council's message to the nation referred to the "present crisis," a section that helped to explain Truman's reference to the United Nations in his letter of thanks. The National Council came into existence at a time "when clouds arising from the war in Korea threaten to darken the entire sky," a time "big" with peril and opportunity. Here the Council's leaders invoked a calling of high moral purpose that bordered on utopian and set the organization on a collision course with the politics of the nation it so hoped to unify:

> Without hysteria, without hatred, without pride, without undue patience, without making national interest our chief end but shaping our policies in the light of the aims of the United Nations, without relaxing our positive services to the other peoples of the world, and in complete repudiation of the lying dogma that war is inevitable, let us live and, if need be, die as loyal members of the world community to which Christ summons us and to which we of the Council are dedicated.

This statement referring to the Korean War was curious on several levels. For one, it was an abrupt switch from the statement's other assertions of organizational purpose; it was much more political than religious, and much more specific than general. For another, reputable Protestants such as Reinhold Niebuhr, professor of ethics at Union Seminary, and John Foster Dulles, a leader in ecumenical circles who would become Dwight D. Eisenhower's secretary of state and crafter of the nation's cold war policy, had long raised questions about Protestant convictions that might lead either to pacifism or reliance upon the United Nations. But there it was, the National Council in its very first utterance to the American people taking a contested and idealistic stand on American foreign policy even while its constitution insisted that the new Protestant agency had no control or authority over its denominational members.

The statement on Korea became a little more understandable, however, in light of an address by O. Frederick Nolde at the Cleveland gathering. An official in the World Council of Churches, Nolde had the task of addressing the "Christian view" of the contemporary international crisis. He had less to say about Christian teaching than about the reasons for supporting the United Nations police action in Korea. In fact his two religious points of departure were that God "makes available strength in proportion to the needs of the hour," and that "world war was not inevitable." From there Nolde offered reasons for supporting the United Nations. He told the delegates to be on guard against eight different dangers. These were hysteria, self-righteousness, unilateral action, false pride, complacency, economic dependence on military production, prejudice, and impatience. That Nolde could not keep vices separate from specific practical considerations indicates how complete his opposition was to direct American military involvement in Korea. The basic thrust of his address was that the United States should not act independently in the international crisis but should do everything in its power to cooperate with other nations. That may have been a plausible argument to make, though many Protestants in the mainline churches took a different view. But it was beside the point of whether Christianity had anything specific to say about the sovereignty of governments, the nation-state, or war. Nevertheless Nolde's concluding affirmation of universal brotherhood was in keeping with the cosmopolitan outlook that had informed Protestant ecumenism for at least a generation. "We must penetrate," he asserted, "the artificial curtains by which we are momentarily separated and experience the bonds of humanity and faith which unite men of different nations and races."

Of course the idea that all the peoples of the earth could be one, and do so through the agency of Christianity, might be construed as old as Christ's prayer for his disciples recorded in the Gospel of John and in the apostle Paul's assertion in his letter to the Galatians that in Christ there is neither Jew nor Greek, male nor female, slave nor freeman. The reason for qualifying Christ and the apostles' desire for the unity of humankind is that theirs was clearly oriented to the church as a people distinct from those outside the church. Yet even a more generous construction of Christian ideals about unity had trouble cohering with the American Protestant version of Christian unity that inspired the National Council of Churches. Here John A.

Hutchinson's *We Are Not Divided* (1941), a study of the Federal Council of Churches, the ecumenical predecessor to the National Council, is instructive about the political (as opposed to religious) conception of unity that guided mid-twentieth-century American Protestantism. Hutchinson's book was not simply an examination of the ideas that animated Protestant cooperation; it came from deep within the bosom of the reigning Protestant intellectuals. It was the fruit of a dissertation in the philosophy department of Columbia University, supervised by Herbert Schneider, with critical comments from theologians at nearby Union Seminary—Reinhold Niebuhr, Robert Hastings Nichols, and Henry P. Van Dusen.

For a study of ideas by a man who secured a job at the College of Wooster on the basis of his Ph.D., and would eventually return to Columbia to teach philosophy, Hutchinson's book was remarkably thin. In one chapter particularly he set out to examine Protestant ecumenism's intellectual apparatus. But at its outset he had to concede that because of the lack of unity among Protestants, owing to denominational differences, ecumenism American style had to tread lightly on any sort of theological affirmation that might offend a particular denomination. Thus the Federal Council had repeatedly declared a "moratorium on theology" and in its constitution explicitly prohibited any effort to draw up a creed or form of worship. Unity would have to come from categories other than Christian ones. Better put, the ideas for unity might come from a provenance loosely Christian but would require serious makeovers to be useful for the practical social and political problems that American Protestants were joining hands to solve.

Hutchinson then described the process whereby Protestants adapted traditional Christian concepts to allow the church to participate in the work of social reform. The Social Gospel had specifically widened and modified "many traditional concepts to make room for new meanings." Sometimes it was not merely modification but outright rejection, such as the church's "attack" upon the distinction between the sacred and secular, and substituting for it the idea of "the sacredness of all life." In other cases the creation of a gospel with social leverage required redefinition. The idea of sin needed to be cast in a social context with a clear distinction between selfishness and service. The doctrine of the vicarious atonement of Christ also assumed a new meaning. No longer was it merely the idea of Christ suffering in place of sinners; it became a "social principle of non-violence and sacrifice to be apprehended and applied in all social relationships." Such refashioning of Christian teaching allowed Protestants to pursue more freely than they had historically the idea that "the purpose of the church [was] to realize the will of God in society." And it gave the church responsibility for the "spiritual and moral welfare of the community" through its dual role as "teacher and judge." Of course Hutchinson was careful to insist that the church's social task did not involve the use of "overtly" political methods or the approval of a state church. Such denials missed the very real possibility that a social gospel might not only redirect the church's endeavors from eternal to temporal affairs (in Augustine's terms, from the City of God to the City of Man) but turn the church into a political lobby. Also missed was the way in which the much-affirmed notion of Christ's Lordship might be at odds with a separation of church and state. When the Presbyterian Robert E. Speer asked Protestant ecumenists, "How great a Lord is Jesus Christ to be? Are there areas of life of which He is not meant to be Lord? If so then He is no Lord of all as we had supposed," a listener might have reasonably concluded that Protestants believed Christ was sovereign over civil government. In which case, didn't the church, as the long history of rivalry between emperor and pope suggested, have a responsibility as teacher and judge to determine public policy?

Still, revision of traditional Christian doctrinal categories was not the same thing as unity, either intellectual or practical. When Hutchinson finally turned to the ideas fueling interdenominational cooperation and church unity, processes better known as ecumenism, the evidence was even harder to find. His concession that the Federal Council's thoughts about its own existence, the differences among the denominations, and church union more generally was "pragmatic, and if one may use the term without derogatory implications, opportunistic," was not entirely propitious even if candid. The attitude to church union by Protestant ecumenists was basically to assume its existence rather than cultivate a coherent argument around which the denominations might rally. The difficulty here was that genuine union or merger of the Protestant denominations would mean the end of work for those denominational officials who had the task of deciding on union. Hence the Federal Council, and later the National Council, became symbols of church unity more than actual mechanisms of union. Protestants could claim through these cooperative agencies to be tearing down the barriers that separated Christ's followers from one another. At the same time they continued to maintain the prerogatives of their particular denominations. If Presbyterians and Baptists could not agree about infant baptism, they could conceivably concur on the best means for Christianizing the American social order.

Even if Protestants could not agree on the teachings and practice of Christianity, their "crusade for brotherhood," as Hutchinson referred to it, endowed the churches with a social program that involved befriending labor organizations and defending collective bargaining, removing barriers between blacks and whites, reducing and eventually eliminating ill-will toward Jews, vigorously defending monogamous marriage and abstinence as the appropriate form of child planning, opposing drunkenness and most forms of alcoholic consumption, establishing standards of decency for Hollywood, attending to problems in rural America, and advocating peace almost to the point of pacifism. Many of these concerns were holdovers from the late nineteenth century when American Protestants first began establishing organizations for denominational cooperation. But the opposition to war was new, especially since the Federal Council had enthusiastically supported American involvement in World War I. Just after the beginning of the Second World War, the Council issued in 1939 a statement that called upon "the churches to pronounce war an evil thing, alien from the mind of Christ." This report recognized that some would fight for "conscience's sake," but even then the conviction should be that war was still evil even if an "inescapable one."

The curious aspect of Protestant ecumenism's understanding of brotherhood and unity was that it left the American churches advocating a view of unity that had trouble differentiating the work of the Federal or National Council from that of the United Nations. Here statements from two different reports that Hutchinson cited are instructive. The first comes from the Federal Council's 1939 statement opposing war:

> We call upon the churches now to seek peace, not for safety's sake of for profit's sake but for Christ's sake and a kindlier world. We could not, and would not, be immune from the world's problems and pain. By generous gift and practical service let us know the fellowship of His suffering in war-torn lands. By trenchant thought let us explore the hidden causes of war. With willingness to sacrfice let us join with others in preparing the outlines of a just peace, or an economic life undisfigured by poverty and greed, and of a world order in which common needs and service of all nations may find a home.

Only two years earlier, at an international gathering of Protestants that prepared the way for the World Council of Churches, a similar sentiment informed hopes not simply for international relations but for a "world Christian community." According to the report of the Faith and Order Conference:

> We desire also to declare to all men everywhere our assurance that Christ is the one hope of unity for the world in the face of

the distractions and dissensions of this present time. Yet we are one in Christ and in the fellowship of His Spirit. We pray that everywhere, in a world divided and perplexed, men may turn to Jesus Christ our Lord, Who makes us one in spite of divisions; that He may bind in one those who by many worldly claims are set at variance; and that the world may at last find peace and unity in Him . . .

Of course church councils were not in the business of issuing statements in favor of war or church divisions. Still, the assumption that Christianity was an elixir that if tasted would cure religious and international strife sounded simplistic, as if the authors of such statements could not see a difference between those matters that forced Christians into different denominations and the ones that led nations to war. Protestant ecumenists had abstracted the ideal of Christian unity from an understanding of the person, community, and denominational purpose that might reasonably recognize the value of differentiation and separate realms of authority, order, and work.

Perhaps Hutchinson himself best summarized the logic behind this version of Christian unity when he wrote about the "church's greatest service." This involved maintaining its own "unique witness" that led "inescapably into such problems as the removal of racial barriers both in church and in society, the maintenance of religious freedoms for all groups, the continuance of mutual church aid through missions and the Central Relief Bureau, and education in such problems as the ecumenical church, peace and disarmament." Here was clearly a tall and ever-expanding order for the church. But the idea seemed to be that because God was on the side of this imperative, resources were abundant. Not only that, but this imperative was also a divine mandate. As Francis B. Sayre, a United Nations official, explained at the opening assembly of the National Council of Churches, the principles of Christ possessed an application wider than individuals. They also applied to nations.

"Since Christianity is the very essence of goodness," he reasoned, "a world society to be enduring must be built upon the uniting and strengthening power of the basic principles which Christ summed up and embodied in his life—whether these be recognized and labelled as Christian, or whether they be tagged as Buddhist or Mohammedan or Hindu, or simply recognized without religious tags as fundamental and eternal reality." For some reason Protestants missed the amazing inconsistency of a religion that would not allow Presbyterians, Methodists, and Baptists to give up their own denominational powers within the United States but now could merge Christianity and any number of Asian religions under the magic of a "fundamental and eternal reality." No doubt an understanding of unity and brotherhood more humanitarian than Christian was responsible.

To assert that the politics of American church unity were simply political may be an overstatement but one with enough accuracy to recognize a nonreligious streak in Protestant ecumenism seldom acknowledged. Throughout American history Protestant denominations invariably considered cooperative enterprises more because of national politics than for Christian motives. Soon after the Revolutionary War, for instance, Presbyterians and Congregationalists entered into a cooperative venture for establishing congregations in the Northwest Territory, the 1801 Plan of Union. Although the Presbyterians and Congregationalists were Calvinists on paper, the greater incentive for collaboration was each denomination's opposition to the establishment of a Church of England bishop in the colonies before national independence and mutual commitments to republican order after the American founding. In fact Presbyterians and Congregationalists first began to convene together almost a decade before American independence because of common opposition to the policies of Parliament. The political nature of this cooperation became apparent when during the first three decades of the nineteenth century each side learned that the other denomination had a markedly distinct understanding of Calvinist theology. This recognition both split the Presbyterian church into strict and Americanized branches and put distance between Presbyterians and Congregationalists altogether by the eve of the Civil War.

After the Civil War, again in response to social and political circumstances, Northern Protestants engaged in their most ambitious era of interdenominational cooperation. The previously mentioned Evangelical Alliance, which gained an American branch in 1867, initiated a string of collaborative Protestant efforts designed to retain the Christian (read: Protestant) identity of the United States. The list of evils afflicting the nation and demanding cooperation were intemperance, Sabbath desecration, atheism, materialism, urban blight, and above all Roman Catholicism. Protestants were particularly alarmed by the rising tide of Roman Catholic immigration to the United States during the late nineteenth century. Perhaps even more glaring was the Vatican's assertion of papal infallibiilty at the First Vatican Council (1869–1870). Protestant church leaders believed they needed a unified religious front if they were to counter Rome's obvious unanimity and control over its church members. Missing were actual considerations of church polity, sacramental theology, or creedal revision that might lead Presbyterians, Baptists, Episcopalians, Methodists, and Congregationalists into a common or generic Protestant church. Instead, what kindled the first formal efforts to establish a Protestant interdenominational organization was a commitment to preserving a Christian nation. The culmination of these Protestant efforts was the establishment in 1908 of the Federal Council of Churches, which took the significant step in one of its first actions of drawing up a Social Creed (see Chapter Four). The denominations may have been divided along theological and liturgical lines, but increasingly they regarded themselves as one thanks to similar convictions about the United States.

Again war proved to be an incentive for ecumenical relations. In 1919, after the First World War, many Protestant leaders hoped to achieve even closer ties among the denominations, moving from a federated to an organic relationship. The 1919 Plan for Organic Union failed thanks to bloated budget proposals and bad public relations campaigns. But the justification for it was not simply fifty years of Protestant cooperation since the conclusion of the Civil War. It was also the fact that Protestants had cooperated so closely during the recent war, both in ministering to soldiers in France and in rallying support for the war at home. If the formal plans for organic union sputtered, the idea that Protestants were unified in serving the nation did not. Hutchinson's book is proof that Protestant ecumenism in the United States, in the form of the Federal Council, drew directly from social and political convictions rather than religious beliefs about Christian unity. The original meeting of the body that in 1950 reconstituted the Federal Council as the National Council of Churches, with its attention to the Korean War and the value of the United Nations, revealed also that church unity among American Protestants basically stemmed from a desire for the church to play an active role in national and international affairs. This may have been a laudable goal, but whether it was actually a Christian one did not seem to dawn on church leaders.

The one time when war backfired on church union came in the decades after the start of the National Council. The Consultation on Church Union (COCU), the most recent and least popular American Protestant ecumenical project, originally drew support from the success of the National Council and the renewed vigor of mainline Protestantism during the 1950s. But the autonomy of the National Council's member denominations remained a problem for some church leaders. The 1960 presidential election proved to be an important factor in demonstrating the problem of Protestant disunity. According to Eugene Carson Blake, the Presbyterian minister and Protestant ecumenist extraordinaire who graced *Time*'s cover on May 26, 1961, when the magazine devoted a feature article to the new Protestant initiative, the contest between John F. Kennedy and Richard Nixon had revealed the fundamental weakness of the church. "Never before," Blake asserted in a sermon before the National Council, "have so many Americans agreed that the Christian Churches, divided as they are, cannot be trusted to bring to the American people an objective and authentic word of God on a political issue." Instead the churches appeared to be "competing social groups pulling and hauling, propagandizing and pressuring for their organizational advantages." Although explicit anti-Catholicism was no longer becoming among Protestants, many observers did sense that Blake's plea for COCU was in response to the election of the first Roman Catholic president, and to rumors of another Vatican Council soon to convene in Rome. The need for Protestant unity in the face of Roman Catholic muscle, almost a century old, continued to motivate ecumenism in America as well as the political fortunes of American Protestants.

Through the 1960s plans for COCU went forward, with Blake playing a key role and the National Council providing the chief constituency for union. By 1970, when the effort produced *A Plan of Union*, only nine denominations had signed on, including two black Methodist bodies, the Northern and Southern Presbyterian churches, the Congregationalists, Episcopalians, Disciples, and two other Methodist denominations. The first page of the plan described these churches as:

> a company of the people of God celebrating the one God, Father, Son and Holy Spirit, moving toward his coming Kingdom and seeking in faithfulness to unite under the Gospel for Christ's mission and service to the world, open ourselves individually and corporately to renewal from the Holy Spirit, struggle against racism, poverty, environmental blight, war, and other problems of the

family of man, minister to the deep yearning of the human spirit for fullness of life.

The problem facing COCU, as its opening declaration implied, was that by 1970 Protestants were even more divided than they had been when Blake proposed the new ecumenical effort. Within a decade, race and gender had become more important as markers of personal identity than denominational labels. As Preston N. Williams, an African-American theologian at Harvard Divinity School, observed in 1972, "to the cultural revolutionaries" of the 1960s COCU represented only one thing: "business as usual." "Given the history of even the liberal Christian church toward blacks, women, and youth," he added, "the failure of COCU aggressively to court the cultural revolutionaries conveys the notion that COCU's phrases are just another set of pronouncements to be more honored in breach than in fulfillment."

Martin E. Marty chimed in about COCU as if it were the last gasp of an old Protestant ecumenism that had experienced cardiac arrest owing to those Americans referred to as "revolutionaries" by Williams. When Blake originally called for a Protestant union, Marty observed, white Anglo-Saxon Protestantism still mattered and "liberal optimism" still prevailed in the mainline churches. Mainline Protestants also imbibed the secular post-Christian utopianism of the time, believing that cities and nations could be governed by wise men. "Few now like to be reminded," Marty wrote only eleven years after COCU's founding, "of a day when they shared hope that 'man in control' would rule, that computers could be idolized or even believed in." In fact COCU came to be the last expression of mainline Protestant confidence in its ability to unify and give spiritual direction to the United States before the reality of race, class, and gender made such national and religious unity look silly if not dangerous. As Marty observed, COCU "set out to overcome 'separation' at a time when symbol-makers now set a new premium on at least strategic 'separation' in various racial, sexual, generational, or other movements." He still believed the unity promoted by COCU was desirable, but it needed a formal expression some distance from the bureaucratic structures and white, male, and American identities that dominated the Protestant mainline denominations.

In the more than four decades since COCU began, Protestant ecumenism has changed course dramatically, even to the point of being an embarrassing reminder of the Protestant establishment's hegemonic demeanor during the century after the Civil War. Gone are the banners announcing "This Nation Under God" at the meetings of church union advocates. Instead mainline Protestants have tried to find reasons other than Christianizing the social order in America and around the world as a basis for church union. But those efforts have proved to be difficult. By 2001 COCU still consisted of the same original nine member denominations, with Episcopalians and Presbyterians backing away from 1999 proposals because of disagreements over the authority of bishops and elders in church governance. The general indifference to ecumenism by most American Protestants, except for those serving on church-relations committees, did not deter COCU from announcing that in 2002 it would change its name to Churches United in Christ (CUIC). Despite the name, the basis for unity, according to one Episcopalian official, had more to do with ending racism in society than among the churches. "The focus on combating racism is surely on target," he said. He also admitted the irony that "racism has divided us and now it unites us." Opposing racism may have been the inevitable outcome for an effort that had once relied upon national unity to inspire Christian ecumenism. Without the political order of the United States to give coherence, Protestant cooperation faltered and needed to find a different rationale, one with equal benefits to society but without clear associations to Protestantism's tainted WASP past. What Protestant ecumenists failed to consider was that social and political differences, as the nation's two-party political system implies, are even more divisive than those over infant baptism, prayer books, and church government.

## *Christian Separatism*

Mainline Protestantism did not speak for all Protestants in the United States and in fact prompted the formation of rival religious and interdenominational organizations. After the 1920s in particular, when conservative Protestants lost confidence in the mainline denominations' ability to police wayward doctrinal views, evangelical Protestants established their own cooperative agencies. One of these was the National Association of Evangelicals (NAE), founded in 1942 and designed to be a rival to the Federal Council and give voice to the many denominations, congregations, and individual Protestants whose views were not welcome in the mainline Protestant institution. Given the explicit competition between the NAE and the Federal Council, as well as lingering bitterness from the denominational quarrels of the 1920s, the antagonism of the ostensibly liberal Protestants to the new evangelical agency was not surprising. The *Christian Century*, the weekly magazine of the mainline, ran as its headline for the story announcing the start of the NAE, "Sectarianism Receives New Lease on Life." Still, what the editors of the *Century* failed to understand was that the effort to unite Protestants in some form of ecumenical cooperative was also responsible for dividing American Protestantism. Not only did some Protestants actually disagree with the mainline's basis for unity, but any conception of Protestant unity would require denominations to relinquish those teachings and practices that had made them a distinct denomination. In effect, Protestant ecumenism had changed the terms of Christian fellowship. For at least three centuries after the Reformation, Protestants had tried to be faithful to Scripture by following its teachings in all aspects of church life. This was the logic that led to the differences among

Methodists, Baptists, Presbyterians, Lutherans, Episcopalians, and Congregationalists, for starters. Each communion believed that its distinct forms of worship, theology, and government were required by holy writ. But with the advent of Protestant ecumenism, that logic was no longer persuasive. The whole of biblical teaching could be reduced to the imperative for Christian unity, with the other matters that separated Protestants falling under the classification of peripheral.

Even if the NAE appeared to be guilty of sectarianism from the vantage of the *Century's* downtown Chicago offices, some Protestant denominations were reluctant even to join the new conservative enterprise. The evangelicals may have had a longer creedal statement, with nine essential articles of belief as opposed to the Federal Council's lone affirmation of Christ's Lordship; but the NAE's list of affirmations was a long way from the creeds of the Reformed, Lutheran, and Episcopal branches of the Protestant Reformation. Consequently some Protestant denominations hesitated to embrace the NAE because its premise for church unity and cooperation was almost as reductionistic as the Federal Council's. If a denomination joined the NAE and agreed to cooperate with other denominations, what did such a decision say about the importance of those specific beliefs and practices that defined a particular Protestant communion? Two Reformed denominations wrestling with these questions at mid-century were the Dutch Calvinists in the Christian Reformed church (CRC) and the conservative—some called them militant—Presbyterians in the Orthodox Presbyterian church (OPC).

The CRC's ecumenical stance was bound up with the dilemmas accompanying an ethnic communion coming to terms with assimilation. Dutch Calvinists had been ambivalent about American forms of piety since they began migrating to the Midwest steadily in the late nineteenth century. Two world wars, however, encouraged patriotism and nurtured a sense of identification with the new homeland. By the 1940s the assimilationists within the CRC took the lead in supporting the newly formed NAE. But by the late 1940s a sufficient number of critics within the church began to raise questions that eroded the CRC's support for the new evangelical enterprise. A major factor was the question of evangelism and preaching. These were tasks reserved, according to some critics, for the institutional church, not to be conducted by some parachurch or cooperative agency. Equally pressing was the theological identity of most institutional members of the NAE. Calvinists were in the minority, and some in the CRC wondered how their denomination could cooperate in evangelism with Protestants who denied the five points of Calvinism. To be a member of the NAE, then, was to abandon those teachings that made the CRC distinct. More important, to be part of evangelical cooperative efforts was to force the CRC to support an agency that was contradicting its own confession of faith. Granted, the five points of Calvinism were not a recipe for interdenominational cooperation. But that was the point. When the CRC withdrew from the NAE in 1951, it was showing that unity as conceived by American Protestants, whether liberal or conservative, made little room for churches still bound to Protestantism's historic teaching.

The story was similar for the OPC, a denomination more resistant than the CRC to assimilationist pressures. Having emerged from the fundamentalist controversy in the Northern Presbyterian church, Orthodox Presbyterians were not reluctant to display their differences with other Protestants. Even so, they too entertained the possibility of joining some form of religious cooperation. The Federal Council was clearly impossible. The NAE appeared to be more congenial because of its opposition to theological liberalism. But the OPC's Calvinism was also an obstacle to joining the NAE, for reasons similar to those used by the CRC. How could the OPC cooperate in evangelism and preaching with Protestants who were not Calvinistic? This did not mean that the OPC (or the CRC for that matter) regarded non-Calvinist churches as non-Christian. It did mean that beliefs about matters such as sin, human nature, and salvation were so weighty that differences prevented union or even cooperation. What was particularly alarming about the NAE to some Orthodox Presbyterians was that the evangelical body appeared to be duplicating the logic of the Federal Council, namely, unifying Protestants in order to carry a bigger stick in national affairs. The OPC regarded the work of the church as distinct from that of the nation, such that common social or cultural causes were insufficient to merit fudging theological norms. No matter what the church's or individual Christian's responsibilities to society were, the OPC's decision to decline membership reflected the conviction that the church's prior duty was to safeguard its own spiritual mission.

These Calvinistic denominations were not opposed to ecumenism per se, only to American ideals of unity. At roughly the same time the OPC and CRC rejected overtures from evangelicals, they joined an international council of churches, the Reformed Ecumenical Synod (RES). Established in 1946 by several Dutch Calvinist denominations in the Netherlands, North America, and South Africa, the RES would eventually attract Presbyterian and Reformed denominations from South America, Asia, and other European nations. This ecumenical body barely caused a ripple within the NAE or Federal Council. It was small, appeared to be sectarian because of its insistence upon Reformed theology, and its American members were bit players on the American ecclesiastical scene. Yet the RES may have been even more ecumenical than either the NAE or the Federal Council, its achievement more unifying. To be sure, it excluded Methodists, Episcopalians, Lutherans, and any number of the other Protestant denominations. But it included lots of non-Americans because the RES's criteria for ecumenism was not political or national but religious and ecclesial. Of course, people uniting for political or national reasons is not inherently a bad thing. But neither is it clear that such forms of unity are either Christian or need to be religiously motivated. If Christianity has more to do with life in the next world than the affairs of this one, then these seemingly sectarian Calvinistic denominations were practicing a form of unity that was more Christian then either evangelicals or mainline Protestants were capable of achieving.

## *Divisive Faith*

Religious diversity and national unity appear to comprise one of the several enigmas of political life in the United States. Despite its wide spectrum of beliefs and religious institutions, America has avoided the religious antagonisms that regularly afflicted Europe, for instance. The religious wars of the seventeenth century were one example of what can happen when diversity of faith teams up with substantial ties between church and state. But the United States, thanks to a political order designed to avoid a repetition of such holy warfare, has managed to accommodate religious differences relatively peacefully. Of course Protestant hegemony made life difficult for any number of non-Protestants and unpleasant for some Protestants who, for example, liked wine with meals or a nightcap. And even if the Civil War was more inevitable than political compromise thanks to Protestant zeal, the case can be plausibly made that America, all things considered, has handled religious diversity remarkably well.

Two explanations may account for America's tolerance toward religious pluralism. One is a secular liberal rendering of the United States that regards the American founding as a brilliant turning point, when religion became a private affair with no bearing on public life. In effect, this interpretation regards the disestablishment of religion as a domestication of faith, thus denying its capacity to divide the body politic.

The other explanation is one friendly to religion and particularly to the faith that became dominant in the United States, namely, mainline Protestantism. In his national best-seller *Habits of the Heart* (1985), the sociologist Robert Bellah and his team of associates wrote positively about the way the largest and oldest Protestant denominations gave coherence to America. "These churches," Bellah concluded, "have tried to develop a larger picture of what it might mean to live a biblical life in America" by relating faith to "the whole of contemporary life—cultural, social, political, economic—not just to personal and family morality." As he went on to explain, the mainline churches were examples of just what sociologists regard as churches, as opposed to sects, in the vernacular of Ernst Troeltsch. That is, a church is a body that "enters into the world culturally and socially in order to influence it," whereas the sect "stands apart from the secular world." Never mind that the American political order and its disestablishment of religion might turn all faiths into sects by denying them political status and government support, thus challenging Troeltsch's churchly status. Bellah and company still regarded the church ideal as one that has and could continue to provide a "religious center" for America. "The church tends to be comprehensive and flexible with respect to society and culture, accepting and attempting to transform social forms and also art, science and philosophy." It stayed close to power "in hopes of Christianizing it to some degree." In effect, the church-type of religious association, exemplified by the mainline churches, imparted to the United States a sense of meaning and purpose. Sectarian religious groups such as evangelicals and fundamentalists privatized faith and denied its relevance to public life, thus inhibiting the ethical and spiritual resolve that healthy societies need.

Bellah's analysis of religion and society was the standard sociological interpretation that underwrote mainline Protestant hegemony. By dividing religious groups into the publicly minded or social-service churches on one side, and the sectarian and culturally isolated sects on the other, assessments like Bellah's kept alive the idea that faith had a vital role to play in public life and that certain religious bodies were more trustworthy than others in their service to the nation. Although he did not say so exactly, *Habits of the Heart* gave the impression that the mainline Protestant churches were responsible for America's ability to tolerate religious diversity. The reason was twofold. First, they were flexible and willing to compromise with aspects of the secular world in order to maintain a position of influence. Second, they were effective in keeping the other religious bodies away from the corridors of power, at least by portraying those other groups as divisive and sectarian. The history of Protestant ecumenism, though not necessarily the best example of Protestant insight, does prove this point. The churches that strove for cooperation and unity were also the ones with the most politically oriented conception of the church. It is not a stretch to conclude that Protestant ecumenism was synonymous with the Protestant establishment because the aim of the former was, as Bellah detected, to provide the United States with a common religious or moral purpose.

Yet the unity that Protestant ecumenists sought was exactly the factor that proved to be so objectionable during the 1960s and after, when various minorities took issue with WASP hegemony in American public life. This is a point that R. Laurence Moore has made effectively. He is especially critical of assessments of religious pluralism that celebrate America's exceptional unity despite real religious divisions. For instance, Moore contends that a genuinely plural religious society would be characterized by aggressive assertions of religious difference because such religious disagreements are "meant to matter." And any such assertion of difference would not unify society but would perpetuate "boundaries between significant groups of people." Moore is one of the few historians of American religion to question the assertion, planted and watered by Protestant ecumenism in America, that "unfriendly feeling is somehow abnormal in a religiously plural society." "Hostility is altogether normal in heterogeneous cultures," he writes, and all the more so, by implication, in religiously diverse ones. This means that Moore disagrees markedly with Bellah's interpretation of American Protestantism as well as the idea that faith may supply the moral bonds for a religiously diverse society. If American Protestantism did provide the spiritual core for the nation, it did so at the expense of religious minorities who had to acclimate themselves to WASP culture in the United States. The "inevitable process of acculturation," Moore posits, "blurs religious distinctiveness behind claims of a common Americanness," and thereby causes particular religions to lose something "vital." One could add that the same point applies to majority faiths like American Protestantism. For by trying to craft a common generic Protestant faith that would unite the denominations and supply the moral purpose for the United States, if not the world, mainline Protestantism also gave up something essential. It forgot about the teachings and practices that were vital to each Protestant denomination, at least at its origin, and assumed that differences over baptism, the Lord's Supper, or conversion were secondary to political, national, or social affairs.

Moore's recognition of the inherent divisiveness of faith, especially in a religiously heterogeneous society, does not prevent him from sometimes appealing to religion's unifying capacity. With Isaac Kramnick, he has denied to Ralph Reed, one of the leading political strategists of the Protestant right, his appeal to Martin Luther King, Jr., as a model for evangelicals' recent ascendancy in electoral politics and policymaking. For Kramnick and Moore, what separates today's Protestant right from King's civil rights movement is "inclusion." If Reed

> can come up with a way to write a pro-family speech, one that will
> be acceptable to the Christian Coalition, that calls upon gays and

straights, feminists and Christian fundamentalists, atheists and Roman Catholics . . . to join hands and sing the words of the great spiritual, "Free at last, Free at last, Thank God almighty, we are free at last," he will have done something that might yet move this nation. But that isn't the message he is even remotely close to delivering.

Interestingly enough, this view of King and Reed is not all that different from Robert Bellah's. In *Habits of the Heart*, Bellah and his colleagues also interpreted King's "I Have a Dream" speech as a fundamentally unifying expression of "America as a community of memory." But if faith is actually as divisive as Moore argued against Bellah's utilitarian construction, how is it possible to view King's appeal to the Bible, Jesus, and the Old Testament prophets as a platform for common action in a religiously diverse and liberal setting? Why isn't it possible to respond to sentiments like King's, in his legendary and moving speech about the glory of the Lord being revealed in the cause of civil rights for African Americans, the same way that Moore responds to Bellah? Why isn't King's appeal also "a tall order" because its religion will not include or "appeal to liberal secularists"? One could easily add, any other nonbiblical faith, or even the biblical ones whose adherents are not particularly inclined to forsake the distinct teachings of their denomination to arrive at a generic Christianity designed to accomplish this-world's political goods.

If religion really does divide, as Moore has helpfully noted, even appeals like King's, as socially worthy and inspiring as they may be, are also religiously divisive. After all, the religion of the Bible, whether Jewish, Eastern Orthodox, Roman Catholic, or Protestant, is clear in teaching that a fundamental difference exists between God's people and those not worshiping and glorifying the true God. The exclusive claims of biblical religion do not necessarily imply theocracy or the exclusion of nonbelievers from even would-be Christian societies. In fact Jewish and Christian thinkers have marshaled all sorts of arguments to render biblical faith compatible with modern conceptions of freedom and political voluntarism. Even so, the exclusive claims of the Bible about the dangers of compromise with unbelief provide a curious basis upon which to try to construct a common faith or unified spiritual mission for a society made up of citizens who do not believe the Bible. Such exclusivity is not simply why some Christians oppose simplistic efforts at church unity and interdenominational cooperation, but also why some Christians and liberal secularists believe religion cannot contribute to the common good that politics is designed to sustain.

# CHAPTER EIGHT

# The Dilemma of Compassionate Conservatism

When George W. Bush announced on January 29, 2001, the creation of the White House Office of Faith-Based and Community Initiatives, he did so without either great fanfare or elaborate explanation. The executive order that established this new office included five points, the first of which came the closest to approaching an argument for a faith-based policy initiative. It asserted the need for such religiously motivated forms of social welfare more than it tried to persuade of their value. "Faith-based and other community organizations are indispensable in meeting the needs of poor Americans and distressed neighborhoods," was how the policy section of the executive order began. The president's formal statement went on to explain that faith-based organizations and relief efforts could not replace the work of government but should be included as partners in the pursuit of "compassionate results." "Private and charitable community groups, including religious ones," the executive order declared, "should have the fullest oportunity permitted by law to compete on a level playing field, so long as they achieve valid public purposes." These desirable public outcomes included "curbing crime, conquering addiction, strengthening families and neighborhoods, and overcoming poverty." The rest of the executive order included White House boilerplate policy verbiage and a fairly long list of functions to be undertaken by the new office. The first item on the list was sufficiently broad to give the faith-based initiative a long leash, pending adequate finanical resources, of course: "to develop, lead, and coordinate the Administration's policy agenda affecting faith-based and other community programs and initiatives, expand the role of such efforts in communities, and increase their capacity through executive action, legislation, Federal and private funding, and regulatory relief."

The person who would try to persuade the nation of the new office's legitimacy and value was John DiIulio, Jr., a professor of political science at the University of Pennsylvania whose own work on crime in inner cities, along with his own born-again experience as a Roman Catholic, had convinced him of the important social services that religious organizations provided across the country. Bush appointed DiIulio to head the new White House office soon after the January executive order, and by late winter the assistant to the president on faith-based initiatives was giving speeches designed to rally support for his new work. One of the more controversial of DiIulio's addresses in his short-lived tenure in the administration was delivered on March 7, 2001, before the National Association of Evangelicals, meeting in Dallas. What made the speech controversial were remarks that revealed a growing division between supporters of Bush over the first word in *faith-based initiative*. Religious purists feared that government involvement with religious social service organizations would place restrictions on the religious component of such assistance. For them, faith was not an extra part of the work, as if one could separate curing drug addiction from faith in Jesus Christ. Rather, in some of the most difficult circumstances, such as those involving repeat offenders in prison and drug addicts, the spiritual component of the social service was crucial to the publicly beneficial result. Religious pragmatists, however, were more willing to live with certain qualifications of religious mission in order that churches and religious community associations might receive government funding that would considerably increase assistance within impoverished urban neighborhoods.

In this debate DiIulio emerged as one of the members of the pragmatic side, and he used his speech in Texas to take a shot at the predominantly white and suburban evangelicals who tended to regard spiritual conversion as crucial to genuine social service. He noted that,

> compared to predominately ex-urban white evangelical churchs, urban African-American and Latino faith communities have benevolent traditions and histories that make them generally more dedicated to community-serving missions, and generally more confident about engaging public and secular partners in achieving those missions without enervating their spiritual identities or religious characters.

When DiIulio added that the NAE needed to "get real" about helping the poor, unhealthy, and prisoners, doubters were confirmed in their suspicions about Bush's choice of a sometimes incautious academic to be the point man for an already contested new federal initiative.

The controversy over faith-based initiatives ended up looking like a tempest in a teapot after the terrorist attacks of September 11, 2001, at which point Bush's presidency hinged on foreign policy. As mere policy the president's faith-based proposal was not terribly novel and would not have generated the controversy it did had partisan politics not kept antagonism from the 2000 presidential campaign burning and hot. Bush's faith-based initiative was essentially a further elaboration of the charitable-choice legislation that Bill Clinton had supported in 1996 as part of welfare reform.

It had provided federal funds for religious social service providers that were not "pervasively sectarian." During the first year of Bush's presidency, however, the debates over government funding for religiously dedicated charitable organizations became a means for either shoring up the president's conservative base or demonstrating the folly of his seemingly naive version of God and country. The faith-based initiative consequently revealed that Bush would govern in a way that was friendly to the religious voters whom he had courted, a revelation that iritated those who had supported Gore and were still smarting from the way the Democratic nominee had lost. But this was a pleasing development for the red-state voters who wanted a president to roll back the onslaught of secularism.

Undoubtedly the opposition to the White House office caught Bush officials off guard, a sign that Bush's knowledge of born-again Protestants was more distant than his own conversion story and remarks about Jesus as his favorite philosopher suggested. The controversy also revealed that federal funding for religion was indeed a constitutionally questionable practice. As with so many church-state issues, faith-based initiatives looked at least like an establishment of religon. This is why both Clinton and Bush had tried, in different degrees, to separate spiritual from physical assistance or welfare. And this is also why the evangelicals implied in DiIulio's remarks objected to what appeared to be a halfhearted effort by the Bush administration. A president who would be so open about his own faith, they thought, would be the one to make a plausible case for faith's personally tranformative powers and so perform the difficult act of separating the spiritual components from religiously motivated social welfare.

In fact the problem with faith-based initiatives went deeper than the constitutional questions regarding church-state relations. As with so many of the examples and arguments in this book, the issue of federal funding for religious charitable organizations begged a fundamental question in pursuit of the legal one. Instead of asking whether the Constitution permitted such entanglement of religion and politics, Bush, DiIulio, and others weighing in should have been asking whether the teachings of Bush's favorite philosopher were compatible with the essential logic of the faith-based initiative. In his speech before the NAE, DiIulio claimed that Americans needed better "networks of social service providers, religious and secular." He added that this need would be greatly diminished "if the church behaved like the church, unified from city to suburb, working across racial and denominational divides on behalf of broken lives and breadless families." Had he known that he was repeating the orthodoxy of the Social Gospel and mainline Protestant ecumenism, DiIulio would likely not have been embarrassed. The reason was his own reading of the Bible. He quoted from the first epistle of John, which asked, "How does God's love abide in anyone who has the world's goods and sees a brother or sister in need and yet refuses help?" Such religious instruction contained only one lesson, namely, that evangelical Christians and organizations needed to "get it done in 'truth and action.'"

The problem that DiIulio failed to address, however, was one that he might have learned from the history of the Social Gospel and the ecumenical movement it inspired. If the apostle John had a different conception of human brotherhood and sisterhood in mind than the liberal Protestant one that regarded God as the father of all men and women, if in fact the early church had a different idea about Christian brothers and sisters and how the church was to care for them, perhaps the meaning of the verse DiIulio quoted was not so obvious. In which case his appeal to "truth and action" may have been simply an appeal to action without truth, because it garbled the meaning of the Bible on the matter of the church's works of mercy.

## *The Great Reversal*

Disputes among the evangelical right's supporters of Bush would appear to conform to the standard two-party analysis of American Protestantism. That view divides the white churches (at least) between the mainline's Social Gospel and evangelicals' individualistic conception of salvation. After all, an important part of the objections that attended the creation of the new office in the White House was the contention that separating faith's positive public consequences from conversion itself was to miss the import of faith. As one administrator in an evangelical drug-rehabilitation program put it, "It is important for these folks to realize that it is 'faith' in faith-based ministries that causes them to be so effective." Bush's policy appeared ironically to be making faith a "casualty" of faith-based initiatives. This argument reflected the alleged classic difference between evangelical and mainline Protestants. While the mainliners equivocated over the importance of individual salvation in the pursuit of redeeming social institutions and the eradication of social evil, evangelicals always insisted that faith in Christ needed first to be evident in individuals, who as the number of converts grew would reform society. DiIulio was at least implying that this difference was inconsequential, that in fact the African-American and Latino Protestant churches, for which the distinctions of white Protestantism were seemingly arbitrary, better understood the socially transforming power of Christianity.

Seldom observed in the whole episode, however, was how all these Protestants agreed with the White House official, DiIulio, that faith is socially relevant and that the church has a responsibility to change society. For instance, as evangelical Protestants explained their objections to faith-based initiatives, they made it clear that their dissent had more to do with implementation than with the White House's conviction that religion was socially useful. Jerry Falwell worried that the Bush initiative could readily be turned *against* evangelical organizations under another administration. Marvin Olasky, one of the original proponents of compassionate conservatism and editor of the conservative Protestant weekly *World*, declared that evangelical Protestants "should never accept money unless evangelism is allowed." Meanwhile Richard Land, head of the Southern Baptist Ethics and Religious Liberty Commission, feared giving federal bureaucrats the power to decide "what is social service and what is ministry." The issue, then, for evangelical critics of faith-based initiatives was not whether Christianity could transform lives and build better communities. It was the degree to which religious organizations would maintain control over their spiritual mission. This was a curious reiteration of the conviction "Let the church be the church," though in this case no one questioned whether the essential cause of Christ was to generate productive citizens and stable communities. If DiIulio was correct that the best sociological studies proved that programs that "encouraged marriage, discouraged divorce, encouraged responsible parenting and discouraged teen pregnancies" were critical to the prospects of needy children, perhaps government should be directly funding churches, not just religious social service agencies. After all, most congregations, whether urban or suburban, fit his description.

Equally revealing in the disputes over faith-based initiatives was the remarkable transformation of evangelical Protestant attitudes toward social action since World War II. What had been a Protestant constituency suspicious of big government, supportive of free markets, and generally opposed to government redistribution of wealth had become, by the presidency of George W. Bush, a body of religious adherents with fewer ties to American political conservatism. Of course, Bush himself has often been the target of political conservatives' criticisms, thus making him the perfect embodiment of contemporary evangelicalism's political equivocation.

Still, the transformation of evangelical Protestantism between 1950 and 2000, from conservative Republican to religiously humanitarian, is fairly remarkable. It points to the dearth of critical reflection, both political and theological, among evangelicals on the significant differences between the responsibilities of the church and the functions of government.

During the 1960s and 1970s, before Republican strategists and pollsters discovered the potential of the born-again electorate, evangelical ideas on politics were predictably right of center. According to Robert Booth Fowler, born-again Protestant leaders spoke and wrote mainly in defense of free markets, balanced budgets, and common standards of public decency; they opposed communism as well as domestic policies that might increase the centralization of America's federal government. This defense of freedom was so strong that many evangelical leaders believed labor unions were incompatible with a liberal society because they impeded free markets. Yet evangelicals were not sanguine about the prospects of the United States. Although they regularly invoked the idea of America's God-blessed status, evangelical spokesmen believed that materialism and hedonism were rapidly dissolving the nation's moral stature. In keeping with these general political instincts, evangelical leaders were also suspicious of social action. On the one hand, progressive reforms threatened to increase the power of government and destroy liberty. On the other hand, tinkering with policy and legislation obscured the fundamental problem of human sin, which could only be remedied through faith. For this reason, before 1980 mainstream evangelical leaders insisted that the church must not be distracted from its primary mission of evangelism to engage in or advocate various social measures.

Some evangelicals dissented from this widespread set of political convictions in hope of making born-again Protestantism more responsive to the needs of the nation. Two evangelicals of note in this regard were Carl F. H. Henry, the founding editor of *Chris-*

*tianity Today*, the flagship periodical of post–World War II evangelicalism, and the evangelist Billy Graham. As far back as his influential book *The Uneasy Conscience of Modern Fundamentalism* (1947), Henry had argued that social concern was not antagonistic to soul winning but an "indispensable element" of Christianity. For this reason he believed that pastors and church members had a duty to be aware and involved politically. But this did not mean that churches should take on the responsibility of social reform. Henry believed that evangelicals did need to adopt a positive attitude to the state and its necessary work of preserving order and implementing a just society. Still, the state's work was different from the church's. While the state pursued order and justice, the church's aims were love and mercy. Thus Henry was critical of churches that had abandoned preaching and evangelism in pursuit of social action. He was also tough on evangelical churches that ignored social evils, but his cautious conservatism placed the primary responsibility for Christian engagement with the social order on individual Christians. Above all, Henry made clear that evangelical political activity and social involvement should "give no quarter to the illusion that Christianity is primarily an ethical idealism engaged in denouncing political and social injustice."

Billy Graham's understanding of religion and politics differed slightly from Henry's and was evident more from his actions than his statements or careful reasoning. Like most evangelicals during the middle decades of the twentieth century, Graham advocated liberty, democracy, and small governmnent, and viewed communism as the bête noire of American ideals. Even so, his conservatism did not prevent him from prodding mainstream evangelicals on race relations in America. In 1953 Graham was a pioneer among evangelicals by holding his first integrated evangelistic crusade in Chattanooga, Tennessee. It became the norm for his subsequent revivals. In the 1960s he also gave his support to civil rights legislation at a time when many evangelicals would have objected, at least out of fear of increasing the size of the federal government if not because of race. Graham also occassionally spoke out on behalf of the poor and later endorsed Lyndon Johnson's War on Poverty. The logic undergirding the evangelist's tentative engagement of social ills was the idea that conversion inevitably leads to the love of neighbor and a concern for the well-being of society. Yet Graham insisted that political involvement had to be kept in perspective, and that the eternal destinies of men and women were more important than the fleeting needs of civil society. As he told one evangelical audience, "Let us rejoice in social action, and yet insist that it alone is not evangelism, and cannot be substituted for evangelism."

For a younger generation of evangelicals growing up in the 1960s and experiencing many of the social protest movements of the era, either as participants or observers, the cautious interventions of Graham and Henry were insufficient to make evangelical Protestant political conservatism appropriately responsive to the needs of women, blacks, and the poor. An indication of this discontent with politics-as-usual came during a small conference over Thanksgiving weekend in 1973, when fifty born-again Protestant academics and church leaders from different denominational backgrounds formulated "The Chicago Declaration of Evangelical Social Concern." The Calvin College historian Joel A. Carpenter argued that this statement signaled a "radical shift" within the evangelical movement. Thanks to this statement, what was once considered political meddling by the church had become axiomatic for evangelicals, namely, that "social justice is one of the central callings of all Christians." "Thirty years ago," Carpenter added, such political involvement would have been regarded as "selling out the gospel" that individual salvation is more important than social transformation. But today evangelical Protestants might disagree about which "policies will get us there, but they agree about the need to pursue 'the righteousness that exalts a nation.'"

The prescriptions for social righteousness, a concept that harkened back to the Social Gospel sentiments of mainline Protestants between the Civil War and World War I, were fairly slim in the Chicago Declaration's brief (fewer than five hundred words) enumeration of grievances. The statement was a mix of confessing evangelical sins for indifference to the economic conditions of the United States and the world, and calls for improvement. The heart of the Chicago Declaration was its longest paragraph, on the kind of justice that God requires of righteous nations:

> Although the Lord calls us to defend the social and economic rights of the poor and oppressed, we have mostly remained silent. We deplore the historic involvement of the church in America with racism and the conspicuous responsibility of the evangelical community for perpetuating the personal attitudes and institutional structures that have divided the body of Christ along color lines. Further, we have failed to condemn the exploitation of racism at home and abroad by our economic system.

For those who paid attention, this statement, even though admitting the failings of its signers, was primarily a rebuke to the standard right-of-center evangelical Protestant politcs. As Carpenter rightly observed, "Evangelical Protestants at the time tended to be seen as Richard Nixon's Silent Majority, the solid backers of the social status quo." In fact, supporting free markets was hardly a voice in favor of the stasis since capitalism has been one of the great engines of change in modern history. At the same time opposing communism, as most evangelicals of the older generation did, was not exactly a conviction far removed from social justice. Still, Carpenter's point is helpful at least in pinpointing a shift in evangelical sensibilities. Christian responsibility came to be seen as involving both personal and social salvation, a blurring of vision that would have important consequences for evangelical attitudes toward politics. The Chicago Declaration was perhaps the first formal statement of post–World War II evangelical social compassion, also noteworthy for its faulting of American conservatives for lacking such sentiment.

The Chicago Declaration was not the only example of evangelicals moving to the left. One of the statement's signers was Ron Sider, then a religion professor at Messiah College, an evangelical Anabaptist school in Pennsylvania, who achieved a measure of fame with his book *Rich Christians in an Age of Hunger* (1977). As the title suggested, Sider was pointing out what the Chicago Declaration had noted, namely that evangelicals were invariably middle class and indifferent to pressing social needs in America and around the world. Like most reform-minded evangelicals, he tried to steer a middle course between the individual and social gospels by affirming that individuals needed to change behaviors that contributed to poverty and that social structures also demanded reform. But the larger message of the book was that fighting such social ills as hunger and poverty was a duty the Bible demanded of all Christians and the church.

At roughly the same time Sider was trying to steer evangelicals in a more progressive direction, Jim Wallis, then a recent graduate from Trinity Evangelical Divinity School in the suburbs of Chicago, was challenging the evangelical status quo with *Sojourners* magazine (originally the *Post-American*) and the formation of a Christian community in inner-city Washington, D.C. Wallis's intent was to break down the walls that divided blacks and whites, poor and middle class, cities and suburbs. For him it was insufficient for evangelicals simply to provide for the poor and hungry. They also needed to identify with people in need because this was precisely what the Bible revealed about God, a deity who so empathized with the impoverished and oppressed that he exalted the humble over the proud. Wallis also created a stir with his 1976 book *Agenda for a Biblical People*, which was as far from Billy Graham as it was from Jimmy Carter. Unlike Sider, who sought a more moderate course, Wallis's modus operandi was radical. "What matters most today is whether one is a supporter of establishment Christianity or a practicioner of biblical faith," Wallis wrote. Like Sider, then, Wallis was appealing to the Bible as a means to call evangelicals to repent of their conservative ways. The proof of such repentance would be found not in correct doctrine or disciplined churches but in the "daily realities of the believer's life in the world." In contrast to the older generation of evangelicals who stressed preaching and evangelism over the execution of good-Samaritan-like deeds, Sider and Wallis were at least putting word and deed on a par, if not elevating the latter, in reaction to evangelicals' erroneous understanding of Christianity.

An ironic consequence of the leftward lurch of the younger evangelicals was that it ended up justifying the activism of the evangelical right that emerged as the dominant born-again political voice after the election of Ronald Reagan. Although the arguments of a Sider or Wallis were designed to produce evangelical Americans not so gullibly loyal to the party of Lincoln, by contending that political involvement and concern for society was precisely what the Bible required, they made it hard to argue that an aggressive conservative evangelical politics was illegitimate. Through a Jerry Falwell or Pat Robertson, who also claimed a biblical basis, evangelicals became an active electoral constituency in pursuit of free markets, small government, increased military spending, and standards of public decency. The Moral Majority may have identified with the platform of the wrong party, but at least it was not guilty of being politically passive. By trying to embody Christian values in its political involvement, from one angle the evangelical right was the outworking of the Chicago Declaration. As Carpenter concedes, the "great surprise" to the younger evangelicals was that fundamentalists and Pentecostals, "two groups not known for their social action," also felt "the pangs of social responsibility." In the case of these Protestants, "warfare against secularism" turned out to be the political outlet.

Lighting the fire of the culture wars was not the only consequence of the evangelical leftward turn. The argument that turned Christ's command to love one's neighbor into leverage for Christians using government to solve the problems of hunger, poverty, and war ended up having as much appeal to the evangelical right as it did to the left-of-center evangelicals who despaired over their fellow believers' endorsement of the Republican party. The man who almost single-handedly appropriated the evangelical reconsideration of the welfare state was Marvin Olasky, since 1983 a professor of journalism at the University of Texas, Austin, and since 1992 the editor of the conservative evangelical newsweekly *World*. In 1992 he published *The Tragedy of American Compassion*, a book that would popularize among evangelicals the idea of concern for those in need and that had genuine resonance with the concerns of Sider and Wallis. Written while a fellow at the Heritage Foundation and published by the evangelical publisher Crossway, *The Tragedy of American Compassion* was perhaps a more effective case for Christian obligations to the poor than anything written against evangelical self-satisfaction during the 1970s. Olasky's argument, for starters, was less religious (he rarely relied in this book on biblical arguments) and more social scientific, thus ensuring a wider hearing even while reaching an evangelical audience through his publisher. He also cut through the partisan nature of the debates over welfare better than the evangelical left had done by arguing that the debate between free markets and big-government welfare programs was stale and no longer fruitful. Like Wallis and Sider, then, Olasky was breaking with the traditional evangelical support for capitalism, at least on the subject of the poor. Where he differed was in his critique of government welfare programs as ineffective and responsible in some measure for perpetuating social pathology. Still, when Olasky concluded that Americans needed to identify with the poor and become involved in their lives (which he did at least to the extent of living as a homeless man in downtown Washington for several days), he was taking a page from the evangelical left's playbook for pushing middle-class born-again Protestants out of their suburban complacency.

Olasky's effort to transcend the partisan politics of welfare legislation did not last long. Within four years he wrote a more mainstream book, *Renewing American Compassion* (1996), which was published by the Free Press and included a foreword by Newt Gingrich. This book was a sign that the Republican leadership recognized a way to use Olasky's ideas toward their own end of welfare reform. Olasky's case against government spending on welfare, and his argument that Christians and religious organizations did a better job in caring for the poor, was—now clear in hindsight—a major component in George W. Bush's program of compassionate conservatism. In his foreword, Gingrich wrote, "Olasky teaches us simply but powerfully to move from entitlement to challenge, from bureaucracy to personal help, and from the naked public square to faith in God." Olasky himself put the challenge forcefully when he claimed that the "major flaw" of the welfare state was "not that it is extravagant," as conservatives had historically claimed, but that "it is too stingy." It provided only material goods without addressing deeper spiritual and personal needs. And the only way to confront those more basic human problems was not through bureaucracy and huge budgets but through the involvement of all Americans in nongovernmental forms of relief, whether personal or institutional. "Now that American society is in dire straits," Olasky concluded, "we need to teach CPS: compassion that is challenging, personal, and spiritual."

Olasky's compassionate conservatism was not the only indication that the earlier call to social action by leaders of the born-again left was finding a home among rank-and-file evangelicals. The National Association of Evangelicals' 2005 statement, "For

the Health of the Nation: An Evangelical Call to Civic Responsibility," gave further evidence both of mainstream evangelicals'
drawing on impulses previously confined to their left-of-center
colleagues and of the evangelical right abandoning conservative
economic policy in the name of compassion. From its founding in
1942 the NAE had maintained a Washington, D.C., office which
initially coordinated relations with the federal government for
member denominations when seeking, for example, the proper
documentation for foreign missionaries, military chaplains, and religious broadcasting. Over time the Washington office assumed
minor responsibilities for lobbying the federal government on issues or measures important to the NAE's membership. During its
first two decades the NAE issued statements that were generally
designed to preserve Protestant hegemony in the United States,
though often by opposing encroachments on the separation of
church and state through state funding of Roman Catholic institutions such as schools and hospitals. In 1951 the association also endorsed a Christian amendment to the Constitution that would
have recognized the "authority and law" of Jesus Christ while also
holding that no ecclesiastical organization would receive official
recognition by the government. Other statements from the Washington office revealed evangelicals' support for the sovereignty of
the United States (as opposed to the National Council of
Churches' support for the United Nations), as well as opposition
to communism and to the age-old Protestant bogeys of secularism
and materialism. During the 1970s Watergate and the Vietnam
War provoked the NAE to be more critical about America in several of its statements while also beginning to take notice of envi-
ronmental concerns and poverty in America. But by the Reagan
era the Republican outlook of the organization was once again obvious, with religious liberty and human rights providing the rationale for opposing the tyranny of communism and Third World
dictators. During the 1990s the NAE also worked with the Clin-

ton administration and Congress to draft the 1993 Religious Freedom Restoration Act. Not until George W. Bush's election in 2000 and his faith-based initiative did the largest and oldest institutional guardian of the evangelical movement adopt a social agenda comparable to the 1973 Chicago Declaration of the evangelical left.

"For the Health of the Nation" was a much lengthier statement than the 1973 declaration. Part of the reason involved an attempt to write an evangelical approach to public policy. The specific policy initiatives in view in the 2005 declaration included perennial conservative favorites such as religious liberty, families, the sanctity of human life, and human rights (based on the image of God in human beings rather than a secular notion of human dignity). Three new policy initiatives also made the cut: "justice and compassion for the poor," preservation of the environment, and peace in the form of advocating the "restraint of violence." By no means radical, this last set of topics was several steps removed from the laissez-faire, anti-Communist strain of Republicanism that had dominated evangelical politics during the three decades after World War II. Furthermore the resemblance between the ideals of the Chicago Declaration and the 2005 NAE statement were not accidental since Ron Sider played an active role in helping to draft the later document. One sign of Sider's influence was the theme of justice, so emphasized that it could function as a verb: "Because we have been called to do justice to our neighbors," the declaration affirmed, "we foster a free press, participate in open debate, vote, and hold public office." "When Christians do justice, it speaks loudly about God" and demonstrated to nonbelievers "how the Christian vision can contribute to the common good and help alleviate the ills of society."

The theme of justice was also evident in the NAE's statement on poverty, which preferred to address the question through the language of a just society rather than through the lens of charity or welfare. The scope of the NAE's proposal was as ambitious as it was—in the language of an older conservative evangelical generation—utopian. Economic justice required a restoration of wholeness in community. Thus the statement urged Christians to become involved in politics in order to "shape wise laws pertaining to the creation of wealth, wages, education, taxation, immigration, health care, and social welfare that will protect those trapped in poverty and empower the poor to improve their circumstances." The restoration of wholeness did not stop at the borders of the United States, however. "We should try to persuade our leaders to change patterns of trade that harm the poor and to make the reduction of global poverty a central concern of American foreign policy."

"For the Health of the Nation" was a moderate statement which could fit relatively easily on the brighter side of the red state/blue state electoral divide. It attempted to steer between the shibboleths of the left and the right while still covering the evangelical ground of the importance of individual responsiblity and the transforming power of conversion both for personal and social reformation. Even so, the NAE's declaration was not terribly far from the same sort of argument that had dominated American Protestantism a century earlier, when the Federal Council of Churches was founded and when Protestants tried to combine commitments to evangelism and revival with a social creed for the churches. Civic engagement needed to include "both individuals and institutions." "While individuals transformed by the gospel change surrounding society, social institutions also shape individuals," and though "good laws encourage good behavior, bad laws and systems foster destructive action." Consequently significant social change required "personal conversion and institutional renewal and reform."

Despite this attempt to walk the high wire of religiously inspired social reform, "For the Health of the Nation" revealed a dramatic shift within post–World War II evangelicalism over the church's involvement with national politics. The greatest indication of change was the loss of conviction that churches should stay out of politics and stick to the business of soul-winning and the exercise of spiritual ministry. The NAE statement quite explictly blurred the line between church and state. In a paragraph describing the kingdom of God, which would be characterized by "justice, peace, forgiveness, restoration, and healing," the declaration added: "We know that we must wait for God to bring about the fullness of the kingdom at Christ's return. But in this interim, the Lord calls the church to speak prophetically to society and work for the renewal and reform of its structures." This was a tall order for an organization that few evangelicals belonged to as individuals but rather through their denominations. The broad mandate went well beyond the older born-again Protestant conviction that made the proclamation of the gospel prior to any other activity the church might perform. Thanks to the logic of compassion, politics and social reform had become for evangelicals as much the Lord's work as evangelism and worship.

## *The Dualistic Challenge*

If through compassionate conservatism, evangelicals were following the trail mainline Protestants had forged a century earlier, they did so also by imitating the older Protestant recipe. That formula combined the doctrines of the kingdom of God and the sovereignty of Christ to yield the legitimacy of religion inserting its moral concerns into all aspects of life. In the evangelical case, the rationale for this move stemmed less from new biblical scholarship or from formal advocates of a Social Gospel as it had in the late nineteenth century. Instead inspiration came from a version of Dutch Calvinism originally articulated by Abraham Kuyper, the Netherland's prime minister during the first decade of the twentieth century. Kuyper's herculean efforts knew no bounds: for starters he founded a university, a church, a newspaper, and a political party. His ideas had gained currency among evangelicals—a group not known for their sympathy with Calvinism—thanks to the rise of a number of academics from Calvin College and Seminary within the ranks of post–World War II conservative Protestantism. Although the influence of these Dutch Americans was most evident in the fields of philosophy and history, Kuyperian-inspired thinkers and institutions devoted considerable attention to welfare reform and charitable choice legislation during the 1990s. The Center for Public Justice in Annapolis, Maryland, was perhaps the most prominent of the organizations. A number of its staff or affiliated writers, such as James Skillen and Stanley Carlson-Thies, produced books and studies that added intellectual depth to the evangelical turn toward social action. Carlson-Thies also served for more than a year on the policy staff of the White House's Office of Faith-Based and Community Initiatives.

The Lordship of Christ over all temporal affairs was arguably Kuyper's most important reason for attempting to return the Netherlands to its former Calvinist glory, and the analogy for evangelical Protestants living through what appeared to be a decadent and secular period of American history was not difficult to fathom. At the opening of the Free University that Kuyper founded, he issued a much-repeated assertion that would inspire Dutch and later American Protestants to believe that their work in the secular world was profoundly religious: "Oh, no single piece of our mental world is to be hermetically sealed off from the rest, and there is not a square inch in the whole domain of our human existence which Christ, who is Sovereign over *all*, does not cry: 'Mine!'" As Jim Skillen explained in the introduction to a 1991 reprint of a pamphlet by Kuyper on poverty, the Dutch theologian and statesman recognized that religion is not simply one aspect of life among other activities but "the direction that human life takes as people give themselves over to the gripping power of either the true or false gods." Religion may "include worship, prayer, and confession of faith," but these activities do not exhaust religion because "at bottom, all of life is religious."

Echoes of this Kuyperian sentiment come through clearly in the NAE's declaration "For the Health of the Nation," which at one point reads:

> We also engage in public life because Jesus is Lord over every area of life. Through him all things were created (Col. 1:16–17), and by him all things will be brought to fullness (Rom. 8:19–21). To restrict our stewardship to the private sphere would be to deny an important part of his dominion and to functionally abandon it to the Evil One. To restrict our political concerns to matters that touch only on the private and the domestic spheres is to deny the all-encompassing Lordship of Jesus (Rev. 19:16).

Whether or not this formulation stems directly from Kuyper, it at least demonstrates that Protestants, whether the mainline or sideline in America, or Calvinists in the Netherlands, invariably resort to the sovereignty of Christ when seeking a justification for participation in public life.

The wisdom of this strategy as a practical approach to public life is certainly open to question, even if it inspires the faithful to see politics as part of their religious duty. The idea that the affairs of civil society or public policy are part of a cosmic contest between the forces of good and evil nurtures a zero-sum approach to government that leaves little room for compromise and raises questions about what to do with nonbelievers and idolatry. Either the state is God-honoring or it is God-denying. But seldom considered in this form of absolute dualism is that the most God-honoring state would at least be one that tolerates only the true faith, with theocracy being a distinct possibility. Nor do the proponents of Christ's Lordship appear to consider that a secular government attempting to be neutral about religion, no matter how awkward such neutrality may be, is fundamentally different and better for Christians than a state that recognizes a God different from Christ and forbids the practice of false religions. In other words, by pitting a religious-friendly state as the opposite of a secular government, the Lordship of Christ outlook fails to do justice to the real genius of the American founding, which was to try to take religion out of the hands of civil authorities and allow believers to practice their faith according to their own consciences. Obviously this left American government unable to appeal to divine will or religious wisdom for its determinations. It also made possible a dynamic where the state would regard faith as something hostile to statecraft, where politics proudly asserted its autonomy from religion's ultimate concerns. Despite these liabilities, an arrangement that allowed Christians to recognize the Lordship of Christ in the religious sphere while leaving it as a matter of speculation for politics did promise a better way to reconcile the claims of God and Caesar than either Christendom's religious establishment or an outright theocracy.

The all-or-nothing logic inherent in appeals to the Lordship of Christ also fails to do justice to the reduced character of Christ's sovereignty in the Christian era. The references in the quotation above from "For the Health of the Nation" about Christ's Lordship all come from the New Testament. But this did not prevent its drafters from appealing also to the Old Testament and the ideals of social justice asserted by Israel's prophets, especially regarding care for widows, orphans, and the poor. The problem with blurring the claims of the Old and New Testaments is that Christ's kingdom in the latter was fundamentally different from the kingdom of Israel in the former. The kingdom of Christ was a spiritual entity, not a political one, and it had every appearance during the church's early history of coexisting with non-Christian empires. In other words, for Christians the equivalent to Israel's theocracy was the church, not the state. The Lordship of Christ, then, was in the Christian

era to be seen and employed within the institutional church. The
state's affairs were to be rendered to the state. This dynamic between church and state was the basis for Augustine's distinction between the earthly and the heavenly cities, and the different goods
that church and state pursued, the spiritual and the temporal respectively.

This Augustinian dualism between the eternal and the temporal, as opposed to the Kuyperian one between good and evil, has
important implications for such concrete realities as welfare and
compassion. If the proper Christian correlation is between Israel
and the church, not between Israel and the modern state, then the
arguments of the Old Testament prophets to care for the poor and
oppressed have their appropriate Christian outlet in the church,
not the welfare state. So far the point would likely gain the assent
of evangelicals such as Wallis, Sider, and Olasky. But unlike evangelical social activists who insist that the church's task is to provide
for the poor and needy wherever they may be found, someone following closely the logic of the church's parallels with Old Testament Israel would say that the church's aid is not for society at
large but ordinarily for her own members. After all, Israel's
prophets were not complaining that the Israelites were not taking
proper care of the surrounding Philistines and Canaanites. The
problem was that God's people were not taking care of their own,
especially orphans and widows. The New Testament reveals a similar concern. The apostles established the office of deacon precisely to take care of the physical needs of Christians, so that pastors or priests could devote themselves to preaching and
evangelism. The first Christians were in no condition to begin to
take on the burden of all the poor in their respective cities since the
church had its own peculiar needs. But aside from the practical realities of the early church, the Augustinian distinction between the
city of God and city of man, overlaid on top of the differences between Israel and the church, suggest that blanket appeals to the

Lordship of Christ for Christian welfare run roughshod over important considerations about the church, its relationship to civil authorities, and the differences between the institutional church's responsibilities and those of individual Christians. The lesson of the Good Samaritan may mean that individual Christians should care for those in need. But that is not the same thing as establishing a denominational agency for welfare or a White House office to promote religious charity.

One group of Protestants particularly careful about such distinctions are Lutherans, largely owing to Martin Luther's Augustinian conception of the two kingdoms. Because of the fundamental difference between law (human efforts to obtain salvation) and gospel (divine provision of grace through Christ), Lutherans have always been wary of endeavors that blur the activity of the state, which needs and requires various kinds of human goodness, and the mission of the church, which is to proclaim the insufficiency of human goodness and the need for divine mercy. With this in mind, the Lutheran Church, Missouri Synod (LCMS) has elaborated a careful set of distinctions that inform the way Christianity and politics ought to be related. On one level an Augustinian concern to protect the uniqueness of the church requires distinguishing between "spiritual" and "civic" righteousness when considering public affairs. If the church confuses the two, it risks confusing the Bible, which is the guide for church life, with reason and prudence, which are the norms for political life. If the church attempts to speak to social ills, its focus should be the "consequence, not the sinfulness" of certain circumstances or policies, in order to protect the distinction between civic and spiritual good. Another distinction the LCMS makes is that between the church as an organization and the church as individuals. The former has the responsibility for proclaiming the word and administering the sacraments; the church's primary responsibility politically, then, is to defend its freedom to accomplish its spiritual tasks. Individual

Christians may and should be engaged as citizens, and this activity "from the bottom up" is the principal way by which the church "works in society."

Finally, the LCMS has developed other distinctions about how the church corporately relates to society. In most cases the church's influence will be "indirect and unintentional," because its religious task involves "no specific design for society" and "no social policy." But this influence will also include a measure of explicit intentionality through the church shaping the consciences of its members, who then seek to carry out their duties as citizens in a way consistent with their moral convictions. On rare occasions the church's influence may be "direct and intentional" when some social issues present themselves "about which the Scriptures speak so explicitly and clearly" that the institutional church is bound to speak. But because this kind of influence "*always* carries the risk of politicizing the church," it should be done infrequently and "only on the basis of clear and unambiguous teachings of Scripture, where the church's *most fundamental* concerns are at stake." The church may also choose to take "direct and intentional" action in the public sphere, but Lutherans generally reject this course because it involves the exercise of civil power, which "has always had a corrupting influence on the church." In fact the LCMS position implies that to take direct action will necessarily compromise the spiritual and confessional identity of the church.

The practical import of these Lutheran and Augustinian convictions has been evident in the LCMS's own guidelines on social welfare policies. In 1969, when the plight of the poor and the promise of the Great Society were prompting younger evangelicals to consider the demands of social justice, the LCMS remained true to its dualistic vision in responding to the call for the church to "become involved in the problems of society." It asserted that the LCMS should "remain alert to the hazard of issuing superficial moral judgments or urging particular forms of action in complex secular matters for which there is no clear Word of God." The 1969 LCMS Synod offered the following reason:

> . . . if our church is to avoid the tragic confusion into which many churches have fallen, it must also be aware of and maintain a fundamental distinction. Words such as freedom, peace, joy, dignity, life, justice, hope, and love have applicability and meaning in both kingdoms, and are indeed gifts of God in both. But the meanings are never equivalent. The history of Jesus Christ crucified dramatizes the difference.

For Lutherans, as it has been for most self-conscious Augustinians, whether Roman Catholic or Protestant, not just the ambiguity of the Bible but the work of Christ placed social reform in a different perspective. If God was ultimately remedying poverty, hunger, and war through the death and resurrection of Christ, the welfare provided by private or government organizations and programs clearly fell into a different category. The difference did not render the work of the state or nongovernmental organizations illegitimate or harmful. But it did mean, as the LCMS affirmed, that the failure of Christians to recognize the difference, from the perspective of the church, was indeed tragic.

## The Tragedy of Compassionate Conservatism

Despite the care Lutherans displayed in protecting the unique mission of the church, American Protestants have regularly confused the temporal and the spiritual. The largest denominations are generally speaking heirs of a form of Protestantism, sometimes known as pietism, that values faith precisely because of its practical utility. Since the origin of pietism in seventeenth-century Germany, which received assistance from the British Protestant revivals of the eighteenth and nineteenth centuries, American Protestants have generally looked for external evidence, such as morally upstanding and visibly pious lives and righteous societies, as indicators of genuine faith. As such, this utilitarian brand of religion has been responsible for any number of Protestant interventions into public life. Not content with a religion confined to sacred creeds, rites, and organizations, Protestants influenced by pietism have insisted that genuine Christianity must be evident in all walks of life, from its private to its public dimensions. To go to church on Sunday is not sufficient for being a good Christian. You also have to wear it on your sleeve, figuratively and sometimes literally, during the week.

The debates over charitable choice and faith-based initiatives, however, have edged this pietistic rationale outside specifically Protestant confines to embrace conservatives from other faiths. One sign of this is Rick Santorum's recent book *It Takes a Family* (2005). In an otherwise sensible and laudable case for careful stewardship of America's cultural, social, and moral heritage as the appropriate task of American conservatism, the junior senator from Pennsylvania displays a measure of confusion when he comes to the topic of faith-based initiatives and charitable choice. The specific issue that complicates the seemingly wide array of social benefits that come with faith-based social welfare programs is the power of such religious organizations to hire employees that embrace the institution's mission. If such agencies receive federal funding and hire on the basis of an applicant's religion, they are in violation of federal rules that forbid all such discrimination. The Catch-22, as Santorum identifies it, is that for a Roman Catholic organization to receive federal funding and be forced to hire non–Roman Catholics is to destroy the very notion of faith-based. At this point the religious organization is no different from the state welfare office since the religious mission is compromised by nonreligious employees.

Santorum refers specifically to the case of Catholic Charities of California, which was sued for not including contraception as part of its health-care coverage for employees. In the decision of the California Supreme Court, the justices refused to grant Catholic Charities the status of a religious employer, thus forcing the organization to comply with state law and include contraception as part of health insurance for its employees. Santorum objects to this decision as a form of discrimination against a religious charity. "The judges of the California Supreme Court are telling the Catholic Church that ministering to the poor is *not* a core value of the church," he writes. "I am sure most Catholics would be shocked to hear that."

But some of those same Roman Catholics might be surprised to learn that some bishops have said of Catholic Charities that this religious charitable agency "is about as Catholic as the motor vehicles bureau." They might also be startled to know that the editor of *First Things*, Richard John Neuhaus, a supporter of George W. Bush and of faith-based initiatives, has faulted Catholic Charities on grounds that match the assessment of the California Supreme Court, namely, that the organization is not terribly religious in carrying out its duties. According to Neuhaus, "rather than trying to promote traditional values and God–fearing behavior, Catholic Charities has become over the last three decades an arm of the welfare state, with 65 percent of its $2.3 billion annual budget now flowing from government sources and little that is explicitly religious, or even values–laden. . . ." "Far from being a model for reforming today's welfare state approach to helping the poor," Neuhaus piled on, "Catholic Charities USA is one of the nation's most powerful advocates for outworn welfare state ideas."

Neuhaus does not disagree with Santorum about religiously inspired welfare or Bush's original plan for faith-based initiatives. The point is that in their quest to affirm the contribution of faith to social welfare, advocates such as Santorum miss an important consideration, which is whether welfare qualifies as truly religious. Indeed, in the case of providing for the basic necessities of life—

food, clothing, and shelter—to tell the difference between a governmental and a religious agency is almost impossible aside from looking at the size of organization's budget or the heart of the person dispensing aid. The act of giving a cup of cold water to a thirsty man is not visibly different when done by a person of faith or a person without faith. Consequently if religious welfare agencies are performing essentially the same services as nonreligious ones, why the need for hiring only people of faith? It could be that such religious service is a means of glorifying God and demonstrating Christian love (which is a plausible religious rationale based on biblical teaching). But why should the state fund the glorification of God or demonstrations of Christian love?

Marvin Olasky recognized the horns of Santorum's dilemma and raised the stakes for faith-based initiatives. Part of his argument involves a reading of Scripture friendly to charitable choice. Compassion was not simply giving those lacking what they wanted or needed. It also required people who would use charity responsibly, not spending handouts on cheap whiskey, not establishing government-sponsored clean needles programs for junkies. The challenge for welfare reform, he wrote, is "to help those who are really in need, and to give them the type of help that can set them on the path to escaping future need." Olasky went on to argue that this path involved not simply job skills, frugality, self-discipline, and any number of other Victorian virtues. It also included faith itself. Here he appealed to the apostle Peter's response to a crippled beggar, recorded in Acts 3. Peter did not "give money (the liberal solution), nor did he proffer a job as if that alone would solve deeper problems (the secular conservative solution)." Instead the apostle healed the man and transformed this "helpless person who looks at passersby hoping to get something from them, to a tiger who walks and leaps . . . praising God." Olasky conceded that those who trust in Christ, whether poor or rich, do not typically experience such dramatic changes, as the miracle narrative clearly implies. Still, Christianity does generate "a change in values, which produces a change in behavior, which normally leads to material improvement." The relationship is not mechanistic. But Olasky concluded that spiritual change invariably leads to physical change.

This was a much more robust form of charitable choice than Santorum's. While the senator from Pennsylvania regarded religious charity largely as the sort of service rendered by public welfare agencies, only in a more personal and involved manner, Olasky saw faith-based initiatives as fundamentally bound up with transforming spiritually the lives of those in need. If Santorum represented the Roman Catholic institutional approach to charity, Olasky echoed the older evangelical conviction that stressed first the conversion of individuals which then led to improved social conditions.

But in each case the effort by political conservatives to harness faith-based initiatives to Republican policy prompted religious conservatives to give up something crucial to their Christian faith as well as to the political order in the United States they hold dear. On the one hand, merging religion and social action invites churches to do simply what the state already does. The church may be smaller, more efficient, and more personal, but because of its size the church lacks the resources of the state, which can feed and house more people. On the other hand, if religious organizations maintain that transmitting faith is crucial to their charitable work, and if they seek public funds for that work, the state will be funding proselytizing. This not only violates the clear intentions of the First Amendment but also the convictions of most conservative Protestants who believe that God's people, not state agencies, should support the Lord's work.

The greater issue is whether Christ and the apostles intended the church to be an agency of social transformation. Even without answering that question, it is safe to conclude that the entanglement of religion and politics through the strategy of compassion has caused religious conservatives, in the name of the love of neighbor, to lose sight of a prior and higher love, namely, devotion to God. For by seeking to make the church responsive to the real physical needs of society, evangelicals have lost the older religious conviction that the church had a work to do, an explicitly spiritual one, that no other institution could perform. Perhaps even more tragic from a Christian perspective has been the accompanying loss of the conviction—thanks in large measure to compassionate conservatism's appeal—that the church's task is ultimately more important than the state's.

# CHAPTER NINE

# A Secular Faith

"Secular" is a scare word to most contemporary religious adherents in America. It is generally taken to mean the opposite of religious, a category or force that denotes the abolition of faith. Soon after the election of Ronald Reagan, many leaders within the Protestant right vilified the constellation of ideas, sympathies, and programs that went under the label "secular humanism." What alarmed many evangelical Protestants then was not so much the noun in that phrase, since humanism whether derived from the Renaissance or the modern version of liberal education was not obviously destructive. But add the adjective "secular" to any noun and you had a clear threat to faith.

The bogey has not really subsided for two decades. In a recent column on efforts to remove the phrase "under God" from the Pledge of Allegiance, Chuck Colson argued that if it were deleted, the change to the Pledge would be "one more step toward the official establishment of secularism as American religion." For Colson, secularism is the equivalent of man declaring his independence from God. "We declare ourselves free from any moral law or governor higher than the imperial self, and so we become gods," Colson wrote. "I cannot imagine a more frightening prospect." Whether or not the Pledge of Allegiance's revision signifies such a damaging outcome, or whether someone might legitimately try to distinguish secular from secularism—that is, what happens to the adjective when it becomes a noun—Colson's rendering of the idea conforms to the common usage of most American Christians, whether it's the noun or the adjective. "Secular" signifies godless, anti-religious, or both.

Yet the word has a much more complicated meaning and history than the contemporary understanding implies, sort of like the word "liberal." Unpacking the meaning of secular is instructive, not simply for explaining the title of this book and its odd juxtaposition of secular and Christianity, but also for unpacking the nature of Christianity and its political consequences. The word is derived from the Latin *seclorum*. Most Americans, even if the classical languages have not been in public schools for generations, should be familiar with this word because it is on every dollar bill printed by the U.S. Treasury. On the left of the side opposite George Washington is an image of a pyramid with the Latin phrase underneath, *Novus Ordo Seclorum*. As already noted, the phrase means "new order for the ages" and testifies to the Founding Fathers' optimism about the new nation. In their conception, the United States represented a new political order in human history, one untried and one that could, if properly nurtured, redirect the future course of human affairs. To American Christians this optimism—some might say hubris—is precisely indicative of the secular. The very idea of creating something *ex nihilo* reveals secularity's anti-religious impulse, because creating from scratch is what God does, not humans. Some might well ask, isn't the phrase on the back of the dollar bill a testimony to secularism's anti-religious animus?

The hang-up here, however, is not with *seclorum* but with *novus ordo*. The former word is far less boastful and much more descriptive than the concept of newness may imply. In Latin *seclorum* typically meant an age or generation, similar to the English words "era" or "period." As such the word accurately signifies a somewhat definite period of time and especially its provisional or temporal quality. A *seclorum* technically represents a period that is likely impermanent, or a stage in history that is passing.

This meaning of the secular is the one assumed throughout this book, underscored by its title and indicative of something crucial about the Christian religion. Despite the relatively common occurrence in church history of Christians attempting to "immanentize the eschaton," that is, to find in contemporary history the perfect realization of divine will, mainstream Western Christianity, both Roman Catholic and Protestant, has opposed such efforts. Church leaders rightly understood that the period of salvation history between the first and second advents of Christ was literally a provisional or in-between time. Aspects of the new heaven and new earth might be evident, but they needed the return of Christ for fulfillment or completion. For instance, Christians knew that the Lord's Supper (Protestant) or Mass (Roman Catholic) was a foretaste of the wedding supper of the lamb foretold in the concluding book of the Bible, Revelation. To think that this Christian rite was the same as one to occur in heaven was crazy. Christianity, accordingly, was always haunted by a sense of being temporary, and it inherited this from recognizing what had happened to Jewish hopes for Jerusalem and the promised land. If the arrangements of Old Testament Israel were provisional, awaiting a Messiah, the arrangements of the church were equally temporary, pending the second coming of Christ. To think of Christianity or the church as true in some sort of absolute or ultimate way, without recognizing that another—the final—stage of salvation history would likely alter Christian teachings and practices, was to miss the faith's secular aspect.

The secular nature of Christianity was not simply relevant to the church's understanding of history but also to its regard for and relationship to the state. On the one hand, the provisional character of Christianity was equally true of the state. In the same way that Christ taught that marriage would no longer be in force in the final stage of history, in the new heavens and new earth, so too the state would one day pass away because it would no longer be necessary. In that golden age, human sinfulness would be completely and forever gone, thus eliminating the need for government to perform its important earthly function of restraining evil and executing civil justice. On the other hand, the church's relationship to the state was deeply intertwined with the periodization or age-diverse character of salvation history. Here the difference between Israel and the church was key. While Israel fused the political and religious by making Judaism the law of the land (for starters), Christianity separated what the Old Testament bound together. The New Testament made no provision for a Christian ruler but told Christians to obey magistrates, even if they were pagan. It did, however, provide broad instructions for rule within the church. Consequently, even though religion and politics were one in the period of the Old Testament, in the new *seclorum* of the church these spheres were divided.

In some ways the Protestant Reformation revealed Christianity's secular side better than Roman Catholicism, despite the insights of Augustine on this point and his high esteem on both sides of the sixteenth-century divide. Protestantism implicitly heralded the kind of confinement of religion to a private or nonpublic sphere that would develop after the American and French revolutions, which formally disestablished Christianity. On one front the Protestant Reformers taught that all legitimate work in the secular world was valuable, thus overcoming the divide between religious vocations and worldly occupations that Roman Catholicism had cultivated through its distinction between the pure work of priests and monks and the less spiritual work of everyone else. Coupled with the Protestant affirmation of secular callings was the doctrine of the priesthood of all believers, which confirmed the value of all believers, whether engaged in secular or religious work. The general thrust of Protestantism was to reduce the church's sway over European society, not merely by dividing Western Christianity but by explicitly questioning whether church authority extended to all the spheres of life implied by the pattern of Christendom or the Holy Roman Empire. Protestantism, then, was not a passive bystander to the secularization of the West but a crucial factor in that development, a factor that stemmed directly from Christian ideas and arguments, not simply from conceptions hostile to Christianity. (Of course, this is not how Roman Catholics saw or see it, but it is strange that contemporary Protestants seem to long for Christian social and political influence in ways that their Reformation canceled.)

The secularizing aspects of Protestantism for daily life were no less true for statecraft. Lutherans developed the Augustinian doctrine of the two kingdoms. It holds that the spiritual and eternal affairs of the church and the earthly and temporal concerns of the state are matters distinct and not to be confused. In turn, the doctrine of the two kingdoms reduced the authority of the church, taking away the realm of civil government from church officials. Calvinists also understood a fundamental difference between the spiritual realities administered by the church and the worldly affairs governed by the state. Calvin even argued that after the coming of Christ, to confuse the two, to mix religion and politics, was to violate the order of the *seclorum*—it was to engage in a historical anachronism and try to reproduce the theocratic administration of Old Testament Israel. Of course both Luther and Calvin still labored in the context of Christendom and were a long way from the religious disestablishments of the late eighteenth century. But by recognizing the markedly different tasks of church and state they were articulating arguments based on Christian teaching, not from anti-clerical prejudice, that would support fundamental aspects of the American and French revolutions' dissolution of Constantine's imperial fusion of religion and politics.

Whatever role Protestantism played in accelerating the secularization of the West, the seeds of the secular were planted early on with the advent of Christianity and its specific teaching about worldly affairs. Despite the objections of America's religious adherents to the notion of secular politics, few scholars who explore even the basic differences between Christianity and other religions have trouble spotting the fundamentally religious character of secularity in the West thanks to the church's peculiar role and doctrines.

For instance, the English conservative and philosopher Roger Scruton assumes that one of the aspects of Western societies that distinguishes them from those in the East or Middle East is the separation of religion and politics and the recognition that "through politics, not through religion, peace is secured." He adds that the Christian separation of religious and secular authority was similar to the Greek. Its classic formulation, for Scruton, came from Augustine in *The City of God* but received even more succinct expression in fifth-century Pope Gelasius I's "two swords" theory, which made the "separation of church and state into doctrinal orthodoxy." Accordingly, God established two powers for earthly government: "that of the Church for the government of men's souls, and that of the imperial power for the regulation of temporal affairs." Scruton concedes that this distinction animated rival claims of emperors and popes throughout the Middle Ages, a rivalry that contributed to the West's unique development and that prompted medieval theologians and philosophers to debate the precise meaning of the "two swords" doctrine. Nevertheless, in Scruton's reading of the West, Marsilius of Padua in the fourteenth century had the last word in *Defensor Pacis*, where he argued that "the state and not the church . . . guarantees the civil peace, and reason, not revelation," governs "all matters of temporal jurisdiction." For Scruton, this secularization of political life was not the fanciful concoction of unpredictable deists like Thomas Jefferson but part of the warp and woof of the West thanks in no small measure to Western Christianity.

In his scholarship on Islamic civilization, Bernard Lewis recognizes that the secular realm is a fundamental difference between Christianity and Islam. Indeed, he has written one statement that is unthinkable either from the lips or keyboards of the Protestant right or their non-Protestant sympathizers: "Secularism in the modern political meaning—the idea that religion and political authority, church and state are different, and can or should be separated—is, in a profound sense, Christian." For most ancient faiths, Lewis observes, religion was part of the civil authority, whether tribe, city, or king. And he admits that some of this older religious tendency carried over into Christendom, where priests "exercised temporal power, and kings claimed divine right even over the church." But these were "aberrations," Lewis maintains. When compared to the major ancient faiths that had some bearing on the West, "Christianity was in marked contrast with both its precursors and its competitors." In Rome, "Caesar was God, re-asserting a doctrine that goes back to the god-kings of remote antiquity." Jews participated in a theocracy in which "God was Caesar." And for Muslims "God was the supreme sovereign, and the caliph his vice-regent." Only with Christianity and in the West, Lewis concludes, "did God and Caesar coexist in the state, albeit with considerable development, variety, and sometimes conflict in the relations between them." As such, within Western Christianity "jurists and theologians devised or adapted pairs of terms to denote this dichotomy of jurisdiction: sacred and profane, spiritual and temporal, religious and secular, ecclesiastical and lay." For this reason, according to Lewis, Christianity accommodated and even encouraged a secular tradition while Islam reacted sharply against secularity. "From the beginning," he writes, "Christians were taught both by precept and practice to distinguish between God and Caesar and between the different duties owed to each of the two. Muslims received no such instruction." The wonder is why present-day Christians in the United States have failed to remember these lessons from their own faith.

Christianity's friendliness to if not encouragement of the secular is just as obvious to those who evaluate not only the differences between East and West, or between Christian and Muslim, but the rise and development of modernity, for some the much feared engine of secularization in Europe and North America. Steve Bruce, a British sociologist of religion, observes that one of the key factors in modernization is another infelicitous word, to which sociology is prone: rationalization. By this he means the eradication of the cosmic order typical of civilizations in Egypt and Mesopotamia, in which distinctions between the natural and supernatural worlds, or between the human and nonhuman, were fluid or nonexistent. In effect the divine was bound up with the cosmos, immanent in and throughout the world. But with rise of monotheism in ancient Israel, God became radically transcendent and other. As Bruce explains, the God of Israel "was so distanced from [his followers] as to be beyond magical manipulation." This deity's laws could be known and had to be obeyed, but he could not be "bribed, cajoled, or tricked into doing his worshipers' will." Bruce argues that in the same way that ancient Judaism introduced a transcendent God into ancient Near Eastern religion, Christianity did the same in the Roman Empire where previously "a horde of gods, or spirits, often behaving in an arbitrary fashion and operating at cross purposes, makes the relationship of supernatural and natural worlds unpredictable." Christianity "systematized" the supernatural and made religion much less a matter of magic than a code of conduct or right response to divine order.

Although Roman Catholicism, in Bruce's scheme, began to remythologize the cosmos and people the universe with angels, saints, and other "semi-divine beings," the Protestant Reformation "demythologized" the world. Bruce is not necessarily contradicting

Scruton and Lewis, who describe the way in which the separation of religion and politics characterized the West even before the sixteenth century. His concern is more narrowly sociological than historical. But it nonetheless carries some relevance for contemporary American Protestants who oppose secularization as inherently antireligious. For Bruce, Protestantism "eliminated ritual and sacramental manipulation of God, and restored the process of ethical rationalization." Historians of science have argued that this sort of rationalization was key to the development of scientific discovery. As Bruce explains, "Modern science is not easy for cultures which believe that the world is pervaded by supernatural spirits or that the divinities are unpredictable," because systematic inquiry into the natural world assumes that "the behaviour of matter is indeed regular." Consequently with Protestantism, the domain over which religion "offered the most compelling explanations" narrowed considerably. The Protestant Reformation's secularizing impulse reduced the power of the church and "made way for a variety of thought and for the questioning of tradition which is so vital to natural science."

Although Bruce does not say so, the same point could be made for the modern science of politics. By reducing the authority of the church in the secular or nonreligious sphere, Protestantism solidified the separation of church and state that had long characterized the West and came to dominate the modern era. Gone was the notion that revelation or churchly authorities govern the civil jurisdiction. Instead, with Protestantism (though individual Protestants themselves may have still operated with a sense of Christendom) came the possibility for the study of and theorizing about politics to emerge as a separate sphere. This does not mean that with Protestantism emerged the first glimmers of social contract theory or a heightened sense of individualism and natural rights. Most Protestants before the mid-eighteenth century defended monarchy and hierarchical social and political order. Still, Bruce's argument does suggest that secularization was a natural consequence of Protestantism, not a mistaken or accidental outcome. If Western Christianity already made room for God and Caesar to exist within the state, Protestantism went even further by demythologizing the temporal sphere and thus providing space for a rationalization of civil jurisdiction. Protestants today who regret or resist secular society do so often because they do not understand more nuanced definitions of the secular. Furthermore they do not appear to understand something crucial to their own faith, something that philosophers, historians, and sociologists have no hesitation in deducing and even applauding. It is that Christianity in a very important sense is a secular faith.

## *The Lure of Christendom*

No matter how obvious the secular tendencies of Christianity generally and Protestantism specifically may be for precise accounts of church and state in the West, modern Christians are reluctant to see the scope of faith reduced. From a general sense that religion deals with moral and ethical questions so basic that it must have something to say about the good society, to more vigorously Christian affirmations about the relevance of the claims of Scripture, the authority of Christ, or the divine origin of the state for politics, American Christians remain dubious about a secular faith. The best version of this reluctance was the assertion of Russell Kirk, the traditionalist conservative who taught and inspired many of today's political conservatives, that all political and cultural problems are at root spiritual problems. I myself, a Christian by profession and a conservative by instinct, have great sympathy for this understanding of the relationship between religion and other spheres of life. But my own study of the arguments made on behalf of Christian scholarship, which in various ways did for knowledge what Kirk described for political and social order, made me suspect that just as human investigation into the arts and sciences may be a human activity distinct from forms of religious devotion and in no way dependent on faith, so too political endeavor may not relate directly to piety.

Kirk's assertion on behalf of faith's fundamental role in society is similar to T. S. Eliot's. For these cultural conservatives, culture inevitably proceeds from cult. As Kirk explains, "A culture is a joining together for worship . . . the attempt of people to commune with a transcendent power." And from this common association in acts of religious devotion, "human community grows." "Once people are joined in a cult, cooperation in many other things becomes possible," Kirk wrote. "Common defense, irrigation, systematic agriculture, architecture, the visual arts, music, the more intricate crafts, economic production and distribution, courts and government—all these aspects of a culture arise gradually from the cult, the religious tie." The danger for Kirk, as it was for Eliot, Christopher Dawson, and Eric Voegelin, was that once the cult withered, the civilization upon which it had grown would also dry up and decay. Although this is by no means an argument about American politics, Kirk's assertion about religion supplying the building blocks for the West and specifically for the American order expresses the instinct of many contemporary American believers who sense that secularization is responsible for so many of the ills that afflict the United States.

The trouble with this understanding of religion's foundational import is twofold. First, it implicitly approaches Christianity from a relatively abstract perspective rather than its actual historical origins. The Christian religion was planted and grew in cultural soils that were already well tilled and flourishing. It did not hatch a new culture or civilization from scratch. Even when it did, its contributions to the West fed off existing arrangements, at least from the Romans if not the Greeks. Second, even more important is the lack of teaching either by Christ or the apostles that the new religion was to be the basis for Christian culture or society. Here the relationship of Christianity to Judaism might explain why Christ would say his kingdom was not of this world. For Christians, the pattern of Israel and theocracy were no longer valid after the coming of Christ. Christians need not try to replicate Israel's legitimate attempt to integrate cult and culture but were permitted to live hyphenated lives, as Greek-Christians, Jewish-Christians, Roman-Christians, and more. In other words, Christian teachings gave no instruction on the establishment of a distinctly Christian culture because Christianity was a religion without a specific land, city, or place. Its teachings transcended the cult-culture relationship as a faith for people from any ethnic background.

Christianity's meager resources for culture formation leads to the second difficulty for Christians who might try to use the relationship between cult and culture as a wedge for faith-based politics. If Christ and the apostles did not leave a blueprint for a Christian civilization, if in fact they lived and died not for the sake of the West but for the sake of God's people no matter where those believers might live, is Christianity really responsible for so many of the achievements that cultural conservatives attribute to Western civilization? One indication of Kirk's answer is his approval of James Reichley's index of eight "value-systems" that might adequately "balance individual rights against social authority" in the United States. Reichley recognized only one such system, "theist-humanism," which Kirk believed most people would recognize as Christianity. Consequently if Americans returned to Christianity's understanding of the human condition and its limitations, the American nation might "restore those common ways of life that we call America's culture." The problem here is that "theist-humanism" is hardly the same as Christianity. In fact the Christian religion is much more than a "value system."

Of course Kirk knew this and was not attempting to diminish Christianity by attributing "theist-humanism" to it. Still, the argument of this book is that using the Christian faith as the basis for culture or politics, by seemingly making it so important, actually trivializes Christianity. The reason is that Christianity teaches far more than human nature, the importance of submission to legitimate authority, or the outline of an ethical code. Those aspects of Christianity were undoubtedly important in the development of the West, its science, politics, and culture. But those Christian ingredients are a long way from what church members confess every Sunday when they recite the Apostles' Creed, or when they hear their ministers grant the assurance of pardon and administer the Lord's Supper. Christianity may have many worthwhile points to make about politics or society, either directly or indirectly, but they are not its main point. Because Christianity does not require a certain form of government, a specific kind of cultural expression, or a distinct way of arranging society, its adherents may legitimately live hyphenated lives that are secular and Christian.

Even H. Richard Niebuhr conceded as much at the beginning of his highly regarded *Christ and Culture*. In a book that has become the standard way for American Protestants to think through their faith's cultural and social significance, Niebuhr confessed something that few Protestants seem to have considered very carefully. Had Jesus "undertaken to reform the religious and national culture, eliminating what was archaic in ceremonial and civil law, he might have been a great boon to his society; but instead of reforming culture he ignored it." In contrast, Judaism was a national life informed by national religion, and Jesus removed all the requirements of the nation's religion and "set up nothing but an ethico-religious system bound up with his conception of the Godhead." In the end, the claims either about culture or politics made on behalf of Christianity may owe more to discomfort with the faith's secular character than with the actual teaching of its founder and its first adherents.

## *Dare to Be a Daniel*

If Christianity is secular, do Christians or the church have no role in public life? The way I typically like to answer this question is to enjoin the common refrain that "It's a free country" and explain that Christians may appeal to religious convictions all they want. But this is a different consideration from whether Christian participation in American politics is appropriate. As I argued at the beginning of this book, most evaluations of the propriety of Christian engagement in American public life have approached the question from the perspective of what the Constitution will tolerate, and whether Christians have grounds for making their religious concerns heard in public life. The question pursued in this book has been whether Christian-inspired policy, arguments, or candidates are appropriate on *Christian* grounds. My conclusion is that such involvement is inappropriate, because using Christianity for political ends fundamentally misconstrues the Christian religion.

As is clear from many of the episodes and themes covered here, American Protestants have not been reluctant to insist that faith has an important role to play in public life, nor have they been shy about acting upon this insistence. Evangelical Protestants are not exceptional in this regard but are simply following the playbook of most English-speaking American Protestants before them. But as the various episodes make clear, Protestants have often misconstrued Christianity to find a publicly relevant religion. Any number of the teachings and practices to which they appealed are capable of a different interpretation and nonpolitical applications. Even if Christian-inspired policy or reforms were appropriate, rare has been the Protestant to argue that the absolute truths of the Bible produce clear political prescriptions. If anything, Christianity teaches some general truths about human nature and political authority that admit a variety of circumstances and policies. Yet if

Christianity has so little to say about politics, and if when it does its meaning is cloudy, what is a Christian to do?

Many American Protestant baby boomers grew up singing a song, "Dare to Be a Daniel." Its lyrics were fairly distant from the actual circumstances of the Old Testament prophet whose tales about withstanding the lion's den of the foreign king Darius turned the doldrums of Sunday School into a brief moment of excitement and wonder. For instance, the song repeatedly talks about Daniel's band, or company of men, who, according to the third stanza, could fell "giants, great and tall." This suggests a conflation of the accounts of David slaying Goliath with Daniel's own administrative and intellectual skill sets. Even so, the refrain of the song pretty much summarized Daniel's import for Christian children: "Dare to be a Daniel, Dare to stand alone! Dare to have a purpose firm! Dare to make it known."

Part of what made Daniel appear so courageous and worthy of Sunday School children's emulation was his remarkable resolve to continue his own forms of worship even when the laws of King Darius made such religious practices illegal. The sixth chapter of the book of Daniel recounts the prophet's famous bondage in the lion's den as the punishment for failing to observe the religious laws of Babylon. Daniel accordingly served as a model of the sort of fidelity and courage to which Christians were also called: no matter what the cost, believing boys and girls were to obey God rather than man. Hence the song's refrain, "Dare to be a Daniel, Dare to stand alone!"

But the fine print of the Daniel narrative reveals another lesson that Sunday School children and their parents seldom considered. It is the account of the Jewish prophet who learned the literature and wisdom of the Chaldeans and excelled in it to such a degree that he emerged as the wisest of the pagan king's counselors. This learning was not simply the liberal arts, as John Calvin tried to explain it, but a language and literature that was infused with false and idolatrous ideas and beliefs, from the perspective of Israel's cult. Just as for the Jewish people, throughout the ancient Near East cult and culture were so thoroughly intertwined that to learn a foreign language and literature was in some important sense an entrance into the religious beliefs of a different God. So greatly did Daniel excel at this learning that he was able, through the aid of his own God, to be a better interpreter of the king's dreams than any of the other Chaldean wise men. In turn, Daniel became the ruler of one of the Babylonian provinces, thanks to his wisdom and service. The fuller account of Daniel, then, the one before and outside the lion's den, is of a man who had assimilated the ways, culture, and customs of a nation whose religion was false from the perspective of the Jewish people. In fact, Daniel and the Jews were in captivity to the Babylonian Empire and had been removed from their sacred land and from the sites of their religious worship. Daniel was in a situation of defeat—his faith disestablished, the empire's religion dominant. Yet he submitted to the ways and ideas of his captors and even excelled at their foreign and pagan culture.

Of course Daniel drew the line when it came to the worship of the God of Israel, thus ensuring that a song would be dedicated to him. For instance, the prophet refused to eat the rich food and drink the exceptional wine of the king's court, not simply because the food may not have been kosher but because the food and wine had been used as part of the worship rites of the Chaldean gods. Consequently Daniel and his Jewish comrades chose a vegetarian diet to avoid being implicated in pagan worship. And he refused to submit to the law of the subsequent king, who forbade all prayers to any god for a period of thirty days. Instead the prophet continued with his daily ritual of prayer in his own home, thus securing his encounter with the lions. So even while Daniel participated vigorously in the culture of his captors, even to the point of becoming a high ranking official, he drew the line at his own Jewish beliefs and practices. As difficult as it might seem, he would be part of Chaldean culture but continue to worship only in the cult of Israel.

This Daniel, the assimilated and devout prophet, may be the best model for American Christians wanting to know how to participate meaningfully in public life. Just as he lived a hyphenated life, so Christians—exiles and strangers, as the New Testament refers to them—may also be called to live lives in which they negotiate competing sets of loyalties and responsibilities. Christ himself appears to have been pointing in the direction of this hyphenated existence when he told his disciples to render some things to Caesar and some things to God. The split duties inherent in Christ's teaching, some belonging to Christians as citizens and others to them as church members, run directly counter to the current quest for individual wholeness that fuels the politics of identity and invites Christians to enter the public square as believers rather than as religious citizens. But Christ's instruction, along with Christianity's historic distinction between the realms of church and state, suggest that the politics of integration are not necessary for followers of Christ. Because Christians are pilgrims and exiles in this world, and long for their true spiritual home, a hyphenated existence is essential to Christian identity. In addition to his teaching about God and Caesar, Christ also told his disciples to live in the world but not to become part of it. On two significant counts, then, Christians have genuine grounds for accepting that life on earth will require negotiating dual sets of duties.

The double-sided character of Christian existence between the advents of Christ is a crucial reason for American Protestants to be more accepting of secular society and politics. Because of a higher set of loyalties and because of hopes for the world to come, Christians can actually be more flexible about America's political affairs than if they believed this world is all there is or will ever be. The otherworldly character of Christianity, in fact, should lower the stakes of politics for those in the church. Of course such otherworldliness may also produce political indifference. But with a properly high estimate of the created order, human nature, and the relative importance of civil society for maintaining order and restraining evil (at least), Christians may fruitfully participate in public life not as a site of redemption but as an essential part of their humanity. Secular politics need not compromise Christian identity. The argument of this book is that secular politics is thoroughly compatible with orthodox Christianity.

For those unconvinced about Christianity's secular character, it may yet be possible to see that participating in a secular polity, obeying the laws of a state that does not acknowledge God, and paying the taxes of a secular government do not contradict or compromise Christian faith. The reason is that God does not require the state to be Christian for it to be legitimate. Which is another way of saying that for thinking through the difficult negotiations of faith and politics, American Protestants should take a page from the book of Daniel. American Protestants have seldom studied that page, but if they had they might have discovered a strategy similar to the one by which the Jewish prophet participated in Chaldean culture, submitted to the Babylonians' laws, and retained his own forms of Jewish devotion and worship. In the same way he participated in Babylonian public life even when it explicitly rejected his God, American Protestants may be able to live contentedly with a political arrangement that claims to be religiously neutral and doesn't require them to abandon their rites, ceremonies, or religious practices. If Daniel could submit to foreign pagan rulers at a time when theocracy was still the norm, the kids—now adults—who grew up singing about the courage of that prophet should be able to live without much discomfort under a secular liberal democratic regime and not feel as though they are being unfaithful.

# A Note on Sources

BECAUSE THIS BOOK is designed for readers with a general knowledge of the debates surrounding religion and American politics, not for specialists in the fields of political science or American religious history, it does not include the standard scholarly apparatus of academic monographs. Those readers curious about some of the scholarly detail that has informed *A Secular Faith* should consult three of my previously published pieces: "Mainstream Protestantism, Conservative Religion, and Civil Society," in Hugh Heclo and Wilfred M. McClay, eds., *Religion Returns to the Public Square: Faith and Policy in America* (Baltimore, 2003), 195–225; "Conservatism, the Protestant Right, and the Failure of Religious History," *Journal of the Historical Society* 4.4 (2004) 447–494; and *Deconctrusting Evangelicalism: Conservative Protestantism in the Age of Billy Graham* (Grand Rapids, Mich., 2004), Chapters One and Two. For those simply curious about the works informing this book, a brief overview of the relevant literature follows.

In addition to the many recent books and essays on religion and American public life mentioned in the introduction, the most noteworthy in my estimation have been: Stephen L. Carter, *The Culture of Disbelief: How American Law and Politics Trivialize Religious Devotion* (New York, 1993); Richard John Neuhaus, *The Naked Public Square: Religion and Democracy in America* (Grand Rapids, Mich., 1984); Garry Wills, *Under God: Religion and American Politics* (New York, 1990); Glenn E. Tinder, *The Political Meaning of Christianity: An Interpretation* (Baton Rouge, La., 1989); Isaac Kramnick and R. Laurence Moore, *The Godless Constitution: The Case*

*Against Religious Correctness* (New York, 1996); and Mark A. Noll, George M. Marsden, and Nathan O. Hatch, *The Search for Christian America* (1983; Colorado Springs, 1989).

The subject of America's Puritan origins, treated in Chapter One, has been almost as vast a topic as New England Puritanism itself. John Winthrop's sermon delivered on board the *Arbella* is widely available, but a fairly easy place to find it is Michael Warner, ed., *American Sermons: The Pilgrims to Martin Luther King, Jr.* (New York, 1999). The definitive study of Winthrop is Edmund S. Morgan, *The Puritan Dilemma: The Story of John Winthrop* (Boston, 1958). Also useful is Francis J. Bremer, *John Winthrop: America's Forgotten Founding Father* (New York, 2003). For the way that some political philosophers have attempted to situate the Puritan vision within the American founding, several of the essays in Thomas S. Engeman and Michael P. Zuckert, eds., *Protestantism and the American Founding* (Notre Dame, Ind., 2004) are helpful. Samuel P. Huntington, *Who Are We?: The Challenges to America's National Identity* (New York, 2004) also makes substantial claims based on America's Puritan origins. For the ideas about the millennium that Puritans bequeathed to later American Protestants, James H. Moorhead, *American Apocalypse: Yankee Protestants and the Civil War* (New Haven, 1978), and Timothy P. Weber, *Living in the Shadow of the Second Coming: American Premillennialism, 1875–1925* (New York, 1979) are good places to start. Augustine's classic formulation of divine intentions and human history is found in *Augustine: The City of God Against the Pagans*, Robert Dyson, ed. (New York, 1998), which includes a helpful introduction and analysis.

The literature on religion and the American founding, the subject of Chapter Two, is also vast. Arguably the best recent book on the topic is Mark A. Noll, *America's God: From Jonathan Edwards to Abraham Lincoln* (New York, 2002). Also valuable are the essays in Mark A. Noll, ed., *Religion and American Politics* (New York, 1990). The text of the Witherspoon sermon cited in the chapter comes from Ellis Sandoz, ed., *Political Sermons of the American Founding Era, 1730–1805* (Indianapolis, 1991), which provides many more examples of Protestant support for the American founding. L. Gordon Tait, *The Piety of John Witherspoon: Pew, Pulpit, and Public Forum* (Louisville, Ky., 2001) provides a wider context for Witherspoon's famous sermon. Other works that interpret the Calvinism of the Revolutionary Era in a conservative manner are Barry Shain, *The Myth of American Individualism: The Protestant Origins of American Political Thought*

(Princeton, N.J., 1996); and David W. Hall, *The Genevan Reformation and the American Founding* (Lanham, Md., 2003). So strong have the associations been between Protestant ideas about liberty of conscience and American ideas about political freedom that no one seems to have felt a need to write about it. But the model for such a study is John T. McGreevy, *Catholicism and American Freedom: A History* (New York, 2003).

The views of Thomas Jefferson and John Adams on religion and morality that introduce Chapter Three may be found in Edward Dumbauld, ed., *The Political Writings of Thomas Jefferson* (New York, 1955), and Charles Francis Adams, ed., *The Works of John Adams, Second President of the United States* (Boston, 1854). On the religious views of the founders, readers should consult Norman Cousins, *"In God We Trust": The Religious Beliefs and Ideas of the American Founding Fathers* (New York, 1958), and Edwin S. Gaustad, *Faith of Our Fathers: Religion and the New Nation* (San Francisco, 1987). Robert Michaelsen, *Piety in the Public Schools: Trends and Issues in the Relationship Between Religion and the Public School in the United States* (New York, 1970); Charles L. Glenn, *The Myth of the Common School* (Amherst, Mass., 1988); and Diane Ravitch, *The Great School Wars: A History of the New York City Public Schools* (Baltimore, Md., 2000) offer historical context on the controversies of religion in public schooling. Readers unfamiliar with historic Protestant teaching on human nature and the difficulty of performing good works may want to consult the Reformed, Lutheran, and Anglican creeds in Jaroslav Pelikan and Valerie Hotchkiss, eds., *Creeds and Confessions of the Christian Tradition*, vol. 2 (New Haven, 2003). For contemporary discussions of Christianity and morality, Gilbert Meilaender provides useful caution against collapsing faith and virtue in *Friendship: A Study in Theological Ethics* (Notre Dame, Ind., 1985), and *Faith and Faithfulness: Basic Themes in Christian Ethics* (Notre Dame, Ind., 1991).

The degree to which Abraham Lincoln believed in divine rule of the United States, the subject that introduces Chapter Four, is best explored in Allen C. Guelzo, *Abraham Lincoln: Redeemer President* (Grand Rapids, Mich., 1999). A good guide to the religious considerations that led Congress to add "under God" to the Pledge of Allegiance is Martin E. Marty, *Modern American Religion*, vol. 3: *Under God, Indivisible, 1941–1960* (Chicago, 1999). On changes in American Protestant theology that occurred thanks to efforts to lend the churches' hand to social reform, William R. Hutchison, *The Modernist Impulse in American Protestantism*

(Cambridge, Mass., 1976), and Gary J. Dorrien, *The Making of American Liberal Theology: Idealism, Realism, and Modernity* (Louisville, Ky., 2003) are reliable guides. Presbyterians like Stuart Robinson, sometimes known as "Old School," who strongly opposed accounts of divine rule that conflated the civil and religious spheres, receive sustained attention in Ernest Trice Thompson, *Presbyterians in the South*, vol. 1 (Richmond, 1963), and James Oscar Farmer, Jr., *The Metaphysical Confederacy: James Henley Thornwell and the Synthesis of Southern Values* (Macon, Ga., 1986). Although I come to different conclusions about the meaning of the Lordship of Christ over the church, Oliver O'Donovan, *The Desire of the Nations: Rediscovering the Roots of Political Theology* (New York, 1999), and John Howard Yoder, *The Politics of Jesus* (Grand Rapids, Mich., 1994) represent some of the diversity among contemporary Protestants in the field of political theology.

American Protestant affinities for democracy, the theme of the fifth chapter, have never been hard to find. The religious training and outlook that informed Woodrow Wilson's own understanding of his political efforts is the subject of John M. Mulder, *Woodrow Wilson: The Years of Preparation* (Princeton, N.J., 1978). On the seeds of American Protestantism's democratic impulse, Nathan O. Hatch, *The Democratization of American Christianity* (New Haven, 1989) is indispensable. Although mainline Protestants in the United States have become less enthusiastic about American forms of democracy, James Hastings Nichols, *Democracy and the Churches* (Philadelphia, 1951) is a good example of the mid-twentieth-century American consensus on Protestantism's ties to democracy. Lyman Beecher, *A Plea for the West* (1835; New York, 1977); Josiah Strong, *Our Country: Its Possible Future and Its Present Crisis* (New York, 1885); Paul Blanshard, *American Freedom and Catholic Power* (Boston, 1949); and Loraine Boettner, *Roman Catholicism* (Philadelphia, 1962) demonstrate the way American Protestants employed democracy against Roman Catholicism. The fundamentalist controversy in the northern Presbyterian church, which accounted for some odd twists in the American Protestant effort to adapt Christian teaching to liberal democracy, receives solid coverage in Bradley J. Longfield, *The Presbyterian Controversy: Fundamentalists, Moderates, and Modernists* (New York, 1993); and D. G. Hart, *Defending the Faith: J. Gresham Machen and the Crisis of Conservative Protestantism in Modern America* (1994; Philipsburg, N.J., 2003). Helpful discussions of contemporary democratic theory can be found in Jeffrey Stout, *Democracy and Tradition* (Princeton, N.J., 2003); Robert Kraynak, *Christian Faith and Modern Democracy: God and Politics in the Fallen World* (Notre Dame, Ind., 2001); Jean Bethke Elshtain, *Democracy on Trial* (New York, 1996); and Stanley Hauerwas, *Unleashing the Scripture: Freeing the Bible from Captivity to America* (Nashville, 1993).

The sixth chapter explores the theme of identity politics and introduces the subject with instances of Roman Catholics running for the highest office in America. Books that explore Roman Catholic assimilation to American political norms, in addition to John McGreevy's mentioned above, are Jay Dolan, *In Search of an American Catholicism: A History of Religion and Culture in Tension* (New York, 2003), and Mark S. Massa, *Anti-Catholicism in America: The Last Acceptable Prejudice* (New York, 2003). On the origins of the religious right and evangelical Protestantism's contribution to identity politics, Lisa McGirr, *Suburban Warriors: The Origins of the New American Right* (Princeton, N.J., 2001), and William C. Martin, *With God on Our Side: The Rise of the Religious Right in America* (New York, 1996) are instructive. I have found David A. Hollinger, *Postethnic America: Beyond Multiculturalism* (New York, 1995) to be especially valuable on contemporary discussions of the self, along with Charles Taylor, *Multiculturalism and "the Politics of Recognition": An Essay* (Princeton, N.J., 1992). Two of the more prominent voices arguing for religion as the core of human identity are Jean Bethke Elshtain, "The Bright Line: Liberalism and Religion," in Hilton Kramer and Roger Kimball, eds., *The Betrayal of Liberalism: How the Disciples of Freedom and Equality Helped Foster the Illiberal Politics of Coercion and Control* (Chicago, 1999), 137–158; and Nicholas Wolterstorff (with Robert Audi), *Religion in the Public Square* (Lanham, Md., 1996).

The degree to which faith functions as a unifying social force is the theme of Chapter Seven. Martin Luther King, Jr.'s views on the topic may be pursued in Clayborne Carson and Kris Shepard, eds., *A Call to Conscience: The Landmark Speeches of Dr. Martin Luther King, Jr.* (New York, 2001), and Kenneth L. Zepp and Ira G. Zepp, Jr., *Search for the Beloved Community: The Thinking of Martin Luther King, Jr.* (Valley Forge, Pa., 1998). Malcolm X's dissent from King's position is available in George Breitman, ed., *Malcolm X Speaks: Selected Speeches and Statements* (New York, 1990). The literature on American Protestant ecumenism is still relatively thin. Samuel McCrea Cavert, *Church Cooperation and Unity in America, 1900–1970* (New York, 1970) is an institutional history written by an insider but covers the basics. The essays in William

R. Hutchison, *Between the Times: The Travail of the Protestant Establishment in America, 1900–1960* (New York, 1990) provide several insights into the inner workings of mainstream Protestantism's cooperative motivations and endeavors. Material for this chapter on the National Council of Churches and the Council on Church Union comes from: National Council of Churches, *Christian Faith in Action: Commemorative Volume, The Founding of the National Council of Churches of Christ in the United States of America* (New York, 1951); John A. Hutchison, *We Are Not Divided: A Critical and Historical Study of the Federal Council of Churches of Christ in America* (New York, 1941); Paul A. Crow, Jr., and William Jerry Boney, eds., *Church Union at Midpoint* (New York, 1972); and Council on Church Union, *A Plan of Union for the Church of Christ Uniting* (Princeton, N.J., 1970). Readers interested in the inability of American Protestant ecumenism to unite Calvinist denominations should consult James D. Bratt, *Dutch Calvinism in Modern America: A History of a Conservative Subculture* (Grand Rapids, Mich., 1984), and D. G. Hart and John R. Muether, *Fighting the Good Fight: A Brief History of the Orthodox Presbyterian Church* (Philadelphia, 1995). In addition to Robert Bellah, et al., *Habits of the Heart: Middle America Observed* (New York, 1988), Bellah's definitive statement on American civil religion is "Civil Religion in America," in William G. McLoughlin and Robert N. Bellah, eds., *Religion in America* (Boston, 1968), 3–23. For an interpretation of American religion that highlights its fissiparous tendencies, R. Laurence Moore, *Religious Outsiders and the Making of Americans* (New York, 1986) is provocative and worthwhile.

The literature on faith-based initiatives and compassionate conservatism, the topic of Chapter Eight, is still being written, but Jo Renee Formicola, Mary C. Segers, and Paul Weber, *Faith-Based Initiatives and the Bush Administration: The Good, the Bad, and the Ugly* (Lanham, Md., 2003), and Amy E. Black, Douglas L. Koopman, and David K. Ryden, *Of Little Faith: The Politics of George W. Bush's Faith-Based Initiatives* (Washington, D.C., 2004) are helpful and supply useful background on the policies of George W. Bush's administration. For evangelical Protestant contributions to these developments, readers should consult Amy L. Sherman, "Evangelicals and Charitable Choice," in Michael Cromartie, ed., *A Public Faith: Evangelicals and Civic Engagement* (Lanham, Md., 2003), 157–172. Mark A. Noll, *American Evangelical Christianity: An Introduction* (Oxford, 2001), and D. G. Hart, *That Old-Time Religion in*

*Modern America: Evangelical Protestantism in the Twentieth Century* (Chicago, 2002), provide overviews of twentieth-century evangelical Protestant politics. For more specific episodes, Robert Booth Fowler, *A New Engagement: Evangelical Political Thought, 1966–1976* (Grand Rapids, Mich., 1982), and Michael Lienesch, *Redeeming America: Piety and Politics in the New Christian Right* (Chapel Hill, 1993) are useful. On the shift of evangelical attitudes toward the welfare state, David O. Moberg, *The Great Reversal: Evangelicals Versus Social Concern* (Philadelphia, 1972); Richard V. Pierard, *The Unequal Yoke: Evangelical Christianity and Political Conservatism* (Philadelphia, 1970); and Ronald J. Sider and Dianne Knippers, eds., *Toward an Evangelical Public Policy: Political Strategies for the Health of the Nation* (Grand Rapids, Mich., 2005) are instructive. The discussion of compassionate conservatism would be incomplete without the author who popularized the phrase—Marvin Olasky, *Compassionate Conservatism: What It Is, What It Does, and How It Can Transform America* (New York, 2000). A Roman Catholic alternative to Olasky comes from Rick Santorum, *It Takes a Family: Conservatism and the Common Good* (Wilmington, Del., 2005).

In my efforts here to lessen hostility to the word "secular" and to recover Christianity's recognition of a secular realm, I have found worthwhile the following: Roger Scruton, *The West and the Rest: Globalization and the Terrorist Threat* (Wilmington, Del., 2002); Bernard Lewis, *What Went Wrong?: The Clash Between Islam and Modernity in the Middle East* (New York, 2002); and Steve Bruce, *God Is Dead: Secularization in the West* (Oxford, 2002). On the importance of Christianity to Western civilization, Russell Kirk, *Redeeming the Time*, ed., Jeffrey O. Nelson (Wilmington, Del., 1999); T. S. Eliot's essays on Christian civilization in Frank Kermode, ed., *Selected Prose of T. S. Eliot* (New York, 1975); and Christopher Dawson, *Dynamics of World History*, ed., John J. Mulroy (Wilmington, Del., 2002) still deserve consideration.

# Index

## A NOTE ON THE AUTHOR

Darryl Hart was born in Abington, Pennsylvania, and studied at Temple University, Westminster Seminary, Harvard University, and Johns Hopkins University, where he received a Ph.D. in American history. He has written widely on religion in American history, including *Defending the Faith*, *The University Gets Religion*, *That Old-Time Religion in Modern America*, and *The Lost Soul of American Protestantism*. He is now director of academic projects and faculty development at the Intercollegiate Studies Institute in Wilmington, Delaware, and lives with his wife Ann in Philadelphia.